I, *the Song*

A. L. SOENS

I, the Song

CLASSICAL POETRY
OF NATIVE
NORTH AMERICA

THE UNIVERSITY OF UTAH PRESS
Salt Lake City

© 1999 by the
University of
Utah Press

Acknowledgment of
permissions appears on
page 299.

LIBRARY OF CONGRESS CATALOGING-IN-PUBLICATION DATA

I, the song : classical poetry of native North America / [edited by]
   A. L. Soens.
      p. cm.
   Includes bibliographical references.
    ISBN 0–87480–590–2 (cloth : alk. paper). — ISBN 0–87480–609–7
(paper : alk. paper)
    1. Indian poetry—North Averica—Translations into English.
I. Soens, A. L. (Adolph L.), 1931–   .
PM197.E3I2 1999
897—dc21   99–21102

For

Jill, Lewie, Ingrid, Chris, Rich, Meg, Rebecca,

and

Bobby, Ben, Allie, Richie, Sophie, and Peter

❧   [That Holiness]

Ἐν αὐτῷ γὰρ ζῶμεν καὶ κινούμεθα καὶ ἐσμέν

Acts 17:28, attributed to Epimenides

CONTENTS

ACKNOWLEDGMENTS

I wish to thank William F. May, Carey Maguire Professor of Ethics, Southern Methodist University, for analyzing this work and suggesting many improvements in its content, style, structure, and approach. His discussion of covenantal ethics and the theology of immanence illuminated many of the poems for me. Professor Paul A. Olson generously read early versions of this anthology, suggested additional poetry, and in his works on American Indian literature, on Chaucer, and on wisdom literature suggested ideas and approaches that helped me understand the poetics of this poetry and enriched my appreciation and enjoyment. Professor Paul Zolbrod, whose understanding of the poetics of Sir Philip Sidney illuminates his work on Navajo and other American Indian oral literatures, emphasized the primacy of performance in the structure, rhetoric, and vision of these poems in his comments on an early version of this anthology. Professor Jean-Anne Strebinger closely analyzed content and form and made many structural and interpretative suggestions that improved the commentary and made the translations smoother and more readable. The subscribers of the Native American Literature list on the Internet carried on discussions that made me reexamine my assumptions and taught me a familiarity with the cultures into which this poetry fits that I could have gained from no other source. I also wish to thank Michael Palmer, M.D., Leonard Gundersen, M.D., and Victor Trastec, M.D., without whom this book could not have been completed. Jill M., A. L. Jr., and Ingrid W. Soens displayed patience and tolerance. Jeff Grathwohl, my editor at the University of Utah Press, was very helpful, trusting that the text would finally come to fruition, in the face of delays, revisions, and interruptions. What is valuable in this book I owe to others. I do, however, with the utmost confidence, claim any errors, grotesqueries, or infelicities as entirely my own.

INTRODUCTION

THIS COLLECTION of poems will introduce readers to the rich and complex classical North American Indian poetry that grew out of and reflects North American Indian life before the European invasion. I have chosen clear, easily readable translations and assembled them around common experiences to tempt readers to read more deeply into this poetry.

Of course, no generalization will hold true for all the classical poems of North American Indians. They spring from 30,000 years of experience, 500 languages and dialects,[1] and ten general linguistic groups and general cultures.[2] Still, the poems from these different cultures and languages belong, after all, to poetry unified by similar experiences and a shared continent. These poems, which share many literary characteristics such as similar images, structures, and settings, reflect light and beauty on each other and increase our understanding as they illuminate one another.

Like all great poems, the classical poems of North American Indians can enrich our lives by helping us take a new look at the world through the poets' eyes. The Pueblo poet who asked Poseyemo to "make the snow bring spring"[3] saw, in drifted snow, the squash and bean flowers spring and summer would bring. Like his fellow poets Robert Frost, A. E. Housman, and Horace, he surprises us with a glimpse of blossoms cocooned in snow. In showing us spring in fallen snow, in snow falling on woods (in "Stopping by woods") or draping the branches of cherry trees (in "Loveliest of trees") or melting in spring (in "diffugere nives"), these poets help us see familiar sights as though for the first time and look again at beauty that habit has led us to overlook or forget.

These poems let us look at our continent through the eyes of an extraordinarily wide range of people: the poets, hunters, farmers, holy men and women, and children who looked at it attentively and with delight before we cut the forests, plowed the tall grass, exterminated the passenger pigeon, and nearly wiped out the buffalo. They help us see what we have long loved as freshly as when we first loved it.

Like all classical poetry, North American Indian classical poetry brings us new insights to enrich the routine wisdom of our own culture. To confirm their resolve when they confronted death, Omaha Hethuska Society soldiers sang:

> This land will last!
> When I am gone, it will last long!
> This land will last long,
> It will endure![4]

Simonides' epitaph for Leonidas and the 300 at Thermopylae expresses the same resolve:

> Traveler, go tell the Spartans that we lie here,
> Obedient to their orders.

The Spartans drew resolve and courage from belief that Sparta would endure. The Omaha singers drew resolve and courage from faith that their land, filled with holiness, would endure. Roman Nose's death song at the Beecher's Island fight[5] and White Antelope's at the Sand Creek massacre, "Only mountains endure," call on the same faith. These poems show us courage in the face of death through new eyes. Drawing courage and resolve from a vision of the holiness filling their homeland, they also suggest a source for that reverence for the land that led Americans to invent national parks.

Most strikingly, however, classical North American Indian poetry brings us flashes of timeless vision and absolute perception: a gull's wing red above the dawn; an otter rising from the water through the morning mist; snowcapped peaks in the moonlight, leading our eyes up to the Milky Way. Such pure vision helps us look outward and focus our attention on what we see; we thus see more clearly and can live more vividly and richly than before. Even if we have never seen a gull's wing redden against the dawn except in an Inuit song, the song can, by way of that wing, lead us to see that spring or summer leaves, red against a low sun, foreshadow the leaves of autumn.

The songs usually embody such vivid flashes of pure experience in the clear and direct language that we also find in the most powerful imagist poems, haiku, and *The Greek Anthology,* even though many of the poems are as structurally and rhetorically intricate as the poems of John Donne, Gerard Manley Hopkins, Andrew Marvell, or William Shakespeare. The anthropologist Alanson Skinner described Prairie Potawatomi poetry as punning, complicated, filled with double or triple allusions, and impossible to reproduce in English.[6] Thus, in his translations, he presented the powerful visions that the rhetoric surrounded in language as simple and pictures as vivid as those filling the Dakota or A'nish'inabeg poems Frances Densmore printed or the Inuit poems Hinrich Rink and Knud Rasmussen translated.

North American Indian classical poetry achieved its vividness, clarity, and intense emotional power partly because the singers made their poems for active use as well as beauty and partly because they made them for singing or chanting (often for performing for an audience) rather than for isolated, passive reading. Making their poetry for singers and performances, the poets chose direct language when they could. Even the most solemn ceremonies, although they often used obsolete or obscure words or phrases to distinguish ceremonial from everyday poetry, also evoked common, daily experience in clear, ordinary words. Familiar words, phrases, and songs called to memory other singers and other times and stirred the emotions that accompanied such memories:

> Some of the songs for this [dance] are very old. I'll sing one for you. It's very old, perhaps two hundred years old. When I was just a little boy at Fort Apache fifty years ago, just old enough to listen to singing, I heard it. There was one very old man who sat by a fire working on arrows and singing it. And while he sang it, he was crying. This song reminded him of the times when he was a young man. That's why I think it is so old.[7]

These poems draw power from action. They always imply singers doing something—performing a ceremony, greeting the sun, grinding corn, or planting squash and beans, for instance—and lure the reader to visualize the action or performance the original audience saw. The mnemonic devices (knotted strings, pictographs, wampum belts, or drawings) that performers often used to help them remember long narrative or ceremonial sequences encouraged the original performers and audiences to remember and visualize earlier performances and thus made performance more vivid. Visualizing a printed poem's setting, singer, and audience as well as its subject will deepen the modern reader's enjoyment and understanding.

The dynamics of performance also influenced the structure of this poetry. The poets often use stock phrases (sometimes drawn from ceremonies) and incremental repetition and variation. Both the formulaic phrases and patterned repetition and variation helped the singer-performer make, memorize, and perform songs. Makers and singers honed such phrases into clear imagery and embodied symbols in undecorated, clear statement and narration. These stock phrases, like the epithets of Homer or the kennings of Anglo-Saxon heroic poetry, reminded the audience of details from ceremonies, myths, and other poems. Incremental repetition also recalled details and images to the audience.

A song from the Tomanpa, an Apache mourning ceremony, exemplifies the effects of such repetition and formulaic phrasing. The Tomanpa contains more than 359 short songs. The songs state isolated details, frequently in ceremonial, ancient, or shaman's words. Often such words did not make explicit narrative sense. Instead they served as an index to the story that the songs recalled to the audience and singer. For example, one song contains two lines, repeated often:

> E<u>mu</u> kayo<u>vb</u><u>ak</u> kange
> Ti<u>yam</u> onge kanga

Three words carried explicit meaning: *mu* (leg), *vak* (step), *tiym* (go). The other syllables, vocables or obsolete or esoteric words, fill out the rhythm. The song reminded the audience that, after burning the body of the culture hero and creator Matevilye, the First People returned to the mountain Avikome. Matevilye's children, Tomanpa and his sister, Qakoisavapona, could not forget their grief, and, *going step* by step on their *legs,* left the people and went south, mourning. Repeating the two lines often recalled the stages of that journey to the audience's memory.[8]

This poetry tended to avoid elaborate descriptions. Familiar phrases and repetition efficiently recalled details that fleshed out the song for both singer and audience. In *Reading the Voice: Native American Oral Poetry on the Written Page,* Paul Zolbrod suggests how such associated details work to evoke memory, emotion, and ceremonial and mythic backgrounds, when he discusses narratives "embedded" in lyrics.[9]

Poets relied on traditional phrases and associations to make their poems. An Inuit singer remarked that his best songs came to him when he left the village, sat alone on a hill, and tried phrases from the songs he liked until he had arranged them into a new song. A Pueblo singer told Frances Densmore that he made songs by fitting well-turned phrases from other songs to the tune he wanted to use. An Apache maker of social-dance songs described his art: "I took some old songs and chose a little from one and a little from another. I used about three and worked one new song out of them."[10] Sioux men composed songs by fiddling around with new combinations of familiar phrases. As Nootka girls, Helen Irving and her best friend, Mrs. Kalopa, made up songs while swinging. Mrs. Kalopa altered and combined proven phrases until the song sounded right.[11]

Of course, such formulaic poetry did not encourage assertive originality. It emphasized tradition: both singer and audience enjoyed hearing a traditional phrase from, for instance, a narrative of origin or emergence, harmoniously adapted to a new healing song, a trickster story, or a hunting or love song intended to bewitch prey into range.

People used, as well as enjoyed, this poetry. As members of medicine lodges and fraternal, sororal, and ceremonial societies, singers used song to persuade the Holiness immanent in the universe and personified in the Holy People to bless their works and days. Songs, like mantras, helped them focus their attention on those powers and that Holiness. They used poetry to introduce candidates to the visions and the Holy Powers that gave the visionary holiness and power. They sang in ceremonies to demonstrate holy power, heal the sick, smooth quarrels and restore harmony, bless the fields, call up rain, encourage growth, ensure plentiful harvests, establish or restore vitality and harmony among the people and their animal relatives, and heal and renew the world itself. Classical North American Indian poetry drew part of its clarity, vividness, and emotional power from this usefulness in ceremonies.

Such ceremonies often required prodigious feats of memory. For example, a Diné *haatali* who supervised performances of Coyoteway sang 161 songs, in a ceremony lasting nine nights. In one song, each stanza repeats and varies a one-line refrain eight times. This line alternates with ten verses and repeats a phrase, "by these he was led," seventeen times.[12] The singer repeated this stanza eight times, varying a word or two, to form an eight-stanza unit. He repeated the eight-stanza unit three times, varying other verses. While singing this 432-line song and following a strict order of variation, the singer also performed approximately 100 ritual movements and oversaw a crew making a drypainting. The crew added details to the painting in time with both the ritual and the song. He repeated this song as songs four, twenty, thirty-five, and fifty-three, with appropriate variations, during the ceremony. Osage, Sioux, Iroquois, Fox, Omaha, Cheyenne, and other nations' ceremonies demanded similar feats of memory.

The people also used poetry to illumine and celebrate everyday life. Song directed their attention to the holiness and wonder that flowed through ordinary events. They sang to greet the dawn and rejoice in the gift of a new day. Women woke their children with song, sang them to sleep, and sang while digging roots, planting, tending gardens, scaring off crows, sizing up good-looking braves, cooking, and greeting guests. Farmers sang to call rain, to bless the fields, to plant and irrigate harmoniously, and to harvest in beauty and plenty. Children sang at play, to scare birds from the fields, and to parody the earnest, or boastful, songs of their elder siblings. The Pawnee boy Eagle feared Thunder and made a song to tell himself Thunder was his friend. Grown up, he sang it as his war song for the courage it brought him.[13]

Obsessed lovers sang to bewitch their targets, brood over the pangs of desire, or rue their affliction. Boys and girls sang to tease and tempt eligible quarry.

Hunters sang when preparing to hunt, calling prey into range, killing, honoring their quarry's spirit, returning home with their meat, and distributing food to those who needed it. Soldiers sang when preparing to fight, scouting, attacking, taunting the enemy, killing or dying, and counting coup. They sang returning from war and when they performed a ceremony such as the Scalp Dance to propitiate the ghosts of dead enemies and wash away the spiritual residue of killing.

Shamans and healers used poetry, as well as prestidigitation, when they showed off their skills and powers in such performances as the Algonkian Shaking-Tent demonstration. Storytellers chanted myths and narratives in the lodges at night. Everyone sang for power and luck when gambling.

Some singers, approaching harmonious death in old age, traveled through the clear light of their homeland, following the route the First People followed when they emerged from the underworld or descended from the sky, and sang farewells to those well-loved places to which the First People had sung greetings.

Classical North American Indian poems, like Virgil's *Georgics* and Hesiod's *Works,* also offered the singer and the audience some practical technical hints or descended from songs that did. Songs not only evoked vivid flashes of harmonious days and beautiful lands, but recalled details that marked the places where the singer and the audience could find fish and game, plant crops, and harvest berries, nuts, roots, and medicinal and ritually useful plants. Songs recalled the configurations of stars or the places of daybreak on the horizon that marked the times for ceremonies, hunting, planting, and harvesting. The songs they sang to prepare to hunt and while hunting often suggested the habits and psychology of their prey.

Such usefulness for hunting, gathering, and farming may be a source of one of the most powerful currents flowing beneath the surface of this poetry: the urge to achieve a selfless attention to the universe and its contents and a determination to see and delight in that universe on its own terms. This determination shaped an ability to pay attention to the Holiness (the principle of movement, life, harmony, and beauty) that filled the world. Nicholas Black Elk, the Oglala holy man, called such selfless attention "attentiveness." To act in ordinary life or in ritual "with a clear mind," "in

beauty," "harmoniously," or in "a sacred manner" required such "atten-
tiveness."

Their songs helped the singers pay attention, not to a transcendent Ho-
liness that spurned our visible universe, but to the immanent Holiness that
saturated it. This poetry led the singers to delight in their world as in a
beatific vision. Thus the Inuit Utitiaq, adrift on the Great Ice, sang a song
that, somewhat grimly, affirmed beatitude when he sang of joy in the ice,
snow, and slush that surrounded him and in the thirst and hunger he felt.[14]
The Ghost Dancers, who sang of a spirit world where the dead lived as
they had in the good time before the European invasion, sought to recall
that world to this, rather than to escape this world to a paradise in the sky.

I like to think that this determination to attend to immanent Holiness
reflects, distantly, the importance of hunting and gathering to the poets.
Hunters needed to pay close, selfless attention to their prey, to its habits,
and to its home to succeed in killing a day's meal. This practice of paying
attention filtered into other songs; Karl Luckert, for example, describes
how Navajo medicine singers used and adapted hunters' songs.[15] Healers
across the continent sometimes used a hunter's vocabulary and hunting
metaphors when seeking to kill diseases and heal patients.

The poets who made these songs inherited symbols and images that
reflected the experiences and ways of life of the waves of hunters and gath-
erers who, beginning 30,000 years ago, crossed from Asia to spread over
North America. These poets drew on a common stock of images, such as
the solitary rock offering refuge or the "visible breath" revealing life and
holiness. Siberian Chukchee hunters called on a medicine stone to carry
them to the safety of an isolated rock when they had to sleep alone out on
the steppes or tundra:

> I am not here.
> I am within this stone.
> And this stone is a big cliff
> In the middle of the Ocean,
> Its sides steep, slippery!
> The spirit who tries to climb it
> Will break his nails
> And slide down into the water.[16]

Such a rock, the primal rock, rises in an Omaha hymn about Creation:
"Suddenly, from the middle of the waters, up rose a great rock. It burst
into flames."[17] Other solitary rocks stand behind Lakota stories about
Devil's Tower as a refuge and the stories about tutelary stones that marked

and protected homelands for the Iroquois and other Eastern Woodland nations.

This protective spire looms behind songs that invoke the primal rocks or mountains that endure while we perish, such as a Cheyenne war song:

> Friends, stone always remains firm.
>   Forward.[18]

At the Sand Creek Massacre (1864), the Arapaho White Antelope sang a death song invoking the primal and enduring earth and mountains:

> Nothing lives long
> Except the earth and the mountains.[19]

The Kiowa attributed saving endurance to the earth and the sun.

> I live, but I cannot live forever!
> Only the Earth lives forever!
> Only the Sun lives![20]

Sitting Bear sang a version of this song,[21] as did the imprisoned Setanka in 1871, just before he attacked a guard, knowing he would die.[22] In 1991, Bertha Little Coyote remembered a relevant song[23] when she heard Frances Densmore's recording of "Old War Song," sung by Elk Woman, in 1935.[24] Howling Wolf sang a similar song.[25] Densmore also heard versions from the Mandan[26] and the Teton Sioux,[27] as did Black Elk.[28] Peter J. Powell cites a similar Kit Fox Society song.[29]

Songs evoking this image of endurance and refuge were so common that they inspired counterpoint songs that made clouds more lasting than rocks and mountains, as a standing wave in a river outlasts any water-drop that flows through it. Two Paiute songs compare the feathers in a dancer's ceremonial headdress and the snow and clouds that cap mountains. The clouds and ceremonial feathers, clothing the Holiness immanent in the world and the dance, outlast the mountains:

> A feather on the hill will remain continuously,
>   But the rocks slide down.
> The crest of the mountain remains forever (2)
>   Though rocks fall continually![30]

An equally vivid image, "visible breath," recurs in poems from across the continent and calls up a spectrum of ordinary sights. Breath rises visibly from a singer greeting a chilly dawn, from the buffalo herd on a cold morning, and in tobacco smoke spiraling up as a singer sings a prayer after drawing on the pipe. The holiness that fills dawn, singer, song, and breath floats in the air, a glowing cloud across the rising sun. In *Black Elk Speaks,* White Buffalo Calf Woman sings:

> With visible breath I am walking!
> A voice I send as I walk.
> In a sacred manner I am walking.
> With visible tracks I am walking.
> In a sacred manner I walk.[31]

The song also evokes (in "visible tracks") the circles of ground-mist that can surround the herd's moving hooves on a humid morning. Charging Thunder added "this red relic" (the sacred pipe) to his version, emphasizing that White Buffalo Calf Woman brought the Lakota the sacred pipe.[32]

Poetry from the Arctic and the Eastern Woodlands alludes to the "visible breath" that clothes a song in chilly air. Orpingalik, a Netsilik shaman, called his song "my breath." In the esoteric vocabulary of the Netsilik shamans, "someone whom smoke surrounds" means "a living person."[33] The Inuit word *anerca* means both "breath" and "song." Ojibwa song mentions the mist rising from a lake, pool, or spring or surrounding an animal (often a tutelary helping a vision seeker), emerging from them into the chilly air. The Prairie Potawatomi identified the dust rising above the buffalo herd with the smoke rising from a ceremonial pipe or the smoke exhaled while chanting a prayer after drawing on the pipe. Visible breath marks the singer, the song, and the holiness that moves in both. It makes the holiness that fills wind and water, dawn and starlight, clear to the attentive watcher, who sees singer and song joined in the holiness that fills the universe.

CLASSICAL NORTH AMERICAN INDIAN poetry reflects ten anthropologically defined areas and cultures. Visualizing these settings can help the reader understand and enjoy the poems from these cultures. The Inuit of the Arctic Culture hunted seal, walrus, caribou, and whale and fished in the northern Arctic, where a shallow layer of sod thawed over the permafrost and melting ice formed bogs in the summer; in the long winter, everything, including the sea, froze.

The Algonkian and Athapascan speakers of the subarctic Taiga Culture, plagued in summer by clouds of mosquitoes and black flies, hunted caribou, deer, moose, musk-ox, woods buffalo, and small game and fished in the forests, lakes, swamps, and rivers south of Inuit territory.

The Siouan and Algonkian speakers of the Northeastern Woodlands hunted deer, fished bountiful rivers and bays, and grew corn, beans, squash, and tobacco in climax forests that stretched from the Atlantic coast to the Mississippi, from the Great Lakes to tidewater Virginia.

The Algonkian, Siouan, Uto-Aztecan, and Tanoan speakers of the Great Plains farmed and hunted horizon-filling herds of buffalo on a vast rolling grassland that offered the buffalo ideal grazing. Woods fringed the rivers. Mountain ranges, isolated upthrusts such as the Black Hills, the Tetons, and the Ten Sleeps, and rifts such as the Badlands and the Palo Duro Canyon interrupted the sea of grass. When the Spanish imported the horse, which enabled the plains nations to follow the buffalo herds, many of them almost abandoned farming entirely. We take our stereotypical picture of the North American Indian from the riders of the plains.

The Penutian, Salishan, Algonkian, and Siouan speakers of the Plateau Culture gathered edible roots and plants and caught salmon, trout, and sturgeon in the abundant fisheries of the intricate river system that drained the Columbia Plateau.

The Na-Dene, Penutian, Salishan, Wakashan, and Chimakum speakers of the Northwest Coast Culture lived in the narrow band between the coast and the coastal mountains, from the Alaskan Panhandle to northern California. The temperate climate and heavy rains (100 inches a year) nourished a rich temperate rain forest. Game and fish abounded; salmon were readily caught. Easily won food gave the Northwest Coast Culture leisure to develop intricate ceremonies and complicated, affluent societies.

Peoples of the California Basin Cultures lived in a cornucopia: acorns and other edible plants grew thickly; deer and small game flourished. The basin supported the densest nonfarming population of American Indians north of Central America. The people identified themselves as members of family-centered villages and spoke more than 100 dialects of Hokan, Penutian, Athapascan, Algonkian, and Uto-Aztecan.

The Uto-Aztecan speakers of the Great Basin lived between the Columbia and Colorado Plateaus and the eastern slopes of the Sierras and the western slopes of the Rockies in arid land, with extreme temperatures and sparse vegetation and game. They depended more on gathering than on hunting the basin's scarce small game and antelope and balanced on a narrow margin of subsistence in small, separated family groups. Their songs contain brilliant flashes of imagistic clarity.

The Pueblan, Yuman, Athapascan, and Uto-Aztecan speakers of the Southwestern Culture farmed and hunted in the mountains, mesas, canyons, plains, and deserts between southern Colorado and Utah and northern Mexico and between the Mojave Desert and central Texas. Desert and Pueblan farming communities depended on dry farming, hunting, and gathering. Hunting and gathering nomads, such as the Navajo and Apache, raided the farmers' fields and the cattle and sheep that had come north from Mexico. They also learned to farm and ranch. The prehistoric Anasazi, Mogollon, and Hohokam had built permanent farming communities with elaborate irrigation systems whose ruins survived and influenced the songs and myths of the Southwestern Cultures.

The Siouan, Algonkian, and Caddoan speakers of the Southeastern Woodlands hunted, gathered, and farmed in the climax forest that included coastal marshes, beaches, grasslands, plateaus, and mountain ridges and extended from the Atlantic coast to Texas's Trinity River and from Virginia to the Gulf. Most communities made their homes in villages along the rivers.

The Indians probably would not have recognized these anthropological groupings. Communities united by a common language or common customs and territory often identified themselves as "the people" or "the real people" and thought of neighbors or outsiders as enemies, at worst, or as allies.

I have organized these poems around common experiences, rather than by the ten area cultures or ten language groups. While none of these cultures or languages exactly resembled any other, and while each created its own poetry, these distinct bodies of poetry shared images, a perception of immanent Holiness, and structures adapted to performance and use in ceremony and ordinary life as well as similar histories and experiences.

The first section, "In a Sacred Manner," contains poetry that describes immanent Holiness in many of its costumes, such as songs, Holy People, daily life, and customs honored attentively. Within and behind these songs sound echoes of a time-spanning chorus of delight in the world and the creating and sustaining holiness that fills the world, the singer, and the song:

> I love my world
> I love my time
> I love my growing children
> I love my old people
> I love my ceremonies.[34]

Such songs help the singers become attentive; the holiness that quickens the singer contemplates the holiness that suffuses the universe through the holiness that fills the song.

The second section, "Thunder," evokes the visible and audible embodiments of holy power, the thunder and lightning that precede and accompany rain, fertility, growth, and survival. Thunder, and the drumming, which represented and embodied it in ceremonies that invoked the power of the Thunder-beings, accompanied lightning and thus accompanied the power the lightning represented. Lightning visibly manifested holy power: lightning embodied the Sacred Predators in hunting fetishes,[35] struck pebbles, concentrated power in them for healing or harming, and marked them for the shamans who sought them.[36]

The poems in the third section come from or allude to the narratives of "Creation and Emergence" that shaped and explained the many ceremonies that brought harmony and healing to the communities and the world. These narratives recounted the origins of the people, the Holy People, and healing and harmonizing power and identified the familiar places where the First People journeyed and where Holy Powers dwelt.

Nearly every community held ceremonies to introduce children into adulthood, men into military societies, and men and women into ceremonial societies and societies of healers. Such ceremonies stated the goals of the society, the knowledge and power the initiate gained, and the immanent holy power and harmony initiation revealed. The songs in the fourth section, "Initiation," come from or allude to such initiatory rituals.

Selfless attention to immanent Holiness brought powerful and healing dreams and visions. In such dreams and visions, avatars of the immanent Holiness revealed powerful songs, plants, and objects. Successful visionaries used the objects and plants and sang the songs, or a song that reminded them of the dream or vision, when they wished to invoke the power it conferred to heal, to hunt, to fight, to prophesy, or to seek further holy power. The songs in the fifth section, "Visions," came from or allude to these dreams and visions.

The sixth section, "The Great Ceremonies," contains poetry drawn from the recurring ceremonies that marked and ordered the annual round of life and brought power, healing, and harmony to the people and the world. Individuals, medicine lodges, or societies usually sponsored such communal ceremonies as the Cannibal, Winter, Ghost, Sun, Dream, Snake, and Antelope Dances and Diné and Midé Healing Ceremonies. Ceremonial or medicine societies produced and performed them to benefit individuals, the community, and the world. The ceremonies could last for a week or longer and sometimes included individual performances by various shamans, as well as group singing and dancing. A trance and a sudden inward gush of coolness often marked the healing the ceremonies brought. Usually they included the display of powerful relics and evoked or recounted origin or emergence stories that explained the roots and power of the ceremonies.

The Wiwan'yang Waci'pi' (Sun-Watching Dance), the "Sun Dance," exemplifies such structured ceremonies. A dream of a Thunder Being, or the desire to heal someone or acquire medicine and power, impelled a Lakota man, woman, or family to sponsor the ceremony. After purification in a sweatlodge, men selected a center pole and women prepared 100 buffalo tongues. The men, as though on a raid, surrounded, cut down, and brought a center pole back to the dance ground and built a lodge before which they prepared a patch of ground on which to put a buffalo skull and in which they made an altar. During the ceremony, dancers circled or approached and backed away from the center pole. Some dancers, after painting themselves, put sticks through muscles in their chests or backs and tied the sticks to thongs attached either to buffalo skulls or to the center pole. They danced and sang until the sticks pulled through the muscles or a medicine man ceremonially released them from their vows. Their songs also served for war, death, healing, and visions.

The Ghost Dance, later and less structured than other major ceremonies, was performed from the western plains to the Sierras. The Ghost Dancers danced as a collection of individuals to heal a world mortally infected by the European invaders. Singing songs from their individual visions, they danced themselves into trances in which they saw the spirit world, learned new songs, saw their dead relatives, and felt the sudden gush of inward coolness that accompanied healing in other ceremonies. Their visions looked back to a world uncorrupted by invaders and forward to a world renewed and disinfected.[37]

Wovoka, a Paiute visionary and shaman, developed the Ghost Dance, modeling it on his visions and a ceremony his father, Tavibo, had invented. Wovoka intended the dance to bring peace, charity, sobriety, and cultural purity. The dance spread to the plains and frightened the army and Indian agents, who feared it as a war dance, forbade it, and used it as an excuse to call in troops to crush any revival of resistance. The massacre at Wounded Knee (December 29, 1890), for which Congress awarded eighteen Congressional Medals of Honor,[38] and in which the Seventh Cavalry took revenge for Little Big Horn, suppressed the dance and ended organized armed resistance to the invasion.

The seventh section, "Medicine," contains poems that shamans, holy men and women, healers, and prophets sang to call holy power to their aid. As they sang, they sometimes entered trances, performed illustrative prestidigitation, and collaborated or competed to edify their future patients. Shamans' and vision seekers' medicine songs evoked the hunter's attentiveness to help hunt and kill disease and to call on the holiness that, wearing Holy Animals, would bring healing power in songs, herbs, stones, and shells.

Shells, herbs, lightning-struck stones, other medicine objects, and medicine bundles contained distilled holiness. The Miami gave tobacco to a medicine stone that brought luck in hunting.[39] Fetishes called buffalo[40] or deer to the hunter. Shamans "shot" pebbles, shells, fetishes, miniature arrows, and other small medicine objects into patients to heal or into enemies to kill. Some of these powerful objects helped bring consenting game and bountiful crops of corn, squash, beans, tobacco, camas bulbs, chokecherries, and piñon nuts; others, in the great ceremonies, helped heal patients and renew the universe.

Section eight, "Love," contains songs that reflect the varied masks love wore. Mothers sang lullabies. Wives lamented absent husbands; husbands, absent wives. Petrel, courting Sedna, sang romantic promises:

> Come to me.
> Come into the land of the birds
> Where there is never hunger,
> Where my tent is made of beautiful skins.
> You will have a necklace of ivory
> And sleep on the skins of bears.
> Your lamps will be always filled with oil
> And your pot full of meat.[41]

So did the bear who married a Haida woman.[42] Some love songs were less romantic; young men imitated and parodied young women, who overheard them and teased back. Some sang charms to enthrall and obsess their targets. Such charms often reflect the suspicion that love based on sexual attraction was ridiculous and dangerous, a form of the power that turned rutting animals, especially males, into slapstick comedians and easy prey.

The poems in section nine, "Hunting," suggest the hunters' skill and their selfless attention to their prey and its habitat. Hunting with short-range weapons such as rocks, curved sticks, spears and atlatls, slings, or arrows requires a concentrated attention and skill. Anyone who spends enough money on rifles, specialized ammunition, telescopic sights, and helicopter rides can slaughter a mountain sheep. To approach a mountain sheep, on foot, closely enough to use a bow and arrow or a spear and atlatl requires that the hunters vanish into the cliffs and summits that the sheep rules. They must anticipate the sheep's movements, stalk and freeze—patient, hidden, motionless.

To kill, the hunters studied the land and the prey with the objective humility and intensity of the scientist and thought deeply and attentively about stories and poems that described their prey and its motives. They learned to focus attention outward on the sheep and the land. They heard the wind and the birds, the fall of stone and water. Hunters listened for the sounds and silences that marked the sheep's approach and learned to sense when to rise, bowstring taut, to catch the sheep nearby and facing away. They hoped to hunt so attentively that they became the relatives, if not the spirit mirrors, of the prey.

Gratitude accompanied success. That a deer, so wary and perceptive that it will start at the fall of a leaf or the passing of a cloud shadow, should come close enough and hold still long enough for a hunter to place an arrow must, sometimes, have seemed unlikely. We are, after all, a noisy and clumsy species compared to deer, slow and vulnerable compared to buffalo. Although many communities thought of prey as relatives, included within elaborate ties of communal obligation, that such a swift, alert, and powerful demicousin allowed the hunter to kill it for food provoked gratitude to the deer, the universe, and the generous holiness that permeated universe, hunter, and deer.

The songs in section ten, "War," encourage enlistment, mock the reluctant, recall victories, bolster the courage of prospective raiders, and call on holy power to help the war party. They invoke the visions and medicine that bring success and state the fighters' resolve. They exult in success, propitiate dead enemies, and mourn the dead. These soldiers were not properly "warriors" (professional fighters) so much as "braves," brave men and women—husbands, wives, fathers, mothers, brothers, sisters, hunters, and farmers who fought when the occasion arose. In most communities, fighting and the discipline fighting required tended to be more or less voluntary. Warrior societies usually did not formally punish those who broke the discipline of an ambush, for example, although they might, among the Omaha, at least theoretically, kill hunters who threatened to break the discipline of the buffalo hunt and spook the herd.[43] Usually, a leader depended on his reputation and community sentiment to persuade young men to follow him.

Section eleven, "Death," contains poems that contemplate old age and the approach of death and dying, mourn the dead, free the spirit of the dead, send it on its journey to the spirit world, and speak for the freed spirit. Behind these songs lies the assumption, often expressed in imagery, that old age and death link us to our universe and the Holiness immanent in it. Old age can reconcile the soldier to death in these poems or can end a harmonious life in beauty. The songs mourn the loss of the dead. Some treat death as a link to the enduring world and a transition through which the spirit merges with immanent Holiness, in clouds and rain as a Katchina, for example, whence it can benefit its living relatives.

The poems in "Rain" (section twelve) celebrate a gift brought by Holy People wearing clouds and escorted by the avatars of immanent Holiness, Lightning and Thunder. The songs come from the ceremonies that called rain and the Rainbringers and from songs and charms that greeted approaching rain and celebrated its arrival. In these poems, rain drenches the earth with outward coolness and brings the community and the world the beauty and health that the coolness drenching their interiors brings the patients, the Ghost or Sun Dancers, the visionaries, and the dreamers.

In section thirteen, "Planting and Harvesting," the poems either come from ceremonies that invoked Holy People and holy power to make seed and fields fertile, rains propitious, and growth and harvests bountiful or reflect such ceremonies and the joy and harmony they sought.

Most of the poets who made the songs in section fourteen, "Dawn," treated the sun as a visible and powerful habitation for the Holiness that filled the universe with movement and life. An Omaha poet sang to dawn as renewing life;[44] a Pawnee, as bringing healing;[45] an Ojibwa, as bringing holy power.[46] The Iroquois poet of the Rites of Condolence identified the ability to greet dawn as a sign of a healed and cleared mind.[47] For healers, dawn confirmed healing. For participants in ceremonies, dawn completed the healing and harmony the ceremonies brought to the people and the world.

LATE EIGHTEENTH, nineteenth, and early twentieth century singers, anthropologists, ethnographers, and poets collaborated to sing, record, transcribe, translate, and print classical North American Indian literature, in the original languages and in translation. Much classical North American Indian literature survived because of the work of Henry Rowe Schoolcraft, Frances Densmore, Alice Cunningham Fletcher, Francis La Flésche, Ella Deloria, Frank Russell, Washington Matthews, Matilda Cox Stevenson, and, more recently, Lawrence Evers, Carobeth Laird, and Donald M. Bahr. They were able to preserve a fraction of the songs the singers knew. One singer, a member of the Turquoise Society, recorded 127 songs. He remarked that he knew twice as many as he recorded. Another singer, from the Northwest Coast, recorded 12 songs of the 80 he knew. This singer said that every member of his 1,000-strong community knew as many songs as he did. Many poems disappeared with his generation. Still, though much was lost, much survives.

No scholar speaks all of the languages in which classical North American Indian songs have survived; thus anyone reading poetry from more than a few of the languages will perforce read translations. The translations vary. The reader who welcomes the variants as offering additional insight into the poetry will usually find the most delight in the poems.

Many of the singers who repeated and varied the laconic verses that formed many of the songs also explained their meanings. Sometimes those who recorded, translated, and printed the songs put the explanations in footnotes; sometimes they incorporated the explanations as expansions in their translations. Alice Fletcher included such expansions in her translation of Tahirassuwichi's version of the Pawnee *Hako*: "[this] English version contains nothing which is not in the original text *explained and amplified by the Ku'rahus*."[48] Others also incorporated details from the singer's explanations into their translations.[49] Such incorporations stated the details that repeated phrases and verses called up for the original audience. These expansions produced varied translations of the same song.

When translators tried to produce in English the beauty they saw in the original poems, they used models they admired. If they admired Romantic and Victorian poetry, as did Schoolcraft and Eloise Streit, they used the techniques and diction of the Victorians and Romantics. If they admired imagists, they used imagist techniques. Thus translations of the same poem can differ noticeably. For example, translators have made several versions of Mary Warren English's Ojibwa song, which may have descended from a seventeenth-century original. Translations vary widely in detail and length, ranging from Schoolcraft's 208-word expansion, through Walter James Hoffman's 114 words, Frederick Russell Burton's 91, Densmore's 78, Burton's 54-word adaptation, to Gerald Vizenor's 12 words. Most of these versions offer details and insights that the others do not and reflect, at one or more removes, the explanations the singers of the originals gave. The different versions hint at some of the depth and richness the Ojibwa song implied to the Ojibwa audience.

Since no English translations reproduce the original poems' harmony and rhetorical ingenuity, I sought translations that state simply and clearly the song's surface and that, like imagist poems or haiku, let the reader collaborate with the song and sense the currents that flow beneath the transparent surface. To make reading easy and clear, I sometimes changed wording, adding "banking" to "tilting wings" and changing "flapping" to "beating" in a Nez Perce poem,[50] for instance, or changed a passive to an active construction. The notes will lead the interested reader to original translations and sources.

North American Indian poetry did not die with the reservation and acculturation, of course. Recently Indian poets have served as shock troops in defending their culture. Poets such as Carter Revard, Emerson Black-horse Mitchell, Kimberly Blaeser, Bruce Ignacio, and Simon Ortiz, to mention a few among many, incorporate classical attentiveness into new songs. They do so in modern forms and contexts, however, and thus work beyond the scope of this collection.

That reader will enjoy classical North American Indian poetry most who reads with an attentiveness resembling the vision seeker's attentiveness, which Nicholas Black Elk recommended to his adopted son, Joseph E. Brown: "[Wachin ksapa yo!]—'Be attentive!'— . . . in every act, in every thing and in every instant, [holiness] is present, and . . . one should be continually and intensely 'attentive' to this [holiness]."[51]

I, the Song

In a Sacred Manner

Modoc

> I,
> the song,
> I walk here![1]

꙳ SINGERS: Mary, Minnie Froben. In this shaman's song, song and singer merge. The song, visible in the singer's breath on chilly mornings or after ceremonially smoking, wears the breath and the singer. Sometimes, song, singer, the Holy Person who gave the vision, and the song that sprang from the vision merge. Walking about, the shaman becomes the song. The singer changes shape in "I, the dog, I walk here!" and, like the continental trickster, Coyote, embodies motion as well as the song and the medicine-power the song brings to bear.[2] These songs, heard and sung rather than read, presuppose action (walking, singing, healing). The notion that a word can exist without the action of speaking, singing, dancing, or healing springs from written language. In written literatures, we see words static and isolated from action, frozen on a page. Aural (heard) literature always implies a speaker or singer. Thus, orally generated origin stories tend not to begin, for example, "Verbum in principio erat . . ." but "Walking about as usual, Coyote saw . . ."

Dakota

> It was a protection predicted for me! (2)
> > A wind wears me!
> > Behold it!
> > It is Sacred![3]

꙳ Lone Man sang this during the Heyo'ka Ka'ga (Fool Impersonation Ceremony). It is stanza 1 of 4. Stanza 2 substitutes *wasu'cha,* hail; stanza 3, *wakan'glicha,* lightning; stanza 4, *malipi'ya,* clouds, for *tate'wan,* wind. A singer sponsored this ceremony after dreaming of Thunder or the Thunder Beings. Holiness, as the elements, wears the singer in the dream and while

3

singing, just as a shaman wears and commands a medicine bird skin or as the song wears the singer in the preceding Modoc song.

Nuchalnulth

Sing your song
Looking up at the sky![4]

༝ Toak, a cheerful old blind woman, sang this song and heartened her listeners. The song implies the sun's warmth on Toak's face as a tangible form of the immanent Holiness in the world.

A'nish'inabeg

My music reaches
To the sky.[5]

༝ SINGER: Ga'tcitcigi'cig. Singers sang this favorite, an archaic song, just before starting a dance. The song rises to the sky and carries the singer to the Holy Powers.

Potawatomi

1.   Everybody sings, (3)
Sings with this world,
With the wind, with the water.
You can hear the water roar.
I sing in the wind, sing to be heard.
I strike my drum. It sings in this world.
I shake my gourd. It sings too.
2. We all sing and dance,
Dance thanksgiving that we have lived so long.
So I sing in the water, sing in the air,
Sing with my drum, sing with my gourd.
We all sing in this roaring water,
As we hear it roar, roar, roar.
3. The Great Manido will help us
Singing, singing, singing!
Singing in this world.[6]

༝ Song 6 from the Human Medicine Bundle Chant. The song, the singer, the dance, and the dancer merge with the holiness that fills the world and delight in that wholeness and unity.

A'nish'inabeg   An overhanging cloud
                            Repeats my words pleasingly![7]

             ꜱ   SINGER: Ki'miwun. A Vision Song.

Inuit   Delightful, the animals,
                            There is no song about them.
                            Words for a song are hard to find—
                            Seals on the ice, down here—
                            When I found a few words
                            I fit them to music—
                            The seals left for their breathing holes.
                            Delightful, the animals,
                            There is no song about them.
                            Words hard to catch—
                            Antlered caribou on the land, down here—
                            When I found a few words
                            I fit them to music—
                            When they crossed the plains.
                            Delightful, the animals,
                            There is no song about it.
                            Words hard to catch—
                            Bearded seals on the ice down here—
                            When I found a few words
                            I fit them to music—
                            When they left for their breathing holes.[8]

             ꜱ   SINGER: Kenusa. A Dance Song.

Potawatomi   Now we all move, moving with this earth.
                            The earth moves, the water moves,
                            The grass moves, the trees, the whole earth moves.
                            We move in time with the earth.[9]

             ꜱ   Stanza 1 of Human Medicine Bundle Chant 1. During this dance, the
                  earth, the water, and the whole world join the dancers.

Inuit

The great sea has set me adrift.
It sways me, like weed in a great river.
Earth and Great Weather move me,
Have carried me away
And shake me inwardly with joy![10]

SINGER: Uvavnuk. This song dependably sent Uvavnuk, a woman shaman, into a trance. She received the song when a ball of fire (a meteor) descended, entered her, filled her with light (the spirit of the meteor), and made her a shaman. The song invokes two Holy Persons, Earth and Great Weather. Such songs, and the healing rituals in which they figured, intoxicated the listeners with joy and led them to admit and forgive sins and relinquish grudges. Such a ritual led participants to see their fellows through a joy that resembles the Diné *hoz'hoh* (Beauty, Harmony). This joy caused them to see and act in harmony. The Ojibwa held a similar ceremonial confession and cleansing.[11]

Konhiak

I am not the waves of the sea,
 Though my branches bend and straighten
  In the wind.[12]

SINGER: Santo Blanco. An Eel Grass Song from the Women's Ceremonies. Eel grass ripened before other plants in the spring. The Seri feasted on this first ripe spring food. Women wearing eel grass crowns sang this song while thrashing eel grass seed with ocotillo poles.

Tohono Au'autam

A black snake goes toward the west.
It travels erect on its tail.
It sings as it goes to the west
And coils around a mountain.[13]

SINGER: Sivariano Garcia. A Vision Song. The original singer took a dream journey, met an Apache he had killed, learned songs to cure the Koop sickness that unpropitiated spirits of dead Apache warriors caused, and gained medicine. He made this song himself. Many songs and stories identify whirlwinds as ghosts. In another Papago song, the snake has become a rain-bringing tornado:

A serpent hangs from the sky with his head over the sea.
  He sways his head to and fro, singing.[14]
The snake wearing a funnel cloud will, when it hits land, bring lots of rain.
This song has turned the dustdevil containing the threatening ghost of the
Apache into a beneficent, if dangerously powerful, rain-bringing tornado.

O'maha

There, wind-spun, I send him!
Going there, wind-spun, I send him!
To the four hills, standing,
  And the four winds!
Amid the winds he goes. I send him.
Amid the Four Winds, standing!
  Ihn! Ihn!
  (Thunder, Thunder.)[15]

Thiku'winxe Turning [the Child] Ceremony, song 2. Four groups of cele-
brants, in cyclonic sequence, take the child and turn him cyclonically at
each of the sacred directions and thus introduce the child, or a candidate
for initiation, to the Holy Powers.[16] The sponsors take the child through
the whirlwinds to a second birth. The whirlwind often evokes death and
rebirth, the dizziness that precedes a vision, and the spirit of the dead. In
the Ghost Dance, whirlwinds led to visions of the reborn earth; whirlwinds
led the Papago scalp-taker to ritual cleansing and rebirth.

Tohono Au'autam

From the west a white wind is coming out.
Stand there and look. It is not near.
It is beside the ocean. There you will see it.
By the reflected light of the sun, you will see it.[17]

SINGER: Harry Encinas. Sung by a Sun Medicine man to other medicine
men searching for a poison tube. Helped by the sun, he could see, as in a
vision, the poison tube (a poison device, planted by an evil shaman to
sicken a village) at a great distance.

Inuit

I see great Mount Kunak to the south!
I watch great Mount Kunak to the south!
I watch the clouds' shining brightness to the south.

Their brightness expands around Mount Kunak
And covers Kunak toward the sea!
Look! The bright clouds shift and change in the South!
See! They reflect beauty to each other in the South.
From the sea they wrap Mount Kunak in bright, changing sheets!
Look, billowing from the sea, they make each other beautiful.[18]

꒰   Arsut's Song. Shape-changing clouds here suggest shape-changing Thunder Beings and Holy People. This song merges the unchanging mountain and the shifting cloud; the lightning-throwing Thunder Beings and the cloud-splitting Grandfather Rock.

Tohono Au'autam

A white mountain far away
At earth's edge stands beautiful!
It has brilliant white arches of light bending to earth![19]

꒰   SINGER: Sivariano Garcia. An Apache spirit led the dreamer on a journey during which he learned powerful songs. Two owl feathers sang this song to him, telling him his journey would end on this side of the mountains. A white mountain suggests snowy peaks and clouds.

A'nish'inabeg

Great piles of clouds
Where I look![20]

꒰   SINGER: Ki'miwuna'nakwad (Rain Cloud). Compare Gerald Vizenor, *Anishinabe Nogamon,* 53.

Diné

1. I am the Slayer of Alien Gods.
   Wherever I wander, before me white forests scatter.
   Lightning scatters them, but I cause it.
2. I am the Child of the Water.
   Wherever I wander, I leave white waters scattered behind me.
   The tempest scatters them, but I cause it.[21]

꒰   Nayenezgani (Monster Killer, Elder Brother, Slayer of Alien Gods), like Ma'ii and the Thunder Beings, converts monsters and wields wind and lightning. The white inner bark of a lightning-blasted tree or forest marks his passage. To'bad'is'ki'ni (Younger Brother) helps him rid the world of dangers and monsters. Dark Thunder and Blue Thunder sing a similar song in Waterway.[22]

Micmac

Death I make, singing! Hey ey-yeh!
Bones I hack, singing!
Death I make, singing![23]

☙ A vengeance song, according to Mary Austin. This song merges singer, song, and arrow in "I," as the medicine song merges singer, song, and power in "I, the Song" above. Silas T. Rand, *Legends of the Micmacs,* collected and published Micmac legends and myths.

Diné

That flowing water! That flowing water!
    My mind wanders across it.
That broad water! That flowing water!
    My mind wanders across it.
That old age water! That flowing water!
    My mind wanders across it.[24]

☙ A hero-hunter, Dsilyi' Neyani, sang this song, looking north across the San Juan River, having disobeyed two instructions: do not hunt to the south and look in the direction you hunt. He looked north to the La Platas (Depenitsa) and his family, sang this song, and attracted the attention of the Holy People, who sent him to be a captive of the Utes.

A'nish'inabeg

In the middle of the sea,
    The vast sea,
    There I sit![25]

☙ SINGER: Na'jobi'tun. The singer, personating a water spirit, a mist, fog, or cloud, or perhaps an otter or snake, sang this song when initiating a candidate into a Midé (medicine fraternity) lodge.

Tohono Au'autam

The morning star is up.
I cross the mountains into the light of the sea![26]

ᴿ   SINGER: Sivariano Garcia. Owl Woman sang this Healing Song toward
morning after a night-long healing session.

Diné

I am the white corn boy.
I walk in sight of my home.
I walk in plain sight of my home.
I walk on the straight path that is toward my home.
I walk to the entrance of my home.
I arrive at the beautiful goods curtain that hangs at the doorway.
I arrive at the entrance of my home.
I am in the middle of my home.
I am at the back of my home.
I am on top of the pollen footprint.
I am on top of the pollen seed print.
I am like the Most High Power Whose Ways Are Beautiful.
Before me, beauty.
Behind me, beauty.
Beneath me, beauty.
Above me, beauty.
All around me it is beautiful.[27]

ᴿ   San'hode'di Begay (Beggar Woman's Son), the son of the Sun, who re-
created the medicine the Gambler took with him when he left the fourth
world, sang this song. The song ends in a beauty and peace resembling the
Inuit medicine woman's "intoxication of joy," which envelops and infuses
those who perceive and act "in a sacred manner," who contemplate the
immanent Holiness with which the Holy People have surrounded and suf-
fused them.

Tewa

Oh Mother Earth, Father Sky!
Your children are we and with tired backs we bring you the gifts you love.
Then weave for us a garment of brightness.
May the warp be the white light of morning.
May the weft be the red light of evening.
May the fringes be the falling rain.
May the border be the standing rainbow.
Weave us a garment of brightness that we may walk fittingly where grass is green.
Oh Mother Earth, Oh Father Sky![28]

ᔓ The warp and weft of the sky loom evoke the fringe of rain that trails from a thunderhead in the Southwest. Merging weaving and coming rain, the images emphasize holiness as continually creating blessing. Plains tribes used another image for the trailing rain: hair trailing down.

Tohono Au'autam

I am on my way running.
I am on my way running.
Looking toward me is the edge of the world.
I am trying to reach it.
The edge of the world does not look far away.
To that I am on my way running.[29]

ᔓ SINGER: Ciko. Ciko dreamed this song, sung in the Wakita, the girls' puberty dance held after ritual isolation. This ritual run toward the horizon brings medicine similar to the medicine brought by the vision quest or salt pilgrimage and reenacts the sun's daily race across the sky.

*Cumberland Sound
Inuit*

Aja, I am joyful! This is good!
Aja, Only ice around me: good!
Aja, I am joyful! This is good!
My country, only slush! Good!
   That is good!
Aja, I am joyful! This is good!
Aja, When, indeed, will this end?
   That is good!
I am tired of watching and waiting!
   That is good![30]

ᔓ Utitiaq, adrift for a week in pack ice when seal hunting, made and sang this song, deliberately seeing and enhancing the immanent goodness in slush and ice. He could see this world in what Black Elk called a "sacred manner." A Haida singer likewise saw and called on the immanent Holiness in his world:

   Ocean Spirit, calm the waves for me
   Get close to me, my power! My heart is tired.
   Make the sea like milk for me!
   Yeho, yeho![31]

Dakota

> The Great Grandfather has said, they say,
> "Dakotas, be citizens," he said, they say.
>   But it will be impossible for me.
> "The Dakota ways, I love them," I said.
> Therefore I have helped to keep up the old ways.[32]

SINGER: Holy Face Bear. The president of the United States, Tunka'shinayapi, contrasts with one of the holiest powers, Grandfather Rock or Mountain, Tunka'shila. The president invited the Dakota to become a *wasichu*. Grandfather Rock gives the power to remain Dakota and live in a sacred manner, following Dakota ways.

Thunder

◌ II

Konhiak

The wind begins
Far off in the sea.
And it blows cold over here
And all over the monte.[1]

◌   SINGER: Santo Blanco. A Wind Song, sung very slowly.

Tlingit

Over there, southeast,
Out to sea, invisible,
It sounds, the Thunder.
You, behind the mountains,
Help us, I beg you,
You, the Thunder.[2]

◌   SINGER: Mrs. Chester Johnson. Mrs. Johnson's mother, a Peace Hostage, sang this Thunderbird Blanket Song at a Peace ceremony in 1907.

Tohono Au'autam

Close to the West, the great Ocean is singing!
The waves are rolling toward me, covered with many clouds!
Even here, I catch the sound.
The earth is shaking beneath me and I hear the deep rumbling.[3]

◌   SINGER: Mattias Encinas. A Rain and Bountiful Harvest (Viikita) Song heard in a dream. Conductors of the Viikita ceremony swung bull roarers, fourteen-inch wooden blades on three-foot ropes, to sound like thunder and assemble dancers.

A'a'tam A'kimult

1. Wind now
   Begins to sing! (2)

13

There, before me,
The land stretches, stretches away before me.
2. Wind's house thunders! (2)
   I roar over the land,
   The land beneath Thunder.
3. Over the windy mountains, (3)
   The centipede wind rippled,
   The wind came running!
4. The Black Snake Wind, (2)
   A song, came running
   And coiled round me![4]

SINGER: Ha-ata. The singer repeated each stanza, repeated lines 2 to the end twice, and then went on to the next stanza.

A'nish'inabeg

From the half of the sky
That which lives there
Is coming and makes a noise.[5]

SINGER: Ga'gandac'. The song came from a dream in which the dreamer heard Thunder, in the sky-half of the universe, warn him of a storm. Someone with friendly intentions made noise as he approached. Hearing the noise, the host put tobacco on the fire, as a reciprocal sign of friendship. Thunder acted like a friendly stranger in this dream. Another friendly "Hello, the House!":

Who sits on the ice
Can hear me singing.[6]

After his vision, Black Elk felt "happy, as though somebody were coming to visit me," when a thunderstorm approached.[7]

Numa

On the peak of the mountain
   The eagle dances,
   The storm bellows.[8]

SINGER: Chuar-ru-um-pik.

Salish

It makes a noise across
   The echo.[9]

ꝫ   SINGER: James Percival. A Sqaip (Tutelary, Guardian Spirit) Song.

Kwagutl

1. Diving from the sky, the Power,
   Striking a whole tribe,
2. Stooping from the sky, the Power,
   Diving, burning the villages,
       Killing all before,
       Heaping the dead,
       Tearing the prey,
   You, Thunderbird,
   Thunderer from Heaven,
3. Stooping from the sky, Power,
   You strike tribe after tribe,
   Gripping the chiefs in your talons.[10]

Bana'kwut

1. He, Thunder, angry
   Because earth parches, dry earth bakes,
   Wants to wet the dried-up earth!
2. He, Thunder, the Rain Chief,
   Lives on the cloud-base.
3. He carries frost;
   Thunder Magician looks like a badger,
   Rain Magician, he, Thunder.
4. He digs through to the sky, lifts his head;
   Then clouds, then rain, then earth, growling comes;
   Thunder comes, lightning comes, snarling comes.
5. He, Badger, alone, white-striped nose,
   Back white-striped.
6. He, the true Badger, the Badger alone,
   The Badger only.
7. He, Thunder Magician,
   Dislikes dried-up earth,
   Hates scratching through it,
   Hates clawing through it.
8. Lifting his snout to the sky,
   Raising his head,
   He makes rain come, wets the earth.[11]

ꝫ   This song merges clouds striped with lightning flashes and the badger's white stripes, the rumbling and snarling of thunder and the badger's growling and snarling. The badger snarls and threatens so plausibly that it has convinced grizzlies to back off, since a fight would be more trouble than winning would be worth.

Diné

My moccasins are black obsidian!
My leggings are black obsidian!
My shirt is black obsidian!
I am girded with a black arrow-snake.
Black snakes go up from my head.
With zigzag lightning darting out from the ends of my feet, I step!
With zigzag lightning streaming out from my knees, I step!
With zigzag lightning streaming from the tip of my tongue, I speak!
Now a disk of pollen rests on the crown of my head.
Gray arrow-snakes and rattlesnakes eat it.
Black obsidian and zigzag lightning streams out from me in four ways!
Where they strike the earth, bad things, bad talk does not like it!
It causes the missiles to spread out.
Long Life, something frightful I am. Now I am!
There is danger where I move my feet. I am whirlwind!
There is danger where I move my feet. I am a gray bear!
When I walk, where I step, lightning flies from me!
Where I walk, one to be feared I am!
Where I walk, Long Life, one to be feared I am!
    There is danger where I walk![12]

Shash, the bear who growls this song, perhaps an avatar of Nayenezgani, accompanied the grandchildren of Etsan'etli on their journey to their homeland and sang this song before attacking the Red Arrow People, who planned to kill the Diné. The song alludes to the characteristics of fetishes made of black obsidian. The maker usually binds a small arrowhead to the back of the bear fetish and sets in blue turquoise for eyes and a jagged line of red coral leading from mouth to heart. The song also suggests ceremonial elements, such as pollen, and the shape-shifting and metaphysical ambiguity that linked good and evil, healing and withcraft, in the Shash, bear, as whirlwind. Bears going underground, hibernating, and emerging in the spring embodied rebirth as well as medicine and long life. Gray may mean grizzled or grizzly.

Kwagutl

> I am the Thunder of my people,
> I am the Sea Monster of my people,
> I am the Earthquake of my people,
>> When I start to fly
> Thunder resounds through the world.
>> When I rage
> The voice of the Sea Bear
> Rumbles through the world.[13]

ᵔ   This War Song invokes the ceremonial masks the people own, as well as the Holy People who lend their powers to the masks and their owners.

Walwarena

> Look! Listen!
>> He grunts on high.
>> The ground shakes.
> At night he makes a noise like thunder.
>> 'I yaka mi ha mi.[14]

ᵔ   A song from the Bear Dance. The singers greatly respected the bear.

Potawatomi

> When you see clouds descend, think of Warrior Chief's flash.
> When Warrior Chief flashes in the clouds, they say,
> "His eyes flash, his flashing eyes!"
> When Thunder roars, that bares them all,
> Those on the side of the road, those who've hidden.
> They hate Warrior Chief's roar.
> That's how Warrior Chief warns them he is coming.[15]

ᵔ   Stanza 2 of the Warrior Medicine Bundle Chant. The medicine bundle chants formed parts of healing fraternity ceremonies and also preceded the public display of the medicine bundle.

Siksika

> I am Iron voice.
> I do not heed.
> Other voiced Thunders heed.[16]

ᵔ   SINGER: Wolf Collar. Prose version: "Brother, I am reckless. I do not listen. I kill anything." Sung by a Young Thunder to a dreamer as a Medicine Song. It cures people struck by lightning.

Tsimshian

> We hear only its large voice,
> A voice like a great brightness!
> The Raven Drum has returned,
>   The Great Cawing,
> The great Voice of the Raven,
>   Covered with pearls!
> Ahead of me, the large voice,
> Nothing but the large voice![17]

꙳   SINGER: Kweenu. This dirge of the Raven Drum Crest alludes to the picture of the raven on the drum played to accompany the song.

Maklaks

> I, Thunder,
> Rumble in the earth.[18]

꙳   SINGERS: Mary of the Klamath Agency School, Minnie Froben. The shaman sang this song when pouring water on the patient.

Tewa

> Far away, in Red River mountains and valleys,
> Buffalo Old Woman, Buffalo Old Man, rise!
> With all your people, get up quickly!
>   With your clouds, rise!
>   With your lightnings, rise!
>   With your thunder, rise!
>   With your rain, rise![19]

꙳   San Ildefonso Buffalo Dance in late January.

A'a'tam A'kimult

> Earth rumbles, Earth rumbles
>   As we beat our basket drums!
> Earth rumbles, everywhere humming!
> Earth rumbles, Earth rumbles
>   As we beat our basket drums!
> Earth rumbles, everywhere raining!
> Pluck the primaries from the Eagle's wing!
>   Point them east,
> Where the large clouds tower,
> Pluck down from the Eagle!

Point it east,
Where the small clouds soar,
It thunders beneath the rain-gods' house there,
   There large corn stands!
It rains beneath the rain-gods' house there,
   Small corn stands there!
   Hitciya yahina-a.[20]

꒱ SINGER: Ka'mal Tkak. The singer sang lines 1–6, repeated lines 2–6, then lines 1–6, lines 1–9, repeated 2–9, and then sang 10 to the end. Paiute thunder and lightning songs also invoke the power of the thunder and Thunder Beings to bring rain.

O'maha

   Grandfather Thunder! far above on high,
The hair, like a shadow, passes before you!
   Grandfather Thunder! far above on high,
Dark like a shadow, the hair sweeps before you
Into the midst of your realm!
   Grandfather Thunder! far above on high,
Dark like a shadow, the hair passes before you.
   Grandfather! dwelling afar on high,
Dark like a shadow, the hair sweeps before you
Into the midst of your realm!
   Grandfather! far above on high,
The hair, like a shadow, passes before you![21]

꒱ This image of hair evokes the picture (more common on the western plains and southwestern deserts than in the East) of drifts of rain dropping from the base of a thunderhead in the distance. The lock of hair also suggests a scalplock, a war-honor and symbol of life, offered to the Thunder Beings to gain protection for a child. Ghost Dancers wore two crow feathers that the spirits grasped to carry the wearer to the spirit world. The dancers tied these feathers to the scalplock. The Sioux pictured Wakan power as a series of wavy lines radiating up from the head. They also used the hand, palm forward, fingers up, moved upward in a spiral to represent Wakan power, in sign language.[22]

Chahiksichahiks

"Child, this that is is good, (2)
This good is yours,

Take it,"
Thunder said quietly, speaking quietly,
"This good is yours."[23]

∽   SINGERS: Effie Blain, Eagle. A War Song. A young man, afraid of thunder,
wept and dreamt that Thunder spoke to him slowly and quietly, saying,
"Don't fear, your father is coming." Thunder then sang this song, which
the boy learned and later sang on war parties. Eagle sang a simpler version
as a War Song.

Maklaks

This is my own, a little boy's song.
    About the thunder I sing now.[24]

∽   SINGER: Sergeant Morgan.

Aa'shi'wi

From where you abide permanently
Your little wind-blown clouds,
Your thin wisps of cloud,
Your hanging stripes of cloud,
Your massed clouds, replete with living waters,
You will send forth to stay with us.
They will come out standing on all sides.
With your fine rain caressing the earth,
With your weapons, the lightning,
With your rumbling thunder,
Your great crashes of thunder,
With your fine rain caressing the earth,
Your heavy rain caressing the earth,
With your great pile of waters here at Itiwana,
With these you will pass us on our roads.[25]

∽   Sung to the Rainbringing Holy People during the monthly offering of
prayer sticks.

Takelma

    Get away from here
With your camas-digging stick.
    Pass from here!
Go to the Mountains

With your sifting pan!
Pass away to Mount Amol'mxadu
    With your camas-stick!
Don't come here with it, not here!
Perhaps your children touch dead peoples' bones
    With their feet.[26]

    This Woman's Song drives off a storm. The digging stick uproots and overthrows camas stalks; the storm, trees. The sifting pan sifts camas root meal; the storm, clouds, and snow.

A'nish'inabeg

Truly the sky clears,
When my Midé drum rumbles for me!
Truly the waters are smooth,
When my Midé drum thunders for me![27]

    SINGER: Gegwe'djiwe'binun'. The medicine drum makes a thunder that smoothes rather than enrages the waters. In the accompanying pictograph in Schoolcraft's edition, a rainy sky arches over a man, standing between two quiet lakes, holding a drum.

Inuit

Ija-ija!
A mighty storm passes around me!
    Ija-ija!
Quiet and smooth lies my sea-path.
    Ija-ija!
What smooths my way before me?
    Ija-ija!
Out of danger, I paddle in quiet water!
    Ija-ija![28]

    An Angmagssalik charm for good weather. The charm appeals to Great Weather, the spirit of the air, to create the condition the singer wanted.

Diné

Thona! Thona!
    A'aaiiyehe oohe. (2)
A voice above, Thunder's voice!
    Within the dark cloud,

Over and over his moving voice sounds!
　Thona! Thona!
　A'aaiiyehe oohe. (2)
　Thona! Thona!
　A'aaiiyehe oohe. (2)
A voice below, Grasshopper's voice!
　Among the plants,
Over and over his moving voice sounds!
　Thona! Thona!
　A'aaiiyehe oohe. (2)[29]

ᴓ   The twelfth Thunder Song in the Mountain Chant. The song summons a rainlike blessing and describes the rain that heals the dry earth with cooling water as the inner coolness heals the patient. The grasshopper sings in many rain and healing songs.

Siehwib-ag

How beautiful they come.
The Rain Gods make a sound up above.
How beautiful! How beautiful!
　That is so.
That is why the raingods will travel
　This year!
How beautiful! That is so!
That is why the rain will fall
　This year!
How beautiful! That is so![30]

ᴓ   SINGER: Anthony Lucero (Pawi'tla).

Shis-Inde

There he runs along!
　Now, Water Youths, to you they start,
They start to you, Water Youths.
　There we are coming,
Water Youths are coming, coming right upstream.
　Fog youths are coming,
In front of the fog, they come.
Where the water stands up straight, next to him,
　The water people come to us.
With water-downy feathers as their feathers,

They come to us!
Holding lightning in their hands.
They come to us![31]

SINGER: Frank Crockett's father.

Tlingit

It always makes me lonesome
When I hear the thunder.
I always think of my brothers
When I hear the thunder.[32]

SINGERS: Goxaq, Mrs. Chester Johnson. Mrs. Johnson's mother sang this Thunderbird Blanket Song at the Peace ceremony in 1907, when she was a Peace Hostage. The mythical boy Goxaq, captured by Thunderbirds, escaped and built a house decorated like the Thunderbirds' Cave. He sang this mourning song.

Shis-Inde

Thus speaks the earth's thunder:
Because of it there is good about you,
Because of it your body is well:
Thus speaks the earth's thunder.[33]

This song blesses the east-facing dancers in the Girls' Puberty Rite.

III   *Creation and Emergence*

Maidu

My world, where one travels by the valley edge,
    My world of many mountains,
My world where one zigzags here and there,
    Range after range.[1]

SINGER: Tom Young. Coyote sings of the as yet uncreated world in which he will travel.

Inuit

Let me remember them,
Call to mind the lands I have reached,
Since I am not trying to find game.
The river Kugyuaq and Pingoq hill,
The river Ukpilik and Kissigaq,
Usungnaqsiorvik and muddy Isoqtoq,
Maqiqsarvik and Mangaqtorvik.[2]

SINGER: Isyagotailaq. A Dance Song.

Diné

Sun's face will be blue.
His eye marks will be black.
His mouth mark will be black.
A level yellow mark will cross his cheek.
His horns will be blue.
He placed it in the sky with a mirage![3]

First Man, First Woman, and Young Wind sing this song while making a sand-painting of the Sun, which they set in the sky when they finish.

24

Lenape   There at the edge of the water, where land ends,
                               Fog was plentiful over the Earth,
                               And there the Great Spirit, the Creator, stays.
                               It began to be invisible, everywhere,
                               Even where the Great Spirit stayed.
                               He created much land here,
                               As well as land on the other side of the water.
                               He created the sun, and the stars of night.
                               All these He created so they might move.
                               Accompanying these good deeds, the wind blew,
                               The sky cleared, and water rippled in many places.
                               All looked bright, for He made islands,
                               And having done so, He remained.
                               Then again, the Great Spirit, a manito,
                               Created manitos, and persons who die,
                               And souls for all of them.
                               Thereafter, He was Manito to young men,
                               To full-grown men, and their Grandfathers.
                               He gave the first mother, mother of persons.
                               He gave fish, turtles, animals, birds.
                               But another powerful manito created powerful men
                               And these water monsters.
                               He created flies and mosquitoes.
                               Everybody behaved, seeing friends everywhere,
                               And was happy, staying with the manitos.[4]

          ᣎ   The "powerful men" created by the second manito were probably magi-
                 cians and shamans.

Kwagutl   What of olden times (2)
                               Shall I tell you, my grandchildren,
                                  Tell you of olden times? (2)
                                  Cloud lay on mountains![5]

          ᣎ   This spell caused cannibal giants to fall asleep.

Noam-Kekhl   This rock did not come here by itself.
                               This tree does not stand here of itself.

There is one who made all this,
Who shows us everything.[6]

꙳ From the last day of the seven-day Kichil-woknam (Obsidian-Initiation).
The shaman presiding gave sleight-of-hand performances after boys' first
drink of water after the ceremony.

Kwatsan

 Howling Coyote took up common dirt
And scattered it toward the sky!
He caused the dirt to become
 Stars and the rainbow.[7]

꙳ SINGER: Alfred Golding. Kwichana Akwa'k (Deer Dance), song 71. Coyote
did not try to sing, but ridiculed those who did, when the First Deer
called for songs and creating power from all the animal spirits.

Salish

Black Bear: Long shall be daylight;
  Darkness long.
Ant: Brief shall be daylight;
  Darkness brief.[8]

꙳ SINGER: John Jack. Ant prevented darkness from lasting six months when
Ant won the contest with Bear.

Tlingit

Raven went up to the head of the Nass
 And stole daylight.
 Pretty soon (2)
He's going to break that box open.[9]

꙳ SINGERS: Frank Italio, Minnie Johnson. One of the Stealing Daylight
Songs. Raven stole daylight and will break open the box holding it.

Nuxalk

My child perished like the sky when it broke.
Go to S'qlwalo'sem of the sky, my child!
Gladden my heart, my child,
Sit down in the mouth of the sky, my child![10]

ꮥ Ku'siut Song. The Guardians put too much wood into their fire and made the sky burst. The sun stopped. Nasnasaka'nix glued the sky back together and wedged a piece of sky into an opening to hold it open for firewood. The sky will not burst again.

Tohono Au'autam

I suffered to the bottom of my heart!
But at last I created a great deal of wind
And at last I created many clouds,
So now I am singing for joy.[11]

ꮥ SINGER: Matthias Hendricks. Elder Brother sang this after creating clouds and winds.

Achomawi

Foam, drift to me!
Bring Foam to me, Wind:
Waves, bring Foam to me.[12]

ꮥ During the Creation, Apponahah, Butterfly Man, sings this song to call Foam, which later becomes earth. The wind and waves drift foam to Apponahah; Foam draws along wind and wave as it drifts to Apponahah.

Hamakhav

I am stirring it around. (2)
It will be dry land. (2)[13]

ꮥ SINGER: Joe Homer. Kwikumat, the Creator, sings this song.

Maidu

In the long, long ago,
Robin Man made the world,
Stuck earth together,
Making this world.[14]

ꮥ SINGER: Tom Young. Robin's Song. Robin Holy Person made a nest. Earthmaker found the nest and built the world on it.

Inuit

Waters become smooth now! (2)
I am hunting for Sod. (2)

Sod, come close to me.
I must spear you
To give land to my people.
O, Sod, come closer.
O, Sod, come within reach of my spear.
O, Sod, become wide land.
O, Sod, let there be room for all.
O, my people, watch me spear Sod.
Come up, O Sod. Come up! (2)
Come up, for the last time, O Sod![15]

ᢂ Raven, creating land, sang this song, modeled on a hunting charm, to the
Holy Person, Sod, who came floating by like a whale. Raven hunted Sod
as the Inuit would a whale and made land for the Kobuk. In the tundra,
the layer of earth above the permafrost resembles sod or turf.

Maklaks

"I take the earth up in my arms
    And whirl it around in a dance!"
On this earth I stand and sing this song.[16]

Ta'n-ta'wats

Where water seeps,
Water, through a valley,
Seeps through a valley.[17]

ᢂ SINGERS: Pete Chile, George Laird. Deer Song fragment. The Deer Song
recounted a journey through the rolling hilly country east of the Colorado
River. Songs such as the Salt, Deer, and Mountain Sheep Songs took all
night, recounted a trip along the boundaries of a hunting territory, and
recapitulated the emergence journeys of the Holy People.

Hamakhav

This is the water, my water.
This is the river, my river.
    We love its water.
    We love its driftwood,
    Its foam wood.
It shall flow forever, (2)
When the weather grows hot,

It will rise and overflow its banks,
It shall flow forever.[18]

    SINGER: Joe Homer. The Yuma Creator sings this when creating rivers.

Karuk

You have been still there for a long, long time.
You will make the power stay fast
And there will be plenty of salmon.[19]

    SINGER: Shan Davis. This prayer, during the World Renewal Ceremony, renews creation by drawing power from the still water in front of Auich crag.

Salish

From now on,
You will be the fire drill,
For those who will be people
From now on.[20]

    SINGER: Jonah Jack. Beaver, having stolen fire, infuses sparks into trees and makes the wood suitable for fire drills.

Ontinonsionni

And this is what Our Creator did.
He decided, "I shall establish various creatures
That will spread their wings from just above the earth
To as far upward as they can go.
And they too will be called animals.
They will begin just above the earth,
And will go all the way into the clouds.
And they too will all have names, the birds with outspread wings."
And with respect to the small birds he decided,
"There will be a certain period when they will stir,
And they will turn back, going back to where it is warm.
And it will become warm again on the earth,
And they will return.
With all their voices they will sing once more their beautiful songs.
And it will lift the minds of all who remain when the small birds return."[21]

᠕   SINGERS: Chief Corbett Sundown, Chief Ellsworth George. The set of
Thanksgiving Chants from which this song comes contains seventeen sec-
tions. Paul Zolbrod analyzes the structure of the entire poem,[22] which bal-
ances references from earth and sky, near and far, concrete and abstract,
and moves from earth to sky, healing, and back to the healed patient. Each
stanza replicates this movement from concrete earthly phenomena,
through celestial objects, to holy forces.

Tewa
               Oh Mother Earth, Father Sky!
        Your children are we and with tired backs we bring you the gifts you love.
            Then weave for us a garment of brightness.
            May the warp be the white light of morning.
            May the weft be the red light of evening.
            May the fringes be the falling rain.
            May the border be the standing rainbow.
        Weave us a garment of brightness that we may walk fittingly where grass is green.
            Oh Mother Earth, Oh Father Sky![23]

᠕   The warp and weft of the sky loom evoke the fringe of rain that trails from
beneath a thunderhead in the Southwest. Plains tribes used another image
for the trailing rain: hair trailing down.

A'a'tam A'kimult
            The world is sung,
            The world is finished.
            The world is sung,
            The world is finished.
            Now it moves, (3)
            Now it stirs.[24]

᠕   SINGER: Visak Vooyim (Hovering Hawk). Chuhwuht (Song of the World).
From the Pima Creation myth. The Creator rolled the first substance un-
der his foot. The ants helped.

Tewa
            There comes the dawn,
            The Universe grows green!
            The road to the underground world is open
            Yet now we live,
            Rising, rising![25]

⟡   Urutu'sendo's (Walking Stick Old Man's) Song. The daughters of Uru
      (the first man), the Blue Corn Girls, floated to the sky in a basket when
      the world flooded. Spider Woman lowered them back to earth after adven-
      tures. They rise, as did the First People at the emergence.

Ka'igwu

              The Spirit Army advances, they say!
              They come with the buffalo, they say!
              They come with the new earth, they say![26]

⟡   Ghost Dance Song. "They say," or an equivalent, customarily introduces
      common knowledge or wisdom in formal narration, legends, or myths in
      many tribal literatures. The formula invokes ceremonial power and identi-
      fies the song as expressing something known by faith. The singers hoped
      that the Ghost Dance would re-create the preinvasion Golden World.

Inuit

              Orphan, you, Little Orphan,
              On the open sea's other side,
              On its beautiful under side,
              Creep carefully there,
              Come out of the sea
                  As a seal! Puh![27]

⟡   SINGER: Nakasuk. The people panicked and threw the little orphan Nulia-
      juk overboard. She became the mother of the sea creatures. The myth, like
      those of Sedna and Takanakapsaluk, may reflect an early practice of human
      sacrifice.

Takhtahm

              Marina, from the West (2)
                  We come.
              With the sacred feathers, (2)
              With the sacred shells, (2)
                  We come. (2)[28]

⟡   SINGER: Rosa Marongo. From the Serrano origin myth. The Holy People
      bring medicine objects that resemble clouds. Dancers in ceremonies re-
      enact the journey.

Tewa

1. Long ago in the North
   Lies the Emergence Road!
   There our ancestors live.
   From there we draw our being!
2. Now we come south
   For cloud flowers blossom here!
   Lightning flashes here!
   Here rain water is falling![29]

ᔓ Santa Clara Turtle Dance Song. During this ceremony, Cloud Kachinas bring seeds and promise abundant harvests and many children.

Akume

There in the West
Is the home of the Raingods!
There in the West
Is their pool!
In the middle of the pool
Rises their spruce tree ladder!
Up from the water
The Raingods draw the life-giving crops.
East from there, where we dance,
They lay the crops.
Up from that place
The people receive crops and life.[30]

ᔓ SINGER: Philip Sanchez (Ho-ni-ya). This Corn Dance (Ya'kahu'na) Song compares the yearly emergence of the corn and rain to the emergence of the First People and the emergence of the healers from visits to the underworld.

Inuit

Glorious, when the caribou herds,
Flocking down from the forest,
Begin to wander northward.
Fearfully they watch
For the pitfalls in the snow.
The great forest herds,
When they spread over the snow,
Glorious!
    Jai-ja-jija!

Glorious, when
Early summer's short-haired caribou
Begin to wander.
When at Haningassoq, down there,
Across the headlands,
They trot to and fro
Seeking a crossing.
    Jai-ja-jija!
Glorious, when the black musk-oxen
Gather in herds down there.
Little dogs they watch for, they do,
When they gather in herds.
Glorious!
    Jai-ja-jija!
Glorious, when the young women
Gather in little herds
And go visiting in the houses—
Then, all at once,
The men down there want to be manly,
While the women simply
Tried to find some little lie.
    Jai-ja-jija!
Glorious, when thick-coated winter caribou
Begin to trek to the forests.
Fearfully they watch
For the little people,
When they move to the forests.
    Jai-ja-jija!
Glorious! The enormous herds
When they begin to wander
By the sea down there.
Down by the shore
The creaking whisper of hooves.
When they begin to wander,
It is glorious!
    Jajai-ja-jija![31]

SINGER: Netsit.

Tsiyame

We, the ancients,
From the middle world below,
Ascended through Sipapu.
Our medicine,
Our songs to the Cloud People,
The Lightning, and Thunder People,
Is like our hearts.
Arrow of lightning, come to us.
We hear the echo;
[The Thunder Beings flap their wings
Amid the Cloud and Lightning People.]
Who is it?[32]

〜   From a Giant Society Rain Song.

Kutiti

1. Come, let's go.
   Yellow and Blue,
   As you come to meet one another,
   We go on, we go right up
   And out into the open spaces.
2. My dears, my dears,
   You yellow corn maidens,
   As you rise up, I see you.
       Then I sing for you![33]

〜   SINGER: Evergreen Tree (Ho'cuke). When this Cochiti Corn Dance Song
speaks of rising and open spaces, it suggests seedlings rising in the fields,
dancers from a Kiva, and the First People at emergence.

Hotcangara

Pleasant it looked, this newly created earth.
Along the entire length and breadth of the earth,
Our Grandmother extended the green reflection of her covering,
And the escaping odors were pleasant to breathe.[34]

〜   The odors escaped in mist at sunrise.

Diné

You say there were no people,
    Smoke was spreading.

First Man emerged first,
>Smoke was spreading.
He brought various robes and precious things, they say,
>Smoke was spreading.
He brought the white corn and the yellow corn, they say,
>Smoke was spreading.
He brought the animals and growing things, they say,
>Smoke was spreading.[35]

SINGER: Hosteen Klah. The *hataali* can sing this song recounting the cre-
ation and emergence of First Man and Woman, derived from the Navajo
Creation Myth, in healing ceremonies. It uses smoke as a kind of visible
breath, like morning mist, and recalls the shamans' visions that lay behind
healing ceremonies, such as Coyoteway, and the Deestii or Crystal Vision
Ceremonies. The second stanza repeats this stanza, substituting "First
Woman" and "many-colored corn."

Shis-Inde

He placed a house here where there was none.
He covered it with the black skin of the deer who come from the East!
He covered it with the white skin of the deer who come from the South!
He covered it with the yellow skin of the deer who come from the West!
He covered it with the white skin of the deer who come from the North!
He caused the black deer horns to alight one after the other on the top of his house.
>He placed a house there.
>He alights there.[36]

SINGER: Antonio. Panther Boy, the primordial hunter, built a hunting
lodge and house for himself and his wife, the daughter of Gaowan, the
Talking Holy Person. This house, like the sweatlodge or the hogan, repre-
sents the world, in this case, the hunter's world.

Diné

>The ladder (8)
From the Emergence Pit,
>The ladder, the ladder,
Talking God climbs with me up the black ladder,
>The ladder, the ladder,
He climbs with the rainbow,
>The ladder, the ladder,
To the edge of the Emergence Pit,

The ladder, the ladder,
Bluebird hums before me,
The ladder, the ladder,
Cornbeetle hums behind me,
The ladder, the ladder,
I, I am Sahanahray Bekayhozhon,
The ladder, the ladder,
Before me all is beautiful,
The ladder, the ladder,
Behind me all is beautiful,
The ladder, the ladder,
The ladder, (4)
The ladder. (8)[37]

SINGER: Hosteen Klah. The second stanza repeats this structure and substitutes Hastcehogan, blue ladder, and lightning. The ladder evokes the reed through which Hastceyalti (Talking Holy Person) and Hastcehogan (Home Holy Person) led the ancients from the last to this fifth world. It also evokes the ladder through the tops of the Kivas in both Pueblo and Anasazi towns. Further, it suggests the shaman's vision-journey, down into the earth through a pit-house smoke hole. Karl W. Luckert and Johnny C. Cook, trans., *Coyoteway,* describe fully a healing ceremonial derived from such a vision.

IV

Initiation

Inuit

> I rise from rest with movements swift
> As a raven's wing beats.
> I rise to meet the day. Wa-wa!
> My face turns from the dark night
> To gaze at the dawn,
> > Now whitening in the sky.[1]

↬ SINGER: Aua. Sung to introduce a child (Kublo's daughter, Kagjagjuk) to life and the Holy Powers on the occasion of her first journey on the sledge.

Ikaniuksalgi

> You day-sun, circling around,
> You daylight, circling around,
> You night-sun, circling around,
> You poor body, circling around,
> You wrinkled age, circling around,
> You spotted with gray, circling around,
> You wrinkled skin, circling around.[2]

↬ SINGER: Susie Tiger. This Medicine Song helps bring a child into the world. The medicine woman then urges the child to come. The singer uses sassafras with this song.

Diné

> Today we are blessed with this beautiful baby,
> > May his feet be to the east,
> > His right hand to the south,
> > His head to the west,
> > His left hand to the north,
> May he walk and dwell on Mother Earth peacefully,
> May he be blessed with good health,
> May he be blessed with various gems,

37

May he be blessed with all kinds of fat sheep,
May he be blessed with all kinds of swift horses,
May he be blessed with many respectful relatives of all kinds.
I have asked all these blessings with reverence and holiness.
    My mother is the earth;
The sky, the sun, and the moon together are my father.
I am the essence of life, which is old age,
I am the source of happiness in beauty.
    All is peaceful.
    All is in beauty.
    All is in harmony.
    All is in happiness.[3]

SINGER: Tom Ration. After the newborn sipped sap (from the inner bark of the piñon) and corn pollen diluted with water, the father took the baby to "an especially nice place where a man of wisdom offered a blessing prayer."

Pomo

To my wife, Good will come!
    To my baby,
Good will come, Good!
My baby will grow up in Goodness.
To my wife, Good to my wife will come![4]

SINGER: Benson. Fathers sang this song eight days after the birth, to introduce the child to the Holy Powers.

Tsimshian

1. Whose little brother am I?
   I never came from Gitksan.
   I came from a long way downriver.
   That is why this child thinks me different.
   Where I walk, I don't recognize my grandfather's village.
   I don't recognize this child.
   That is why this child is different.
   Whose little brother am I?
2. Whose little brother am I?
   I carry in my grandfather's crest,
   The Double-Headed-Person!
   I will stand it in the middle
   Of my small house.

All the people will see it,
    All the chiefs.
Whose little brother am I?[5]

꙳   SINGER: Weerhae. Weerhae's family sang this ceremonial lullaby in a family
    feast when first showing the child to relatives.

Kwagutl

When I am a man,
Then I shall be a hunter, O Father!
    Ya ha ha ha!
When I am a man,
I shall be a harpooneer, O Father!
    Ya ha ha ha!
When I am a man,
I shall be a canoe-builder, O Father!
    Ya ha ha ha!
When I am a man,
I shall be a board-maker, O Father!
    Ya ha ha ha!
When I am a man,
I shall be a workman, O Father!
    Ya ha ha ha!
That we may want for nothing, O Father!
    Ya ha ha ha![6]

꙳   SINGER: Workingman. A father sang this song for the child, to infuse in
    him the song and the power to accomplish the future the song pictures.

Hamakhav

Facing East   Sun, life-giver,
                As you rise,
                See our home this day!
                Give this boy a good life.
                Let this boy bring good to his people.[7]

Kwagutl

Father: You were given by good fortune to your slave,
            You were given by good fortune to your slave,
            To come and take the place of your slave.
                Wa ya ha ha!

<blockquote>

Son: Oh Tribes, now hide yourselves!
I have come to be a man and my name is Hellebore!
   Wa ya ha ha!
   Already the cedar withes are twisted
That I shall pass through the mouths of the heads
   That I take in war
   For I am true Hellebore!
I'll take princes' heads in war when I come to be a man
That I may have your names, as my father has done,
   Who has your names for his names.
   Wa ya ha ha![8]

</blockquote>

SINGER: K'ilem. A warrior father sang this for the birth of his first son, named after the Skookum root (*Veratrum eschscholtzii*), which was used, in conjunction with cedar, to treat sore backs and constipation.

Tewa

Sun! Morning Star!
Help this child to become a man.
I name him Rain-Dew Falling!
I name him Star Mountain![9]

Kwagutl

Grandmother: Our Treasure came here to dig clams
For her mother and her old slave!
   Ahe ahe ya!
Our Treasure came here to dig clover
For her mother and her old slave!
   Ahe ahe ya!
Our Treasure came here to dig cinquefoil
For her mother and her old slave!
   Ahe ahe ya!

Child: O mother, make me a basket that I may pick
Salmon berries, salal berries, and huckleberries
   For my old slave!
   Ahe ahe ya!
Let him who is to be my husband get ready
So he may be ready to help my mother and my old slave!
   Ahe ahe ya![10]

SINGER: Workingman. For the birth of a daughter.

Tohono Au'autam

Baboquivari is there on the east side.
It has white blossoms on it.
Toward that mountain I am on my way.
I am running to join the singer.[11]

᠀ SINGER: José Ascencio. Wakita (Girls' Puberty Ceremony) Song. The song alludes to a ritual race, imitating the sun's daily race across the sky. The girl had to stand up all night. The sun gave the girl endurance; the girl reaffirmed the sun's power.

Diné

My little one, she runs out. (4)
The White Shell Girl, she runs out.
Having shoes of white shell, she runs out.
Having leggings of white shell, she runs out.
Having a blouse of white shell, she runs out.
Having a feather of white shell, she runs out.
The sacred words, your girl, she runs out.
Before her, all is beautiful, she runs out.
Behind her, all is beautiful, she runs out.
My little one, she runs out. (4)
The Turquoise Girl, she runs out.
Having shoes of Turquoise, she runs out.
Having leggings of Turquoise, she runs out.
Having a blouse of Turquoise, she runs out.
Having a feather of Turquoise, she runs out.
The sacred words, your girl, she runs out.
Behind her, all is beautiful, she runs out.
Before her, all is beautiful, she runs out.
My little one, she runs out! (4)[12]

᠀ SINGER: Hosteen Klah (Left-Handed). During puberty ceremonies, and other ceremonies, participants ran races that paralleled and affirmed the sun's daily race.

Ipay

Striped Quail, speckled Quail,
Dove, bleeding.[13]

᠀ The tattooist sings this while tattooing a girl's face, as a sign of womanhood.

A'nish'inabeg

> The ground trembles as I start to enter.
> My heart fails me as I start to enter
>   The spirit lodge.[14]

> SINGER: Be'cigwi'wizans. Lines 1–2 are repeated six times. Midé Healing Songs, by mentioning trembling ground, evoke earthquake, the buffalo herd, thunder, and the Thunder Beings. Shamans took such Healing Songs from their visions. The Midewiwin sang the first verse as they marched around, the second and third after they entered the Midé Lodge. The leader imitated a Spirit Bear, Ma'kwa Man'ido, one of the Powers behind Midé power.

Noam-Kekhl

> This is from the Creator.
> I show you what He did.
> I do not do this myself. He taught me.
> If you believe this, it will be well with you!
>   People will be good to you!
>   Believe what I say![15]

> When, during the Kichil-woknam (Obsidian-Initiation), the presiding shaman dug four times into proven dry ground and then dug a foot-deep hole, into which water flowed, he chanted this poem.

Ontinonsionni

> We wait in the darkness!
> Come all ye who listen,
> Help in our night journey!
> Now no sun shines, now no star glows.
> Come, show us the pathway.
> The night is not friendly;
> She closes her eyelids.
> The moon has forgotten us.
> We wait in the darkness![16]

> The first song in initiating a new member into the Negarnagarah medicine society. The initiation recapitulates the myth describing the origin of the Little Water Medicine. In the myth, of which Harriet Converse gives several versions, birds and animals resurrect a "Doer of Good," who brings back songs and a ritual to his people. These songs and rituals recount the sequence in which animals brought help to the resurrection, at night. The

animals who brought help represent the totem clans, the Night Birds, the Wolf, the Buck and Doe, the Bear, the Hawk, and the Eagle. The initiate can heal using the power, songs, and medicine bundles and objects belonging to the society.

Ipay

> I am singing.
> Eastern bird, I sing,
> Western bird, I sing,
> Grouse, I am singing,
> I am a man.[17]

This song came from a vision during the Boys' Puberty Ceremony.

Kwagutl

> By Numiye (4)
> I was taken around the world.
> By Numiye (5)
> I was taken around the world.
> By magicians,
> By Numiye. (4)[18]

During the Winter Ceremony and the initiation of the Wild Hamats'a into the more or less disciplined Cannibal Society, the society's chorus sang this song to the candidates.

Kwagutl

> The earth will tilt where it is.
> The floor will throw us off where it is.
>   He will shout,
>   The Grizzly Bear,
>   The Great One,
> Hu u! Nun! hin! Nun! hin![19]

The Cannibal Society initiate imitated the bear while singing this Nane (Grizzly Bear) Song. Bear Dancers guarded the dance house and enforced the privileges of the Hamats'a. Those who violated these prerogatives were once killed. Nanstalihl-Pa'hpaqalano'siwi (Pa'hpaqalano'siwi's Grizzly) tears up flesh for Pa'hpaqalano'siwi or Nan-kohlila (Grizzly Bear Unrestrained). "When the Great Grizzly Bear cries, 'Hu u! Nun! hin! Nun! hin!' the people will fall in fright as if thrown from a tilted plane."

Akume

I am going to ask, ye-a ye-a,
I am going to ask.
I am going
Toward the east
On the shell trail,
Toward the east
Where the water of life lies,
Where the sun rises,
Bringing life, health, and happiness
To the earth.[20]

ᔆ A candidate for initiation into one of the ceremonial societies sings this
song, while carrying a prayer feather during the initiation.

Tiwame

He begins to move,
The man who will do the whipping.
　He moves.
　I am the man.
　I open my eyes.
Now I am a member of the Shalak.
It is my right and duty
To take the place of a spirit
With my mother, the Bear.[21]

ᔆ The singer sings this very old Domingan Shalako song before he whips the
candidates with a yucca whip. The officiant gives four strokes to the per-
sonators of the hero-twins, Masewi and Oyoyewi, to the candidates, and
then to the members of the society, each kneeling by a stone cougar. The
society "traps" new members: catches them intruding on Shalako prayers.
This society of hunting medicine men wears bear-paws in treating the sick
and snatching at witch spirits. They also use fetishes and shell bracelets.
Their crystal gazers test the tutelaries of the aspirants to membership.

Tewa

1. Here and now we bring you, oh our old men,
　Sun Fire God, Northern Blue Cloud Person,
　Sun Fire God, Western Yellow Cloud Person,
　Sun Fire God, Southern Red Cloud Person,
　Sun Fire God, Eastern White Cloud Person,
　Sun Fire God, Dark Cloud Person Below,

Sun Fire God, All Colored Cloud Person Above,
Here now, we bring you your special prayer stick,
We make you an offering of sacred meal,
A little bit for all, we make you these offerings!

2. Stand ready, then, to walk at dawn
With the rain upon the Northern mountain top,
Upon the Western mountain top and the great lake,
Upon the Southern mountain top where the Tshu people sit,
Upon the top of the Eastern Great Dawn Mountain,
Upon the top of the Sky-Universe Mountain!
Upon the top of the Mountain Sitting under the Earth,

3. Bring cloud flowers bearing rain!
Set cloud flowers upon the far Northern mountain top,
Set cloud flowers there upon the Western mountain top,
Set cloud flowers there upon the Southern mountain top,
Set cloud flowers there upon the Eastern mountain top,
Set cloud flowers there upon the mountain top Below the Earth,
Set cloud flowers there upon the mountain top Above the Sky,
Set cloud flowers there, bearing rain!

4. There, on the middle mountains, first lay fogs.
That is why from there to San Juan pueblo, ready at dawn,
You bring your lightnings, your thunders, and your rains together,
Changing the fields lying between!
That is why the wide plains now revive!
That is why the hills of the plain now revive!
That is why your drying lakes,
Your lakes where they are lying, now revive!

5. May all tame animals increase and all children,
For we are all little people to be loved by the gods
As far as the sound of our Great Mother's breathing reaches!
Even to the Utes, Apaches, Navajos,
Kiowas, Comanches, Cheyennes, even to all, cloud flowers!
To the Mexicans, even to them it reaches!
To the Americans, even to them the sound
Of our Great Mother's breathing reaches!
So now the Gods love them, and they each other!
That is why we expect to find our food here, we mortals!
May you place good summers and good harvest days and nights!
For all may they place
The same good days and nights of harvest.[22]

ᴈ   Initiation Chant of the Kwirana K'osa (Clown) Society. These Delight
Makers police and parody ceremonies. Herbert Spinden, *Songs of the Tewa*,
gives the Tewa text.

Tohono Au'autam   Reed Mountain stands up at the West.
There an eagle arises. The flat land resounds.
Narrow Mountain stands up at the East.
There a hawk cries. The mountains echo.[23]

ᴈ   Eagle Killer Initiation Song.

A'nish'inabeg   Spirit, a spirit, you who sit, who sit here!
The fog gusts from place to place
Whence the wind blows.
I see you are a spirit, and am dying!
I am trying you, the Bear.
The bird, the crow's skin, makes me a spirit.
Thunder is the White Fire Bear.[24]

ᴈ   SINGER: Sikas'sige. This song initiates a candidate into the fourth degree of
the Midé. The sponsor shoots the candidate with a *mi'gis* (a medicine shell
or stone). The candidate "dies," becomes a spirit, and resurrects with a
new power and name. The pictographs show a manido controlling fog, a
Bear Man'ido, and a Thunder Being. White Bear Man'ido is one of the
most powerful of the manidos. Fire suggests lightning.

Meshkwakihugi   We shake the mane of this huge buffalo (3)
Here, on this earth of ours![25]

ᴈ   SINGER: Kinaya. White Buffalo Ceremony, song 28. The dancers sang this
song. When the buffalo was about to bless the lodge members, the origi-
nator, or a visionary, his mane shook.

A'nish'inabeg   When the waters are calm
And fog rises,
I will now and then appear![26]

꙳ SINGER: Na'jobi'tun. Midé Ceremonial Closing Song. The accompanying pictograph shows an overcast sky and a manido (a water spirit, male beaver) emerging from a circle.

Tsistsi'stas

My Grandfather gave me
The rawhide thong to tie,
The songs to use,
And the long sinew cord to tie the toes.
My Grandfather, medicine power ties me!
My Grandfather gave me a medicine whistle.
My Grandfather gave me a tipi;
The medicine wind rocks it back and forth on the earth.
My Grandfather gave me a medicine rattle!
My Grandfather gave me the night!
My Grandfather gave me everything on this earth.[27]

꙳ SINGER: Bob-Tailed Wolf. A Shaking Tipi Song. The medicine man sang this song while being tied, preparing for the Shaking Tipi performance, recounting how he gained his medicine power. The medicine man and his helpers erected a small tipi. The audience and the helpers bound the medicine man tightly, as helpers bound Harry Houdini. Placed inside the tipi, the medicine man summoned spirits who freed him from his bonds, sang Medicine Songs, flew about the inside the tipi, and shook it.

Hamakhav

Come and stand beside me, boy,
And I will teach you how to cure sickness.
I blow my breath over the sick one and he is well.[28]

꙳ SINGER: Awheyama. A long-bearded tarantula sang this in a vision, in the mountains where Awheyama built a house. The tarantula put a hair on the ground to represent a patient. Honyavre, the mirage bug, sang a similar song to him, in a similar vision, when he was a little boy.

Pahodja

We bring health, power, and prosperity
    To our new son.
He shall live to be white-headed
    And carry a cane.[29]

ᎧᎧ Calumet Adoption Ceremony Song. By joining the society, the initiate was reborn.

Dakota

> You cannot harm me.
> You cannot harm one
> Who has dreamed a dream like mine,
> One who has seen the buffalo in their lodge
> And heard them say,
> "Arrows cannot harm you."[30]

ᎧᎧ Brave Buffalo tested this song by having his friends shoot arrows at him, then bullets. Medicine power derived from the Holy Powers and visions and could inhere in lucky objects, including songs, ceremonies, stones, and fetishes. Luck derived from visions. The warrior who had dreamt a lucky dream could fight without fear.

Shis-Inde

> 1. I come to White Painted Woman,
>   By means of long life I come to her.
>   I come to her by means of her blessing!
>   I come to her by means of her good fortune!
>   I come to her by means of all her different fruits!
>   By means of the long life she bestows, I come to her.
>   By means of this holy truth she goes about.
> 2. I am about to sing this song of yours,
>   The song of long life.
>   Sun, I stand here on the earth with your song!
>   Moon, I have come in with your song.
> 3. White Painted Woman's power emerges, her power for sleep.
>   White Painted Woman carries this girl!
>   She carries her through long life!
>   She carries her to good fortune!
>   She carries her to old age!
>   She carries her to peaceful sleep!
> 4. You have started out on the good earth!
>   You have started out with good moccasins!
>   With moccasin strings of the rainbow, you have started out.
>   With moccasin strings of the sun rays, you have started out.
>   In the midst of plenty, you have started out.[31]

꒱   The fourth song sung by masked dancers at sunrise of the fifth day to end the four-day-long *gotal* or *gans* puberty ceremony for girls. The Arapaho ask for similar gifts for their girls, in a similar ceremony.

Aa'shi'wi

Now this day, our child, into the daylight, you will go out standing,
  Preparing for your day, we have passed our days.
When all your days were at an end, when eight days were passed,
  Our sun father went in to sit down at his sacred place.
And our night fathers having come out standing to their sacred place,
  Passing a blessed night, we came to day.
Now this day our fathers, Dawn Priests, have come out standing to their sacred place.
Our sun father having come out standing to his sacred place,
  Our child, it is your day.
This day, the flesh of the white corn, prayer meal,
  To our sun father, this prayer meal we offer.
May your road be fulfilled. Reaching to the road of your sun father,
  When your road is fulfilled, in your thoughts may we live.
May we be the ones whom your thoughts will embrace,
  For this, on this day, to our sun father, we offer prayer meal.
  To this end: may you help us all to finish our roads.[32]

꒱   Often reprinted, in various forms, this chant carries the subject from meeting Holy Powers through life to death and transformation into a helpful Holy Person.

Maidu

Look at the poppy flowers,
Growing fine.[33]

꒱   SINGER: Pablo Sylvers. From the Girls' Puberty Ceremony.

V

Visions

LAMENTING

Suquamish

How shall I get clams?
How shall I get mussels?
How shall I get elk?
How shall I get fish?
How shall I get wealth?[1]

꒳ SINGER: Jacob Wahelchu. Lamenting before seeking a vision. The singer swam the narrows to an island and dug with his hands, for two nights, seeking a vision. In his vision he saw a man-spear and a man–war-club.

Ikaniuksalgi

They take us beyond Miami.
They take us beyond the Caloosa River.
They take us to the end of our tribe.
They take us to Palm Beach, coming back beside Okeechobee.
They take us to an old town in the West.[2]

꒳ SINGER: Susie Tiger. Paul Olson identifies the water surrounding Grand-father Rock as the "water impossible to cross" that separates us from the Holy People's world.[3] Such water flows in the Caloosa in this song that mourns the removal of the Seminole, driven from their home in the Everglades. This song laments the world before the white people infected it, the original world, the spirit world, the real world. John Swanton cites a Creek myth that places Spirits, Death, or Evil in a town in the West.[4] Florida cowboys drove herds across the Suwannee from Old Town to Gainesville.[5]

Tlingit

The pole drifts, drifts away.
The sandbank falls, falls down.

At himself that Raven looks,
Looks at himself.
Pity the Raven.[6]

⌇   SINGER: Mrs. Frank Dick. The Raven House Post fell down and drifted
when a riverbank fell in. A raven hopped on the floating post and looked
down at the raven carved on the post.

Micmac

Our country, now lost,
Seems clearly, to us,
As though it were spread with boughs!
Yoogwaaegen'!
Yoogwaaegeno!
It seems clearly, to us,
Our country, now lost,
To be blue, like the clear blue sky![7]

⌇   SINGER: Susan Christmas. Badger, a shaman and something of a trickster,
sings this song in a version of the Star-Wives story, when an irritated hus-
band is about to throw him off a cliff. His spine survives, and he regener-
ates. The song evokes the shaman's descent to the underworld; Badger
sees the world from above as green, like the surface of the water from
above; from below, as blue, like the surface of the water from below. Some
languages used the same word for "blue" and "green."

Nanbe

My home over there, My home over there,
My home over there, now I remember it!
And when I see that mountain far away,
Why, then I weep. Alas! What can I do?
What can I do? Alas! What can I do?
My home over there, My home over there.[8]

⌇   A Nambe Pueblo song. San Ildefonsans sing a similar song. This song, like
one Nayenezgani sang and many Ghost Dancers sang, envisions home and
a preinvasion Golden Age in inviolate home territory.

Tlingit

1.   I am going to die
Without seeing Daqlawe'di's children anymore.

That is nothing if I lose lots of property!

2.   It is only crying about myself
That comes to me in song.[9]

     SINGERS: Tsaka'k, Dekina'ku. This song, composed about Kulttsa'xk, a Koske'di, predicts death, mocks greed, and laments, suggesting the formal lament that often preceded the formal search for a dream or vision.

A'nish'inabeg

Sometimes I go about pitying myself
As the wind carries me across the sky.[10]

     SINGER: Ga'gandac'. The singer dreamt of a stormy sky and thunder, sounding like Midé drums. Pitying himself, he lamented. His lament led the Holy Powers to send him power in this vision of a Thunder Being. This song is often anthologized (e.g., Astrov, *Anthology,* 46; Chapman, *Literature,* 285; Day, *Sky Clears,* 148; Levitas, Vivelo, and Vivelo, *We Wait,* 31; Bierhorst, *Trail,* 130. Vizenor, *Nogamon,* 54). Ki'miwun (Rainy) dreamt similarly and won a similarly powerful song:

As the wind carries me about the sky.[11]

Yokuts

Motsa: Friend, friend, I dance,
          Holding a bunch of feathers in my hand.
Coyote: I am coming to meet you, friend!
          I am going to take you up north
            To the rainbow.[12]

     SINGERS: Motsa, Josie Alonzo. Motsa, a powerful shaman, sang this song to call his tutelary, Coyote, when he wanted to dream for more power. In the song, Coyote says what Motsa wanted him to say.

PREPARING

A'a'tam A'kimult

1. Now the Butterfly Song begins!
   Both sides dance to and fro
   Until the dust rises!
2. The Butterfly Bird
   Begins to sing his many songs!
   I run to the house
   Where the dust rises close to the walls.

3. I now begin the song.
   I heard the song as I ran.
   I join in the singing.
4. The Cat-tail Leaf Woman
   Begins to sing with me!
   I join the circling dancers,
   Singing and beating my chest.
5. Toward cloud-topped Matcipan Mountain,
   In clouds, I drift, singing!
   Toward cloudless Ka'matuk Mountain,
   Unclouded, I drift, singing!
6. To Dead Mountains Standing,
   Hurry! Run! Arrive!
   There you can see, younger brother,
   How the winds run and pass across!
7. There, at Ma-ayal Mountain
   In the clearing before the Magician's House,
   There a woman laughs.
8. Down the slopes of Crooked Mountain, singing!
   Down Crooked Mountain,
   That wears a headdress of foam,
   We have run for blue water.[13]

SINGER: Ki-iwa. A Butterfly Song (Hahakimam Nyoi). On the Papago salt pilgrimage, the seekers passed several mountains, arrived at the ocean, and raced up and down the shore along the surf to achieve a vision. This Pima song moves from a ceremonial dance through a vision of the journey itself. It moves outward, from the dance to meet a cousin of one of the Wild Women who sang outside ceremonies, then over the mountains to the sea and to the race for a vision.

Havasuwapay

A fresh wind in that land.
A strong wind in that land.
Girls circle around.
Girls dance in a circle.
   A cool wind.[14]

Teyadjava dreamt that he heard girls sing this song in a strange land. He sang it in the Yimaga dance, to bring rain, and as a Social Dance Song.

Konhiak   Watch me dance!
I raise myself above the water!
The wind that blew around me
     Blows under me now.
So I do not drop down on my beach.[15]

꙳   SINGER: Santo Blanco. The Mirage's Song from the Women's Ceremonies.
Tiburon island, in mirage, seems to rise and float above the water, as if
wind were blowing under it.

Sanpoil   Only one being, their horse,
All night they dance for it,
     The ghosts!
All night it rattles.[16]

꙳   SINGER: Cultus Charley.

Cowlitz   *Bear:*   I dance on the swamps,
          On every swamp.
Elk: I dance on all the mountains,
          On five mountains
          I have a dancing ground.
Deer: I run if they try to kill me.
          To my five mountains
          I run away and leave the people.[17]

꙳   SINGER: Mary Iley. Animals' Tamanaos Songs. When Rabbit sang the
house pole into life and motion, the singers fled the house and became
tutelary animals.

THE VISION

Achomawi   Sky above.
Dust whirling.[18]

꙳   SINGER: I'nuwi (Old Chocolate Hat). This dreamer's song, like other
Ghost Dance songs, uses the image of dust whirling up to the sky in a
dustdevil, a thermal, for power and spirit.

No-ochi   On a mountain
                                 The noise of the wind.[19]

            ℘   SINGER: Sidney Blueotter (Sa'vapaatsuk).

Tohono Au'autam   Now I am ready to go.
                                 The ocean wind from far off overtakes me.
                                 It bends down the tassels of the corn.
                                 The ocean wind hurts my heart.
                                 Beautiful clouds bring rain upon our fields.
                                     The outspread water!
                                 Running along it, I seized the corn.
                                     The outspread water!
                                 Running along it, I seized the squash.[20]

            ℘   A Salt Pilgrimage Song, chanted after salt is purified. These salt purifica-
                   tion songs resemble corn planting and growing songs. The pilgrims ran
                   along the shore, hoping to trigger a vision. The pilgrims' ceremonial lan-
                   guage uses "corn" for "salt." Like all Papago ceremonies, this pilgrimage
                   sought rain. In another version, the rain-bringing ocean wind breaks down
                   the squash leaves.

Pestamokatiyak   We are the stars who sing,
                                 We sing with our light.
                                 We are the birds of fire,
                                 We fly across the heaven,
                                 Our light is a star.
                                 We make a road for spirits,
                                 A road for the Great Spirit.
                                 Among us are three hunters who chase a bear:
                                 There was never a time when they were not hunting.
                                 We look down on the mountains.
                                 This is the song of the mountains.[21]

            ℘   The Seven Stars sing this song. Many myths and stories include the seven
                   stars. For example, Hiawatha had seven daughters, whom Osinoh, a sha-
                   man, killed in order to send Hiawatha to meet Deganwida, cure Adadarko,
                   and found the Great League.

A'nish'inabeg   Beautiful as a star hanging in the sky
                  Is our Midé lodge.[22]

SINGER: Na'jobi'tun. The star hanging above the Midé Lodge, the Thunder Beings' nest at the top of the center pole of the Sun Dance, the tree house attributed to the shamans Osinoh and Adadarko in the Hiawatha myth, the eagle's nest, and the medicine nest the Yokuts sing about when redirecting the power of the Rolling Head all house holy power. The drawing that accompanies this song, of the star above the Midé Lodge, contains two poles, suggesting two candidates. The stars and the Milky Way often suggest the path the spirits take to the Holy People.

Kasogotine   In a single glance
                  From among the spirits,
                  I will see the great buffalo.[23]

A prehunting or prewar song. Emile Petitot, *Traditions*, remarks that "spirit" means both "harlot" and "spirit." The combination suggests the Wild Women who, like the Maenads or Bacchantes, sometimes figure in hunting origin myths and in fertility ceremonies.

Meshkwakihugi   The buffalo move about with light. (4)
                  They drift slowly with dim light.
                  They, the buffalo, move with light,
                    Slowly.[24]

SINGER: Kinaya. The Twenty-third White Buffalo Song. Long ago, when a herd of buffalo were standing together at night, there was a flash of light. In the morning, there was just dim light.

Chahiksichahiks   He said, "Unreal the buffalo is standing."
                  "Unreal the buffalo is standing," he says!
                    He said, his sayings,
                  "Unreal the buffalo is standing, (2)
                  Unreal in the open prairie standing!" (2)[25]

SINGER: Wicita Blain. Sung in the Buffalo Dance. From a vision that included a spirit buffalo. "Unreal" here means "unordinary, holy." A man watching a scattered herd saw a buffalo lie down. He dreamed of the buffalo that night. The buffalo promised medicine and the power to prophesy. Another warrior implicitly compared his "ordinary" life to the Holy People's life:

> Let us see, is this real, (3)
> This life I am living?
> You Holy Ones who dwell everywhere,
> Let us see, is this real,
> This life I am living?[26]

A warrior, going alone on a raid and unlikely to return, sang this song. Herbert Joseph Spinden attributes it to the Pawnee.[27]

Tohono Au'autam

> A little gray horned toad
> Came out of the darkness.
> Right round he twisted,
> Stretched out his neck,
>   And spoke to me.[28]

Yokuts

> Now I, in lightning, move![29]

SINGER: Josie Alonzo. The tutelary appeared in light, or lightning, singing this song.

Numa

> Feathers on the mountain endure;
> Rocks slide down.[30]

Clouds crown the mountains as feathers crown ceremonial figures. This song reverses the convention that makes rocks the most enduring creatures.

Miwok

> Dancing on the world's rim![31]

This Costonoan Dance Song reflects a vision of Holy People dancing on the horizon, against the sky.

No-ochi

We are playing
Along the shore.[32]

∿ SINGER: Kanav. Kanav's uncle dreamed this old Dream Song and sang the
song when he was alone thereafter.

Wintu

Above we shall go,
Along the Milky Way we shall go,
Above we shall go,
Along the flower path we shall go![33]

∿ SINGER: Harry Marsh. "Flower path" alludes to the Milky Way.

Achomawi

These are the spirit shadows of flowers.
The left is the spirit of red flowers;
The right, the spirit of wavering flowers.
The left is the name of the world;
The right is the name of the air.
Ah'mah, wahm'nah, nah'neyo.[34]

∿ During Edechewe's journey to the sun and moon, Ah'mahl (Shadows of
Beautiful Flowers) sings this song in a field of flowers, waving in the wind.

Chahiksichahiks

Spring is opening.
I can smell the different perfumes
Of the white weeds used in the dance.[35]

∿ SINGER: Mark Evarts. This song may allude to the hallucinogen and poison
jimson weed, *Datura stramonium*, whose seeds produced visions, when
they did not kill. *Datura* speaks as a Holy Person in a Papago couplet:
Datura: The lizard weed is like me;
It has yellow blossoms.
Lizard weed: The *Datura* is like me;
It has white blossoms.[36]
Datura killed fewer than another ceremonially used hallucinogen, loco
weed (*Astragalus* and *Oxytropis*). More probably, the song alludes to early
blossoms.

Wintu   Above the place where the minnow maiden sleeps
                                             At rest, her fins moving gently in the water,
                                                 The flowers droop,
                                                 The flowers rise again.[37]

                              ᵔ   Flowers, which appear in most Wintu Dream Songs, carry associations
                                             with stars, the Milky Way, spirits, and whirlwinds. "The minnow maiden"
                                             may allude to or name a constellation.

A'a'tam A'kimult   Cactus blossoms swaying back and forth,
                                             Way over, far away, they grow,
                                             Way over, far over desert ridges.[38]

                              ᵔ   SINGER: Hal Antonio. A Pima Huhuwuhli (Wind, Medicine) Nieh (Song).
                                             Probably the stick cholla cactus, which resembles Anasazi and Hohokam
                                             stick-figure petroglyphs. Swaying, which reflects the action of the wind,
                                             often suggests spirits or the holy power the wind embodies.

Numa   The spirit,
                                             The spirit
                                             Is swaying and singing.[39]

Wintu   Above they will go,
                                             The spirits of people, rhythmically swaying,
                                             Swaying, dandelion puffs in their hands,
                                             The spirits of people, rhythmically swaying.[40]

                              ᵔ   SINGER: Jim Thomas. Thomas, a shaman, sang this Dream Song in a
                                             Dream Dance, during which the women swayed rhythmically, with bent
                                             elbows, forearms pointing forward, and waved white flowers or cloths
                                             while the men danced in a circle around the fire. He introduced the dan-
                                             delion seedheads, which, he said, represented the spirits, which float away.
                                             The song became customary at funerals.

Hamakhav   The sun is set;
                                             It is dark, night-crazy;

Anyone who dreams of these crazy nights
    Will steal and rob.[41]

    ᵔ   SINGER: Perry Dean. Tortoise narrative, location 6. Matavilye's two young sons, after burning his body, move to the West and sing. The chanted narrative recounts the sons' journey, marking the Mohave's territory and recounting the myths that happened at each location.

Havasuwapay

Wolf, my father, said something I did not like.
He asked for one of my wives.
So I'm wandering around here,
Where the Bighorns sleep!
My body feels strange, ticklish.
I'm wandering about here,
That's what I'm doing.
My body feels strange, ticklish,
So I'm wandering around here,
Where the Bighorns sleep.
My hands feel strange;
They are dark, like Bighorn hooves.
My hair spirals and grows:
I have mountain sheep horns.
My youngest wife gives me boiled beans,
    And I eat them.
I imagined that; it was not true!
Instead I take the tips of cactus blossoms,
    And I eat them.
My oldest wife gives me boiled pumpkin,
    And I eat it.
I imagined that; it was not true!
Instead I take the tips of the grass,
    And I eat them.
Oh, my women, what have they done to me?[42]

    ᵔ   SINGER: Sinyella. Miracle Boy (Forms Itself), having won a race and Bluejay wives, wanders off on his mythic journey, kills the Bluejay people, and sings this song when he turns into a mountain sheep, after his father has offended him by asking for one of the two women.

Ontinonsionni

4. Yeidos. I see it walking,
         The song.
13. It goes, it goes here,
         My song.[43]

☞ From a Round Dance. The song, like the Modoc shamans' songs, walks in the persons of the singer or the dancers.

Wazhazhe

Amid the earth,
Renewed in green plants,
Amid the rising smoke,
I see my grandfather's footprints as I wander from place to place.
I see the rising smoke as I wander.
Amid all forms visible, I see the rising smoke as I move from place to place.
Amid all forms visible, I see the little hills in rows as I move from place to place.
Amid all forms visible, I see the spreading blades as I move from place to place.
Amid all forms visible, I see the light of day as I move from place to place.[44]

☞ SINGER: Tsezhin'gawadainga. The Ninth Buffalo Song, the First Corn Song. The people sing individually, at the signs of earth awakening from winter. The singers see mist rising from sun-warmed earth and from the buffalo hoofprint left by Holy Power. The mist, the breath of the earth revived by the sun, rises like the smoke from the pipe, the prayers the smoke carries, the song to the sunrise on a chilly morning, and the dust that marks the herd. The song may, in "the rising smoke," allude to the practice of burning dried corn stalks in the fields for their fertilizing ash. This mist shows visibly the holiness that fills the corn, beans, and squash, as well as the earth.

Chahiksichahiks

There it comes! (3)
The expanse of earth is wide!
My brother the fox said, "See the expanse.
The White Foxes know
The expanse of earth is wide!"[45]

☞ SINGER: Wicita Blain. A Wolf Society Song (29). This very old song recalls living in Nebraska, where kit foxes lived. A war party found a fox singing this song.

Inuit

Joy, joy, joy, joy!
I see a little shore spirit,
A little aua.
I am also Aua,
The shore spirit's namesake.
Joy, joy![46]

ᕐ Aua sang this song to summon his helping spirits, a shark and an aua (shore spirit).

O'maha

An invisible one moving there makes a noise; (2)
Therefore, over the earth a noise!
An invisible one moving there makes a noise,
     A noise of living creatures![47]

ᕐ Honhewachi Honorary Chiefs' Society Song. The song refers to the serpent that represents life as it moves through the short grass prairie. We cannot see the snake, or the wind, but can see the grass sway when they pass by. The serpent moves as does the lifegiver the sun and makes noise like the lifegivers rain and wind. The noisy serpent may also, perhaps, hang from a thundercloud and sway like a tornado.

Diné

Far beyond he appears;
Now Slender Horn appears.
His antlers become him.
     Now he appears.
Far beyond he appears;
Now Swollen Horn appears.
His horns become him.
     Now he appears.[48]

ᕐ This song describes a vision in which the prophet in the Mountain Chant saw a black bighorn standing on a rock.

No-ochi

The high mountains, (2)
We will climb them. (2)
We will plant our feet in the land!
There our Great Power lives![49]

꙯   "A favorite of mountain indians, who live where peaks reach 'the home of
the Great Spirit,' " according to E. L. Young.

Inuit

    1. I rise, I rise among spirits,
       I see the phantoms of the dead!
    2. Child, great child,
       Child-master of the air,
       Come down, great infant spirit.[50]

꙯   SINGER: Netsit (Copper Eskimo). These two charms, old combinations of
mysterious words, offer some details from the vision or dream that origi-
nally inspired them.

A'a'tam A'kimult

    Sun, up there,
    Standing up there in the West,
    You are telling me something!
    Your rattle, your magic gourd rattle
       Resounds in the West.[51]

꙯   SINGER: Sutatki. A Badger Medicine Song, fourth in a sequence. The
singer repeated the second line, then repeated lines 2–5, and repeated the
resulting stanza four times. The sun's rattle, thunder, promises eventual
rain and ritual power. It recalls Elder Brother, the Creator, who made
water and rain, and a ritual and visions that recalled this rain-making. A
Papago shaman sang a similar vision:

    1. Do you see, my younger brother?
       Now I sit down! My gourd rattle moves in a circle.
       Evening rushes out and goes sifting down over there.
    2. Do you see, my younger brother?
       Now I sit down! My gourd rattle moves in a circle.
       Morning rushes out and goes shining over there.[52]

This shaman saw Elder Brother performing a ritual, singing a song, which
he learned. The gourd, moving in a circle, moves in a way peculiar to
Elder Brother. The shaman moves the gourd horizontally when he sings
without words, vertically when he uses words. This ritual circling motion
ties Elder Brother to other agents of change, Coyote, Whirlwind, and the
Thunder Beings, resembling as it does the whirlwind that they all wear
from time to time.

MEDICINE FROM THE VISION

Tlingit

1. For the last time I look at
My fathers' land.
What Wolf will pity me?
2. Sorrow you gave to my hands,
Tecqwedi-child, my husband,
When you left me!
3. Why don't I dream of you,
Kagwantan-child?
It is all right
If I don't dream of you.[53]

SINGER: Emma Ellis. Ellis composed stanza 1 at eleven, when her father, mother, and grandfather drowned, and she heard the waves sing this song. She wrote the second stanza after her first husband, Dick Peterson, died.

Inuit

1. What I wonder,
Does the lovely south wind, thinking,
Whisper?
About the pensive little people
Who live north of us,
About them it whispers!

. . . .

5. What, I wonder,
Thinking about the point over there
That I used to stroll over
About the big antlered caribou bulls,
As I wander!
6. What, I wonder,
Thinking about the big herds
That stood out like mounds
I used to watch for?
The multitude of black musk oxen
I watched for, yes,
Those I used to watch for![54]

SINGER: Tatilgak. Qingordleq's Song. Stanzas 2–4 substitute east wind–inland behind us, north wind–south of us, down there, west wind–right in

the fjord there, invoking the winds in cyclonic order. The people forgot
the first singer, but remembered his song.

Hidatsa

My Father says
"When the wind blows,
I will go with it."[55]

෴   SINGER: Lean Wolf. The singer, carrying chokecherries, sang this Bear
Medicine Song when starting for the place where he would cure a patient.
The first owner heard the song in a vision.

Chahiksichahiks

I say, "There she stands, there, in the woods."
There she stands, (4)
Alone with the wind she stands,
There Cedar Mother stands.
Her song springs from the coming of the wind.
    There she stands. (4)
Alone with the wind she stands.
    Attentively I prayed
    That my Mother might come.
Now I say, "There she stands, Cedar Mother,
That I might live in Goodness."
Now she has stopped among the trees,
    The woman of exceeding beauty.[56]

෴   SINGER: Big Star. Song 2, the Bear Ceremony. A war party lost their sacred
bundle, lost the horses they had stolen, and lost many warriors in an am-
bush. Mad Bear, wounded, was treated by a bear and healed by the ever-
green Mother Cedar Tree in a vision. She gave him the Bear Ceremony
Songs. She drew her power, and immortality, from the moon.

Nimipu

Banking on tilting wings,
Wings beating, beating, beating,
Banking on tilting wings,
Pursuing through song,
Wings beating, beating, beating,
Soaring on tilting wings.[57]

⌇   Singing this Nez Perce song helped an aspirant gain a vision. In the original vision, the low sun struck a canyon wall. A browsing fawn saw the eagle soaring and ran. The eagle sang "Onatuihnanis." The fawn stopped to listen, transfixed. The eagle stooped, and smaller birds came to the feast. In the vision Eagle said, "I am all-powerful among birds. Other birds and animals know me and fear me. Like me, you shall be powerful. Like me you shall have the wisdom and strength to become a leader of your people. My name is Eagle–Who Knows All Languages. Your name shall be my name."[58]

Siksika

>   The ground is our medicine;
>   It is powerful.
>   The wind is our medicine.[59]

⌇   Blackfoot Buffalo Bull Society Songs. From a vision of Buffalo.

Carrier

>   Nipili, hold my hand, (2)
>   I hold the rope that holds up the earth.[60]

⌇   SINGER: Uzakli. This Medicine Song cures dream sickness. In his vision, the owner saw Nipili and an angel in the sky. This vision probably substituted a winged angel for an earlier winged Holy Person.

Diné

>   O'wo ha'ha'ye'halagai!
>   From the shore of the red river
>   No light comes because of his dust!
>   From where Abalone Woman planned a journey to you,
>   No light comes because of the dust!
>   From the shore of wide river,
>   From where Buffalo Woman lumbers toward you,
>   No light comes because of their dust!
>   From the shore of Sa-mee River,
>   From where Horned Chief lopes toward you,
>   No light comes because of their dust!
>   From the shore of Fall River,
>   From where the Buffalo Calf bunch dances toward you,
>   No light comes because of their dust!
>   A'ye'halagai![61]

~ From a Buffalo Song that recalls a vision of Buffalo and the Flintway hunter's myth. The song pictures the herd emerging from its dust cloud, its breath, and the earth's visible breath.

Carrier

A thunder receding into the distance
    Seized me.[62]

~ An old man, believing that any of the animal Holy People can seize a person, who then becomes a healer and visionary, fainted after a black eagle swooped toward him. A feeling of impending hysteria preceded the swoop. He woke the next day, after he dreamt he entered a great tunnel in the mountain, and came out with this song.

Kasogotine

Look! See how we all fly back
To warm and fertile lands.[63]

~ SINGER: Lizette Khatchoti, a female shaman (Peaux-de-lièvres). When the Trumpeter Swans leave for the south in the autumn, they bugle this song among the clouds.

Kwagutl

Yahana,
    I went standing
At the foot of a mountainous cliff,
    Taken by someone,
        Ahihe,
Falling down constantly,
Falling down constantly.[64]

~ A Matum (Invisible Flyer) Song. Matum gave a young man quartz crystals and the power to fly through the air. The Matum dancer wears a row of five crystals, or mica-covered wood, along the crown of his head.[65]

Diné

This dream I dreamt, (2)
Miraculously brought me,
Today it will not happen!
Today it has not happened.[66]

ᘐ   SINGERS: Pinetree, Other Trees Extend Down. If Talking Rock (a rock formation in Echo Canyon, eroded into a face) sends a warning dream,[67] Rock Arch (Rainbow Bridge) can avert the threatened event.

Hamakhav

> I blow my breath at the darkness
> And it disappears like a mist before the sun
> And day comes.
> When you sing this song
> And blow your breath at the darkness
> It will disappear.[68]

ᘐ   SINGER: Awheyama. Brown Buzzard promises healing power in a vision.

Hamakhav

> 1. Tell it everywhere
>   To the sea!
> 2. Butterfly created,
>   He made himself.
>   He cannot be
>   Killed!
>   He dreamed well![69]

ᘐ   SINGER: Mahtsitnyumeve. Coyote gave Qwaqaqta, a doctor for eyes, healing in the dream this song evokes.

A'a'tam A'kimult

> In the white Morning
> I entered the ruins.
> In the white Morning
> I entered the Magician's House.
>   I came there,
> My heart a flame, shining with power!
> Under the lofty feather roof
> He increases his magic power, singing!
>   He moves slowly there,
> My heart a flame, shining with power![70]

ᘐ   SINGER: Virsak Vai-i. Makai Nyoi (Magician's Song). A Healing Song that came in a vision, during which the healer gained power from Earth Magician. His heart became a flame when it embodied that power.

A'nish'inabeg

What are you saying to me?
"I am arrayed like the roses,
And beautiful as they."[71]

SINGER: Na'waji'bigo'kwe. A Midé love charm and Healing Song. Roses in Midé ceremony, song, and pictographs represented the harmonious healing power of choral song.[72] This song implies that the song wears the singer. It also served as a love song.

VI The Great Ceremonies

Natinnoh-hoi

> This time only you will see me.
> When they dance at Takimildin
> Fog will cover the base of the mountain
> Toward the south!
> I watch from there!
> Thus, when the time comes,
> They will dance it thus!
> Whoever dances thus will think of me.[1]

SINGERS: Senaxon, McCann. Kixunai sang this song in a vision, instituting the Jumping Dance and Ceremony. Ceremonial societies usually produced the communal ceremonies. They usually alluded to an original ceremony derived from a vision.

CEREMONIES FOR RAIN

Sitsime

> In Sipapu,
> Inside of the house of the Rain-Men
> The head Rain-Man speaks:
> "Now you are ready to go out,
> You Rain-Boys and Girls;
> It will rain all over the world,
> Over the South, over the East,
> All the rains will come to the people
> Below the clouds.
> All the little children
> Carry pretty flowers
> And throw them down from the sky;
> These flowers are the best clothes
> We can wish;
> It is all over the world."[2]

A Chakwena Kachina Dance Song.

Hopitu

There in the west, at the house of the clouds,
At Sipapuni, center of the world, is a cloud altar.
There rain rises, rain goes out from there,
The four younger sisters, those Rain-God Maids.
Water Cougar is there with something on his face,
    A streak of rain-clouds.
Water-light, moon-light water, will be there.
Lightning, thunder, rain-rumbling-thunder!
    Hiwai! Running water!
    Hiwai! Rushing, running water!
Yellow Corn, Blue Corn, my Mother
    Will wake us among the houses![3]

A Snake Dance Choral Song. The snake men enter and circle the plaza, face each other, and sing before handing out the rattlesnakes.

Tsiyame

White Floating Clouds,
Clouds like the Plains
[Bring the earth water.]
Sun, Moon,
Cougar, Bear, Badger,
Wolf, Eagle, Shrew,
Maasewe, Elder Warrior,
Uyuuyewe, Young Warrior,
Samaihaia, Northern Warrior,
Shinohaia, Western Warrior,
Yumahaia, Southern Warrior,
Ahwahaia, Eastern Warrior,
Peahhaia, Zenith Warrior,
Sarahaia, Nadir Warrior,
[Ask the Cloud People
For rain for us.]
Medicine water bowl,
Cloud Bowl,
Sacred Water Vase,
[Send the earth water.]
I make a meal road,
The ancient road,
The ancient road of meal,
[For my song.]

> White Shell Bead Woman,
> Who lives in the sunset,
> Mother Whirlwind,
> Creator Father,
> Yellow Northern Mother,
> Maker of good thoughts,
> Blue Western Woman,
> Red Southern Woman,
> White Eastern Woman,
> Pale Yellow Zenith Woman,
> Dark Nadir Woman,
> Speak for us to the Cloud People.[4]

Sitsime

> Yellow butterfly, Green butterfly,
> You who dance among the flowers![5]

     An old Rain Ceremony Song.

TO BRING FERTILITY

Konhiak

> 1. The plants are growing.
>   They are green now
>   But they are all coming into flower.
>   Soon will be the New Year
>   So let us dance.[6]

     SINGER: Santo Blanco. Women's Fiesta Song. Women's Dance Song. In the Women's Circle Dance, in May, when flowers bloom, each woman took the part of a flower. Each painted her flower on her face and danced, wearing flowers in her hair and a wreath of leaves. The dancers placed fruit and flower baskets in a circle outside the dance ground. The singer, an old man, the only man participating, stood in the center. Then little girls formed a ring, around them, the maidens, then young matrons, and outermost, the old women. During the dance, each dancer left her ring, danced to her plant, and returned with her fruit or flower.

Nanbe

> Avanyu, Storm Snake Old Man,
> Come here now, for we are dancing!
> Bringing your rain, you arrive now.[7]

∽ Nambe Sun-Rain Dance. Avanyu, a horned serpent flashing lightning from his mouth and feathered with clouds (the storm god glimpsed through thunderheads), threatened to flood the world. The hero-twins killed him with arrows and left his body as the ridge at Nambe Falls. Water still pours from his mouth. At San Juan, races accompany this ceremony. San Juan dancers sing this song as part of the Man Ceremony, Sen Poen. The ceremony links symbolic human sexual intercourse and the earth's fertility.[8]

Zuni

From where you stay quietly,
Your little wind-blown clouds,
Your fine wisps of clouds, your massed clouds,
You will send forth to sit down with us;
With your fine rain caressing the earth,
With all your waters,
You will pass to us on our roads.
My fathers, add to your hearts.
Your waters, your seeds,
Your long life, your old age,
You will grant to us.
Therefore I have added to your hearts
To the end, my fathers, my children:
You will protect us.
All my ladder-descending children
Will finish their roads.
They will grow old.
You will bless us with life.[9]

∽ A ladder leads into the Kiva, a men's society clubhouse and chapel. The descent also alludes to Sipapu, the hole through which the First People emerged into this world and which leads to the spirit world. The song suggests death and rebirth. The First Coyote Medicine Bringer took such a journey to meet the Coyote Holy People and bring back the healing Coyoteway Ceremony to the Navajo.

RACES AND PUBERTY CEREMONIES

Tewa

Old Sun Man,
Stand ready at Dawn on Cactus Ridge!
Old Moon Man,
Stand ready at Dawn on Cactus Ridge!

> Stand ready at Dawn,
>> Ready to go to San Juan!
> Stand ready at Dawn,
> Ready to run the Eagle Tail Rain Standing Road!
> Little White Twins, from Stone Man Mountain,
>> Stand ready at Dawn,
>> Ready to go to San Juan,
> Ready to run the Rain Standing Road at San Juan!
> Great Night Star Man,
>> Stand ready at Dawn,
>> Ready to go to San Juan.[10]

ꝰ The races, which accompany many ceremonies such as puberty ceremonies, imitate the daily course of the sun and strengthen the sun to run its daily race from dawn to sunset.

A'a'tam A'kimult

1. Singing, to the Magicians' houses,
   My shining magic, lifted,
   Stands as I sing.
2. The Wild Women first came running
   Holding blue flowers!
   Running from the dawn!
   Whispering as they file in!
3. I run the crooked trail.
   I run the crooked sunset trail.
   I run to the Rainbows,
   With swinging arms I go there.
4. Bright Dawn appears there,
   Bright Dawn, there in the sky,
   Dimming the Pleiades!
   To the Moon the Sun appears,
   Rising, rising high!
5. Bluebird came running with many women!
   They ran carrying clouds on their heads,
   All running, clouds atop their heads!
   Shaking their clouded heads, shaking us!
6. Gray Spider Magician
   Ties the Sun as the Moon rolls on,
   Stops there, turns and rolls back!

See his green cane
Rising higher![11]

᠅ SINGER: Ki-iwa. The Middle Run Song (O-ota Vapai Nyoi) at a feast. The
song marks a course from dawn to sunset. Dawn brings clouds, the Wild
Women from the fertility myths, and Spider Magician's power to make the
fields green. Gray Spider orders the fabric of the creation. He laces earth
to sky, makes a frame of sticks, covers them, in speech, and makes an offer-
ing to propitiate the dead in the Scalp Song.

Konhiak

I run a race
With a man who is very fleet.
With us runs an old man
    Who is fleet-footed,
And an old woman
    Who is very fast.
My young companion
Runs evenly with me,
And we reach the line together.
The old man is close behind.
He is winning when the woman shouts
And he staggers and falls dead.
The old woman crosses the line.[12]

᠅ SINGER: Santo Blanco. In this ritual race from a vision, the Old Woman,
the earth, masters a competing power or shaman. An appropriate vision or
dream, or the desire to heal someone or to acquire medicine and power,
often led a man, woman, family, or society to ask for an initiation cere-
mony or to vow to sponsor a dance.

A'a'tam A'kimult

The Wild Woman rose and ran,
    Around me here, she ran,
    Beating the air and her breast.[13]

᠅ SINGER: Juan Thomas. Toatcita Nyoi (Medicine Song). The Wild Women
sang in the darkness surrounding ceremonies at night. Dancers represented
these ceremonially promiscuous women in some of the puberty and fertil-
ity dances. The Wild Women sing, or accompany, badger, black lizard,

owl, and gila monster songs.[14] The Wild Women enjoy hearing the singing, and their enjoyment helps cure the patient.

BRINGING SOCIAL AND PERSONAL HEALING

Kwagutl

    1. I come to see you, ghosts.
      Why do you make this clamor,
        Ghosts, who drive us mad?
      Why make the house reverberate,
        Ghosts, who drive us mad?
      From the beach,
      Why call us from the beach,
        Ghosts, who drive us mad?
      Coming from the beach,
        Famous ghosts who drive us mad!
    2. They come out of the ground from you,
        Ghosts, who drive us mad!
      The voice of Hunger comes from you,
        Ghosts, who drive us mad!
      We come to get Plenty from you,
        Ghosts, who drive us mad![15]

This song and the ceremony originated in a journey to the underworld, where the spirits taught the visionary secrets, the dance, and medicine. In the dance, the dancer summons ghosts and sinks into the ground. Voices, of people speaking through buried kelp tubes, rise from the ground, imitating the ghosts' voices. The dancer rises from the ground in a similar dance, four days later.

Kwagutl

    Do not yet truly eat. (2)
    By and by you shall truly eat,
      When you eat with me!
    The food refuses to go down your throat!
    I have become Pa'hpaqalano'siwi,
    I have become the good Hamats'a.[16]

SINGER: Gwa'kwils. A Hamats'a sang this during a Body Eating Contest. During the Winter Dance, members of the Cannibal (Ha'mats'a) Society initiated the candidates, who had spent a month or more alone in the wilderness acting as wild carnivores, scavengers, and cannibals. The initiated Hamats'a acted as members of the medicine society and no longer bit people, except when they fell into a ritual frenzy, sparked by hearing personally taboo words. The Kwakiutl probably elaborated their Winter Dance more than did other Salishan-Wakashan communities. Edward S. Curtis says that the performers faked the body and mummy eating and slave killing that marked Cannibal Society Dances and Ceremonies. Franz Boas gives many instances of the stage devices and illusions the Kwakiutl used in such ceremonies.[17] Pa'hpaqalano'siwi, a man-eating being, appeared to those chosen to become Hamats'a or play any other part in the Winter Dance. Pa'hpaqalano'siwi moves like the wind and snatches up bodies as does a tornado or whirlwind. Several Holy People serve Pa'hpaqalano'siwi: Kwahqaqalanohsiwi (Pa'hpaqalano'siwi's Raven) tests food by pecking out the eyes of prey; Kyenkalatlulu, a woman, finds bodies for Pa'hpaqalano'siwi and offers him her arm to bite; Hohhuq, a monster bird, crushes skulls; Nanstalihl-Pa'hpaqalano'siwi (Pa'hpaqalano'siwi's Grizzly) tears up flesh for him. Other helpers are Kaloqutsuis (Curved Beak of the Upper World), another huge bird; Kominaka, a very large woman, who plays Raven; and Nunhltsista (Senseless), impervious to fire, enraged by fire.[18] Irving Goldman discusses the man-eater societies at length.[19]

Nuxalk

> I was taken around by Kominaka,
>   There, around the world.[20]

༄ The Maiden Warrior sings this song given by Kominaka (Rich Woman), a Holy Person in the second order of importance in the Winter Dance.

Kwagutl

> Where the copper hair,
> Where the ice hair is spread,
> There is the supernatural.[21]

༄ This Crest Origin song, sung in the Potlatch Ceremony, recalls the myth of two boys, whom G'itgoo'yim led into the forest, where they played with salmon for four days, became supernaturals, and gave this song to the Crest Owner.

Tsimshian

> Who will chase me into the sky?
> . . . .
> Are you trying to break the pillars of the sky?

Who will run with me into the sky,
You fake chiefs imitating real people?
Who will follow me through the hole,
    Through the hole in the sky,
Through the great, bright mirage beyond?
    Who will imitate me
When they see my white footprints,
    White as Raven's in the snow,
    White as Raven's. (2)[22]

SINGER: Weehawn. The chief danced to this Raven Frog Phratry's Chief's Song and shook eagle down from his head, as a sign of peace and friendship during Peace Dances and Ceremonies.

Kwagutl

1. The Ho'xhoku's voice is heard
     All over the world.
   Assemble at your places, Dancers!
     At the edge of the world
2. The Raven's voice is heard,
     All over the world.
   Assemble at your places, Men!
     Dancers at the edge of the world.
3. The Hamats'a's voice is heard
     All over the world.
   Assemble at your places, Men!
     Dancers at the edge of the world.[23]

A Hamats'a (Cannibal) Song summons the dancers in the Winter Ceremony. The Ho'xhoku, a long-beaked bird into whom a youth who has seen Baxbadualanuxsi'wae or his entourage transforms, fractures skulls and eats brains. The Raven (Qoa'xqoaxualanu), another of Baxbadualanuxsi'wae's entourage, scavenges the eyes from bodies Baxbadualanuxsi'wae has devoured. The name Baxbadualanuxsi'wae (First to Devour Men at the River's Mouth, or Ocean, or Stream Running North) suggests that the ocean was the first cannibal.

Tlingit

1. Ravens, he is your Stone Canoe,
     Your feelings, Buffalo House People!
   Where is the Raven?
   In it, he can go safely to land.

2. The Paddlers know him,
   Your river marker, Ravens.
Be happy,
   Below, the sound is heard.[24]

෯   SINGERS: Kuckena, Frank Italio. A Peace Dance Song. The Peace Hostage, like the medicine Stone Canoe or the buoy, ensures peace and thus makes journeys safe for the Kagwantan. The spirits speak from below and support peace.

Dakota

        The meadowlark, my cousin,
           A voice, soars in the air.[25]

෯   Sung by the conductor in the Oglala Lakota Hunka Ceremony, during the symbolic capture and adoption of the *hunka* (captive) into the Hunkayapi, for whom the ceremony was performed. The ceremony formed bonds among the Hunkayapi as strong as those formed among warrior societies, without forming an organization. The ceremony worked almost as did adopting a captive into the tribe. The conducting shaman, invoking Meadowlark, claimed power to produce fidelity. By mentioning the lark's voice in the air, this song claimed and produced a fidelity that pervaded the camp. In this song, lark's song wears the lark.

Tsimshian

        I will sing the song of the sky!
        Down it flies the owl,
           Spiraling like a whirlpool!
        This song is all the songs of those wearying,
        The tired salmon panting in the swift current,
           The whirlpools.
           I walk around
        Where the swift water runs into whirlpools.
        They talk rapidly to me, hurriedly.
           The sky turns over.
           They call me.[26]

෯   SINGER: Tralahaet. This ancient Chief's Song preceded the distribution of gifts in potlatches.

Maklaks   I am the South Wind's magic song
                             And sweep over the earth.[27]

                 ꝫ   SINGER: Sergeant Morgan.

Zuni   That our earth mother may wear a fourfold green robe
                                 Full of moss,
                                 Full of flowers,
                                 Full of pollen,
                             That the land may be thus
                             I have made you into living beings.[28]

                 ꝫ   This chant accompanies consecrating and dispatching the prayer sticks that
                     please the rainmakers.

Qwulh-hwaipum   Sound of the drum, sound of the heart,
                                 My brothers, my sisters.
                                 I am meeting you.
                             I am meeting you at the dance.[29]

                 ꝫ   SINGER: Tom Bill. John Arthur Brown quotes Smoholla's post-Anglo ver-
                     sion, in which the pure of heart would hear bells sound at the ending of
                     the world.[30] Drums rather than bells figured in the original ceremony and
                     songs.

Inuit   Look, they come,
                             Gaily dressed in fine new furs.
                             Women, women, young women!
                             See, wearing mittens,
                             They hold gulls' wings high,
                             And their coat tails wave
                             As they sway!
                             Women are here, women, young women!
                             No mistaking when they stride forth
                             To meet the men
                             Who joyfully await
                             The prize of victory in the contest![31]

⌁ SINGER: Orulo. Orulo, an Iglulik woman, sang this song, part of the *qulunertut,* a contest including a song contest. Half the women waved gulls' wings; the other half sang a song from which this section comes. The half that tired lost and had to stride over to the winners, who surrounded them, while the men tried to kiss them. Groups danced to celebrate success or to ask for help in hunting and to stage contests in archery, poetry, invective, and other demonstrations of skill.

Numakaki

My tail rattles,
My ears rattle,
Each end rattles,
My whole body rattles!
My face is striped!
My back is striped.[32]

⌁ SINGER: Wolf Head. This is a Skunk Society Song, which recalls a story in which Coyote and Skunk deceive prairie dogs, leading them away from town in a dance to eat them, as the Walrus and the Carpenter did the oysters. Little girls (ages eight to thirteen) of the Skunk Society danced, walking in line singing, each holding the dress of the girl ahead. The little girls pretended to be skunks or prairie dogs or both. Often they mocked warriors who regarded themselves overly highly. The Skunk Society did not encourage male self-satisfaction.

SUN AND MEDICINE LODGE CEREMONIES

A'nish'inabeg

Cool water he will give me to drink,
Man'ido, when he sees me.[33]

⌁ SINGER: E'niwub'e. Man'ido's gift of cool water produces the interior coolness that the Sun and Ghost Dances and the Blessingway of the Navajo also confer. E'niwub'e's grandfather sang this for him and other boys returning from their fasting vigil. As he sang, water sprang from a hole in the center pole.

Neshnabek

1. Go and get the cedar pole,
   Stand it in front of my house, in the ground.
   "The man everlasting" is to be with us for as long as the earth lasts.
   It stands for a mortal man, standing in this world forever.

2. Dance around this pole and thank Ka'kak,
    Who makes his nest in the top of this tree, a man,
    Who will stand here as long as the earth shall last!
    As long as the earth shall last,
    Ka'kak will make his nest in the top of this tree.[34]

ᚫ   Duck Hawk Clan Chant 8. This cedar centerpole stands for Wi'saka's
      brother who, when killed, turned into a tree. The cedar and the cotton-
      wood suggested rebirth. In a version of the myth of the wise and foolish
      wishers, one who wishes for immortality becomes a cedar; another, a rock.

A'nish'inabeg   The receding sound (2)
                         Of the nest,
                             I listen to it![35]

ᚫ   SINGER: E'niwub'e. E'niwub'e's grandfather sang this song when E'niwub'e
      had blackened his face to go on his fasting vigil. Some Sun Dancers set a
      pole, perhaps twenty feet long and six or eight inches across, with two or
      three stumps of branches left at the top, in the middle of the Sun Dance
      ground.[36] Often the dancers hung ceremonial objects such as a buffalo
      head, eagle feathers, or fetish figurines high on the pole or at the top.
      These ceremonial objects tended to evoke the Thunder Beings and suggest
      the thunder rolling over and past the dancers.

THE SUN DANCE

Dakota   Look! The Buffalo stand.
                      I make them![37]

ᚫ   "I make the good spirits of all game come and watch!" The Holy Animal
      People help the Sun Dancer. The singer saw these Wakan Persons in a
      vision related to the Sun Dance and heard this song, which invokes the
      medicine given in the vision. The song also evokes good hunting in a cere-
      mony that evolved from a Hunter's Dance into a War Dance and then into
      the healing Sun Dance. Having dreamed of a Thunder Being, or desiring
      to heal someone or acquire medicine and power, a man, woman, or family
      vowed to sponsor the dance.

Assiniboin   Thunder hovers close about
                                      This Wakan tree.

      ᧂ   A Make a Home (Watichaghe) Ceremony Song. "Home" refers to the "nest" built for the Thunder Being at the top of the sacred tree, the center pole of the lodge. After preparing a sweatlodge and purifying themselves in sweatlodge ceremonies, plains Sun Dancers selected a center pole for the dance. Acting as though on a raid, the men surrounded, cut down, and brought back to the dance ground the center pole, to which they attached medicine objects. The plains dancers often put objects recalling the Thunder Beings into a "nest" on the center pole. The Potawatomi, the Ojibwa, and the Cree also built nests for the Thunders on the center poles of their ceremonial grounds.

Ka'igwu   Father! You give us this cedar because you love it.
                                      Every other tree dies, and grass:
                                      But this tree, it does not die in winter,
                                      Its leaves do not drop off in the fall.
                                          We think you love it.
                                      You take care of it. You keep it always green.
                                      You give it a good road. I want you to smell its smoke.[39]

      ᧂ   A chant or prayer to the sun. Sun Dancers carried green cedar, because as an evergreen it symbolized rebirth and long life, as did the cottonwood. Some dances used cedar as the center pole, some cottonwood. In some Sun Dances, the dancers carried sage, also an evergreen.

Dakota   Thunders brought me down to earth!
                                          Clouds blowing in every direction
                                              I come through![40]

      ᧂ   The owner and singer dreamt, as a boy, of a nest descending, carrying him. The Thunders did not tell him the dream's meaning, as they should have, and he did not know to sponsor a Sun Dance. He led a disastrous life until a clown (a *heyo'ka*) interpreted the dream and told him he must sponsor a Sun Dance. Usually the Sun Dance recalled details from myths or visions and brought the sponsors and the dancers power, medicine, long life, and visions.

Nimic

That we will dig out the Great Rock in beauty;
That that Great Rock will go out from its place;
That those visible here will go out in beauty from this place;
 I pray.
 That is ended.[41]

♪ The celebrants sang one version of this song while preparing the altar within the lodge, another while preparing the *thi'aya,* the mound containing a consecrated buffalo skull, facing the entrance of the lodge. Songs such as this link the Great Rock embodying creation and endurance: the Holy Person Iya, for example, with the buffalo on the plains or the deer in the woodlands.

THE GHOST DANCE

THE DANCERS SANG each line of the Ghost Dance (Wanagi Wachipi) Songs twice, unless otherwise indicated. The Ghost Dancers danced to heal a world mortally infected by the European invaders. The dancers felt the sudden gush of inward coolness and the cataleptic rigidity that accompanied healing in ceremonies such as the Sundance or Nightway. In their vision, the dancers looked back to the old world, free from invaders, and forward to a new world, disinfected.[42]

O'maha

My friend, this is a wide world
We're traveling over,
Walking on the moonlight.[43]

♪ An Omaha woman heard this song, a Ghost Song but not a Ghost Dance Song, in a dream and placated the ghosts by throwing bread to the four winds in the morning. The Omaha often saw ghosts as whirlwinds walking a foot or so above the ground. In a Caddo myth, Coyote made death eternal by barring a dustdevil containing a spirit from entering the lodge and returning to life. "Now whenever anyone meets a whirlwind or hears the wind whistle, he says, 'Someone is wandering about.' "

Ka'igwu

The Ghost army advances, they say!
They come with the buffalo, they say!
They come with the new earth, they say![44]

♪ The dance, the Ghost Dancers hoped, would trigger the return of the preinvasion world and the disappearance of the invaders.

Kadohada'cho   E'yehe'! Children!
                     Come on, Caddo, we are all going up
                     To the great village—
                     With our father above, (1)
                     Where he dwells on high—
                     Where our mother dwells—![45]

          The Ka'dohada'cho included the Wichita, Pawnee, Arikara, and Kichai in
          Texas and Louisiana.

Tsistsi'stas   Well, my children—Ehe'e'ye'!
                     When you meet your friends again—Ahe'e'ye!
                         The earth will tremble—E'ahe'e"ye'!
                         The summer cloud (1)
                         Will give it to us.[46]

          The summer cloud, or thunderhead, evokes a Crow–Cloud–Thunder Being
          complex of associations and images.

Inuna'ina'   The cedar tree,
                     We have it in the center
                         When we dance.
                     We have it in the center.[47]

          The cedar, like the cottonwood, carries power. As an evergreen, it brings
          long life. The Micmac, in the common story of four wishes granted, say
          Glooscap changed the man who wished for long life into a cedar.[48] Some
          tribes made the cedar the center pole in the Sun Dance. The shaggy cedar
          acquired additional holy power from resembling the shaggy buffalo; once
          Indians visiting Washington asked for tufts of buffalo hair and cedar limbs
          to use in ceremonies there.[49] Cedar smoke protects from lightning and
          sickness.[50]

Numa   Tall, the cottonwoods, the cottonwoods grow tall, (3)
                     They grow tall and leaf-covered, green and tall. (3)[51]

          For plains and desert tribes, the cottonwood marked water. Its peeled bark
          fed horses, and from its roots people made Kachina dolls and ceremonial

objects. Black Elk made a cottonwood the symbolic center of a sacred dance and of the nation.[52] The Shoshone and Crow Sun Bear Dancers made a cottonwood pole the center of their Sun Dance.[53] The cottonwood evoked memories of life before the invasion. Levi Young prints this, without the Ute original, as a "song to the Cottonwoods."[54]

Inuna'ina'

The seven venerable Chi'nachichi'bat priests,
     I weep for them.
I weep for the Ba'qati wheel.[55]

The singer saw preinvasion games, priests, and camp in a vision of a Golden Age. References to gambling and hoops allude to the sacred hoops, such as the hoop that Black Elk saw, which bound the people together and, when broken, marked defeat. These Water-Sprinkling-Old-Men, the Chi'nachichi'bat priests, carried medicine bundles, and their lodge of seven priests served the tribe as its most honored ceremonial association.

Ka'igwu

I scream because I am a bird!
 I bellow like a buffalo!
  The boy will rise![57]

SINGER: Pa-guadal (Red Buffalo). Sung at a dance at Walnut Creek, 1893, under the prophet Pa-ingya, to resurrect Red Buffalo's recently dead son. Red Buffalo's father was one of the "buffalo doctors" who imitated the buffalo's bellow in their war cries. Red Buffalo claimed to have inherited his father's powers. He composed this song in a trance, in which he saw his father, the Father, and the Crow.

Inuna'ina'

Little boy, the coyote gun,
 I have uncovered it—Ahe'e'ye'!
  The sheath lies there![58]

SINGER: Nakash (Sage). In his vision, the singer saw a dead little boy visiting him on sentry duty outside the camp. Sage saw himself as one of the middle-aged *gaahi'na,* "coyote men" (pickets), stationed on the hills near camp. The *gaahi'na* wore white buffalo robes, painted with white clay, and carried the coyote gun, a club decorated with feathers and sheathed in bear gut, when on duty. They slept alone on the hills outdoors and sought visions. The Ghost Dance Songs often include such intimate, emotionally powerful, quotidian events. Shaman-sponsors sang these songs to initiate or reintroduce into dream power the warrior who had taken a scalp and been purified. Extraordinarily valorous warriors used the shield and club. The Papago linked ancient forms of medicine weapons (the Eagle shield, the war-club) to purification after scalp-taking, medicine that brought power in war, but also to domestic medicine, the power to bring rain.[59]

Inuna'ina'

> The Crow woman,
> To her home, she is going.
>   She will see it.
> Her children,
>   She will see them.[60]

❧ Composed by Mo'ki (Little Woman), wife of Grant Left Hand, son of Nawat (Left Hand), of the Southern Arapaho. She took the name "Crow Woman," messenger of the spirits. Her two children had died. In a trance during a Ghost Dance, she met and played with her children in the spirit world. She told her husband, who went to the next Ghost Dance. In his vision, his dead little boy rode behind him on his horse over the green rolling prairies of the ghost world. Nawat and Mo'ki went to every dance thereafter, for a chance to play with their children and talk to dead friends. The Kalispell tell a similar story, about a chief who lost his son, fell into suicidal despair, and received a prophetic vision and bullet-proofing medicine.[61]

Dakota

> Mother, come home!
> My little brother goes about crying!
> Mother, come home![62]

❧ From a vision in which a young woman saw her mother in the spirit world, her family as it was before her mother died, and the Golden World before the invaders killed it. Curtis calls this song one of the most popular sung in the Ghost Dance.[63] Harry Paige heard Nancy White Horse sing a version at Soldier Creek, South Dakota, in July 1964.[64]

Dakota

> "I made moccasins for him,
>   For I love him,

To take to the orphan.
Soon I shall see my child!"
    Says your mother![65]

꩜   The singer made moccasins for her dead child, whom she had seen in a
    vision, and carried them during the dance.

Inuna'ina'
The seven crows—Hi'a hi'ni'ni!
They fly about the carrion—Hi'a hi'ni'ni![66]

꩜   A vision of a successful buffalo hunt in the Golden Age—friends cutting
    up meat and seven crows hovering for food, suggesting medicine power
    like that accompanying the seven venerable Chi'nachichi'bat priests in
    Arapaho songs 43 and 44. Four signified great Wakan power; seven signi-
    fied lesser, but still great, Wakan power; songs and stories mention seven
    crows, seven priests, seven stars, and other sevens.

Inuna'ina'
How bright the moonlight
Tonight as I ride with my load of buffalo beef.[67]

꩜   SINGER: Yellow Horse. The emotional impact of such a song appears more
    clearly when highlighted against an Omaha White Buffalo Ritual song,
    IV.9, in which the successful hunter tells his son to help him dress out the
    buffalo.[68] Black Elk describes the joy of such a hunt.[69] This song memorial-
    izes a vision of dead friends in the spirit world preparing to go on a great
    buffalo hunt. In the vision they came back in moonlight, their ponies
    loaded with buffalo meat, able to live in a sacred manner. Arapaho hunters
    sang a similar song.

Dakota
"Give me my knife
I shall hang meat to dry"—Ye'ye!
    Says the grandmother—Yo'yo!
"When it is dry,
I shall make pemmican!"
    Says the grandmother—Yo'yo![70]

꩜   Making pemmican (buffalo meat dried, mixed and pounded with berries
    and fat, and stored in hides) triumphantly climaxed the successful buffalo

hunt. The hunt entailed weeks of practical and ceremonial preparation. After the hunt, making pemmican required communal effort and cooperation. A large store of pemmican helped the people survive through the winter. This song evokes a preinvader Golden Age, in which the Grandmother (earth in human form) prepares pemmican and fills the world with buffalo. When the singer sang this song, hide hunters had killed nearly all the buffalo on the continent, and no one could make pemmican anymore.

Ka'igwu

> I mash the berries!
> Travelers come, they say!
> I stir, I stir the berries!
> I lift them with a buffalo horn spoon
> And carry, carry them (to the strangers)![71]

These berries, the "best fruit," do not grow in southern (Kiowa) country, but in the North, whence the Sioux drove the Kiowa. This vision evokes a pre-Sioux as well as a pre-*wasichu* Golden Age. The Kiowas' yearning for the edenic North resembles the yearning that drove the Northern Cheyenne to follow Dull Knife and Little Wolf in their trek north, which Mari Sandoz recounts in *Cheyenne Autumn*.

Inuna'ina'

> There is a good river,
> Where there is no timber,
> But thunderberries are there![72]

In a vision, the singer saw people camped by a permanent river, fringed with berry bushes, probably the black haw, that bore sweet berries, scarce in the South. The Okanagon viewed the serviceberry (*Amelanchier alnifolia*) with the same affection.[73] Like the haw, the serviceberry resembles an exceptionally sweet currant. People used these berries to make pemmican.

Tsistsi'stas

> I waded into the yellow river,
> Into the Turtle river, I waded.[74]

Perhaps the River of Many Turtles, the St. Croix. Turtle supports the universe in many mythologies. Algonquin tribes honored Turtle as a symbol of earth, often addressed her as "mother," and made the Turtle Clan the most prestigious. They called Mackinac Island *michilimacinac,* "the Island of the Great Turtle," and made their favorite bowls from turtle shell.[75]

Tsistsi'stas

> My comrade—I'yahe'yahe'e!
> Let's go play shinny—Ahe'e'ye!
> Let's look for our mother—Ahe'e'ye!
> Our Father tells us to—Ahe'e'ye![76]

SINGER: Mo'ki. In a vision, Mo'ki called to a dead girlhood friend, seeing her as she was alive. Shinny, a woman's gambling game, appears in both myth and ritual. "One's sicun may inhere in anything . . . even in things used to gamble." Our mother alludes both to Mo'ki's mother, evoking nostalgia for a happy childhood, and to the earth, evoking yearning for a preinvasion Golden Age. Mo'ki (Little Woman), wife of Grant Left Hand (Nawat), became a leader in the Cheyenne Ghost Dance movement.

Inuna'ina'

> My children, my top—
> It will win the game![77]

In a vision, the singer met a boyhood friend who had died young. The singer spun tops with him (using a whip or quirt) as they had when children. The top's humming suggests the humming of the earth before the advent of the new earth; its spinning, the whirlwind.

Numa

> The rocks ring. (3)
> In the mountains they ring. (3)[78]

The singer explained this song as evoking the roaring of a storm in the mountains. The wind gives voice to the enduring rock. In some stories, the wind saves the trickster from a vengeful rock.

Numa

> Fog! Fog!
> Lightning! Lightning!
> Whirlwind! Whirlwind![79]

This song uses symbols for powerful Holy Beings. Clouds, lightning, and rain suggest Holy People; the whirlwind, ghosts. In a Navajo Bear Song, the bear calls himself "whirlwind" and carries lightning and danger. A Zia Rain Dance Song asks Mother Whirlwind to intercede with the Cloud People. In signs and pictographs, jagged lines represent lightning, wavy lines Wakan, Manitu (Algonquin), or Orenda (Iroquois) power and Holy People.

Numa

> The snow lies there—ro'rani'! (4)
> The Milky Way lies there![80]

꙳ The Paiute danced at night. The Sierras looming in the West, nearby, snowcapped in the moonlight, offered a visible bridge to the Milky Way, the road that spirits took to the spirit world and along which they would return to bring the new world. Wovoka, prophet of the second Ghost Dance, was Paiute.

Ka'igwu

> That wind
> Shakes my tipi
> And sings a song for me![81]

꙳ "Tipi" can stand for the sky-covered earth, the camp of the band or tribe, or the medicine hoop. Plains shamans often demonstrated their power in the Shaking Tipi performance, in which they sang Vision Songs inside a medicine tipi, while freeing themselves, Houdini-like, from bonds. The tipi shook during the ritual and echoed with the voices of dead shamans, or Wakan beings, and the sound of sacred stones bouncing off the interior walls.[82]

Numa

> The wind stirs the willows. (3)
> The wind stirs the grasses. (3)[83]

꙳ The Paiute ground and boiled wild millet seed (*wai'va,* the sand grass of Nevada) into a mush. Like other Ghost Dance Songs, this one recalls an emotionally powerful memory of preinvasion daily life.

To Heal the World

Yokuts

Leave me a little of the sun!
Do not devour it altogether from me!
    Leave me a little![84]

ɔ   Sung to the moon to reverse an eclipse.

Karuk

This world is cracked.
But when I pick up and drag the stick
    All the cracks will fill up
And the earth will become solid again.[85]

ɔ   SINGER: Francis Davis. In the World Renewal Ceremony, the singer sang
this song while dragging a stick to fill lines scratched to represent cracks in
the world.

Tiwame

The dance is finished;
They crowd around the ladder.
All who take part say,
One man speaking after another,
"We hope we'll have good crops!"
"We hope we'll have watermelons."
"All over the world
[Holy Love] is spreading."
"When we go to rest tonight,
We expect to feel joy in the morning."
"May the wild animals flourish
    All over the country."
"May we have plenty of parched corn."
Someone hearing says,
"They say most precious words,
Most beautiful things."
People say, "How can he say such blessed things?
He must have them from his fathers.
He learned them well—most fitting things."
"When we get to our homes,
The next evening we shall talk about it."

"What a good dance that was,
Everybody feels better."
"We wish we could have it oftener,
But it is fitting only once a year."[86]

ᴄ⌒ The K'eres word for the highest, most sacred, most pleasant, and best
good possible, for which I use "Holy Love," has no satisfactory English
equivalent.

Walwarena

Hear that which sounds!
Listen to the sound of the world.
   It will always be.
Why does the world rumble so?
Why does the world roar so?[87]

ᴄ⌒ SINGER: Fernando Librado. Sung in the Seaweed Dance. The dancers imi-
tated the movements of seaweed. This song, evoking the crash of the surf,
addressed the rising Pleiades.

Ipay

10. Water rolls in,
     Pounds in,
     Waves pound in.
12. Eagle is swooping! Look!
     Eagle is flying! Look!
13.   Colored, (2)
       Red colored,
       My eagle![88]

ᴄ⌒ Eagle Dance Songs. Ocean talks to Eagle. Eagle talks and finally, sunset-
colored, swoops toward the surf.

Walwarena

   Clear the way!
Clear away the dirt that obstructs.
When I step forth with pride,
   The feathers fold up!
   I am a creature of power.
I stand and begin to walk

To the mountain tops,
To every corner of the world.
   I am a creature of power.[89]

꙳   SINGER: Fernando Librado. Bear Dance Songs. The people found the "feath-ers" or fur of this fierce beast in all corners of the world and respected the bear deeply. The dancer moved very quietly and respectfully to all four cor-ners, extending the *plumero,* a feathered wand.

Ipay

1. I dance using the feather skirt,
   The Sun,
     My rattle.
2. Around my head, my *nitceyo,*
   As I dance
In the eagle feather skirt.[90]

꙳   Whirling Dance Songs. The dancer, clad in a ceremonial eagle feather skirt, invokes sun power and the tutelary *nitceyo.*

Karuk

You, Kashoknan, Sandy Bar and Stony Bar,
You have been sitting here from the beginning.
   The World has tipped.
   Now I will straighten it.[91]

꙳   SINGER: Shan Davis. The singer burns a *Syringea* and tobacco mixture. During this ceremony, the singers moved their song over their land, heal-ing and renewing specific places.

Diné

[You who dwell] in Tse'ghi,
In the House Made of Dawn,
In the House Made of Evening Light,
In the House Made of Dark Cloud,
In the House Made of Male Rain,
In the House Made of Dark Mist,
In the House Made of Female Rain,
In the House Made of Pollen,
In the House Made of Grasshoppers,
Where Dark Mist curtains the doorway,

Where Zigzag Lightning stands high on top,
Where Male Rain stands high on top!

    Oh Male Holy Person!
With your moccasins of dark cloud, come to us,
With your leggings of dark cloud, come to us,
With your shirt of dark cloud, come to us,
With your headdress of dark cloud, come to us,
With your mind wrapped in dark cloud, come to us!
With the Dark Thunder above you, come to us soaring,
With the shaped cloud at your feet, come to us soaring,
With the far darkness made of the dark cloud over your head, come to us soaring,
With the far darkness made of the male rain over your head, come to us soaring,
With the far darkness made of the dark mist over your head, come to us soaring,
With the far darkness made of the female rain over your head, come to us soaring,
With the zigzag lightning flung out high over your head, come to us soaring,
With the rainbow hanging high over your head, come to us soaring!
With the far darkness made of the dark cloud on the ends of your wings, come to us soaring,
With the far darkness made of the male rain on the ends of your wings, come to us soaring,
With the far darkness made of the dark mist on the ends of your wings, come to us soaring,
With the far darkness made of the female rain on the ends of your wings, come to us soaring,
With the zigzag lightning out high on the ends of your wings, come to us soaring,
With the rainbow hanging high on the ends of your wings, come to us soaring!
With the near darkness made of dark cloud, male rain, dark mist, and female rain, come to us!
    With the darkness on earth, come to us!
With these I wish the foam floating on the flowing water over the roots of the great corn!

I have made your sacrifice! I have prepared a cigarette for you!
Restore my feet for me,
Restore my legs for me,
Restore my body for me,
Restore my mind for me,
Restore my voice for me!
Today, take out your spell from me,
Today, take away your spell for me!

Away from me you have taken it!
Far off from me it is taken!
Far off you have done it!
    Happily I recover!
Happily my interior cools!

Happily my limbs regain their power!
Happily my head cools!
Happily my limbs regain their power!
Happily I hear again!
Happily for me it is taken off!
    Happily I walk!
Impervious to pain, I walk!
Feeling light within, I walk!
    With zest, I walk!

In beauty, abundant dark clouds, I desire,
In beauty, abundant dark mists, I desire,
In beauty, abundant plants, I desire,
In beauty, abundant pollen, I desire,
In beauty, abundant dew, I desire!
Happily, may fair white corn to the ends of the earth come with you,
Happily, may fair yellow corn to the ends of the earth come with you,
Happily, may fair blue corn to the ends of the earth come with you,
Happily, may fair corn of all kinds to the ends of the earth come with you,
Happily, may fair possessions of all kinds to the ends of the earth come with you,
Happily, may fair jewels of all kinds to the ends of the earth come with you!
    With these before you, in beauty may they come with you,
    With these behind you, in beauty may they come with you,
    With these below you, in beauty may they come with you,
    With these above you, in beauty may they come with you,
    With these surrounding you, in beauty may they come with you,
        Thus in beauty you perform your tasks.

    Happily the old men will look on you,
    Happily the old women will look on you,
    Happily the young men will look on you,
    Happily the young women will look on you,
    Happily the boys will look on you,
    Happily the girls will look on you,
    Happily the children will look on you,
    Happily the chiefs will look on you,
    Happily the chiefs will look on you!
Happily as they scatter in different directions, they will look on you,
Happily as they approach their homes, they will look on you,
Happily, may their roads home be on the trail of pollen,
    Happily, may they also return!

With beauty before me, I walk!
With beauty behind me, I walk!
With beauty below me, I walk!
With beauty above me, I walk!
With beauty around me, I walk!

In Beauty, it is finished!
In Beauty, it is finished!
In Beauty, it is finished![92]

Prayer of the First Dancers, from the Nightway. Talking God (Hastceyalti) dwells in Tsegi, both a specific place, a hogan, and the world roofed with sky and walled with rainbow. Probably the Native American poem most widely known to Anglos. Readers often compare it to Psalm 23. It gave N. Scott Momaday the title for his first novel, *House Made of Dawn*. The *hataali* (singer) performs the Kledzhe Hatal (Yeibichai) (Night Chant) to heal a patient or harmonize a group. This song describes the approach of a rain-bringing thunderstorm, its arrival, and its passage to carry rain and harmony to the rest of Dinetah. The Holy Persons embodied in the storm also bring healing. The healing rain concentrates in the patient, bringing interior coolness, and then spreads out to the participants, the audience outside the hogan, Dinetah, and the universe. The Sun Dance also produced this feeling of interior coolness, of being drenched inside with cool water. The patient repeats this song to the Pollen Thunder Being, line by line, after the *hataali*. Repetition and incremental change characterize not only relatively short songs, but entire rituals. In Coyoteway, for example, a nine-night ceremony, the *hataali* repeats an unraveling song three times in a sequence of 161 songs. The song itself repeats an eight-stanza sequence three times, varying four words. Each stanza repeats a phrase, "by these he was led," seventeen times.[93]

Medicine

CEREMONIES AND SOCIETIES

Modoc

As a head only, I roll around.
I stand on the rim of my nest.
I am enveloped in flames.
What am I? what am I?
I, the song, I walk here.
I, the dog, stray, in the north wind I stray.
I am about to shoot an arrowhead.
  I am a bad song.
  The earth I sing of.[1]

SINGERS: Mary, Minnie Froben. Kroeber, *Handbook,* combined these lines (each line a separate song in Gatschet, *Klamath*). These songs, sung before or while the healer sucks out disease and blows it to the winds, include many common images associated with medicine: the powerful Rolling Head (line 1) figures in stories (similar to stories about rolling rocks) that pit one power against another. The Burrowing Owl, a prophesying person, contracts its body and seems to roll, walking around on the prairie. The nest (line 2) recalls the songs of the Crane and Fire Mantle and the nest of the Thunder Beings, surrounded with lightning (line 3). The song that wears the singer (line 5) evokes both shaman and Holy Person. The stray dog (line 6) calls on the power of the Trickster as a wandering coyote. Shooting feathers, shells, stones, or miniature arrows (line 7) enabled the healer to attack and remove the disease. Grandmother Earth (line 9) heals and transforms. The bad song (line 8) evokes the malevolent power attributed to shamans and implies a contest between the healer's good song and the witch's bad song.

Kwagutl

I was taken to the foot of Quartz Mountain.
I was taken to the foot of the Mountain,
Whence Quartz came rolling down to me.
It flew with me, carried me
To the end of the world,
    To the cloud,
Me, the child of Ma'tem.[2]

ᔭ This Ma'tem song alludes to a myth in which a youth, struck by his father, wandered, seeking death. He jumped into a river above a log jam then off a cliff. He arrived at Na'oalakoa (Quartz Cliff) in a rain of crystals and, covered with crystals, climbed the mountain. The Ma'tem, a supernatural bird who lives on a steep mountain and can confer the power of flight, gave him that power. He flew for four days and found he had flown for four years. He turned into a white eagle, evaded capture by his tribe, visited the ghosts, who can resurrect, and brought his people Ghost Medicine and healing ceremonies.[3]

Hamakhav

The Night Bat, rising, flies!
I tell it. I sing it.[4]

ᔭ Raven sings this song during the hero-twins' creating and emergence journey. The healing ceremony in which it occurs recapitulates their journey.

Konhiak

I am in the dark, but I know darkness.
    It does not trouble me.
The dark is the same as the light.[5]

ᔭ SINGER: Santo Blanco. Men's Ceremony. The Spirit of the Cave sings through the Old Woman.

A'a'tam A'kimult

Pitiable Wild Woman as I am, in the early evening,
My heart flowers.
In the evening, Wild Woman as I am,
My heart flowers with the singing.[6]

ᔭ SINGER: Sutatki. Tciataki Nyoi (Gila Monster Song).

Numa   Over the land at night
                                        The music drifts slowly.[7]

Yurok   We Holy Persons, well,
                                        The world and we Wogies
                                        Pretty much support each other,
                                        So I think you shouldn't be afraid
                                        Of what's happening here.[8]

                    ᠊᠊   Dancers, worn by Holy People, sang this Wogey Song in healing cere-
                          monies.

Neshnabek   1. Now I sing my power song, power given me.
                                           I take a rotten tree fallen in the woods.
                                              I stand it up.
                                           I go west of that tree, look back, and it is green.
                                           Green all over. That is the power, the power I have!
                                              The power he gave me.
                                           I stand it up, stand up the rotten tree, and it has leaves.
                                           I walk to the tree, put down tobacco.
                                           I sit to its east, smoke my pipe, and give thanks.
                                        2. A Powerful gift he gave me.
                                           To resurrect something dead, renew it.[9]

                    ᠊᠊   Stanzas 1 and 2 of Wolf Bundle Chant 2. The Winnebago Trickster met a
                          dead tree at the edge of a swamp, thought it a man holding out his arm,
                          and imitated the tree for a day and night. In a Cherokee story, a hunter,
                          adopted by bears, saw his bear mentor killed. The hunter looked back, on
                          his mentor's instructions, to see him rise from the bones and skin and go
                          back into the woods. This tree may also evoke the pole at the center of the
                          Sun and Ghost Dances.

Wazhazhe   "With what shall they adorn their bodies as they tread the path of life?"
                                           It has been said in this house.
                                        The crimson color of the God of Day who sits in the sky,
                                           They shall make their sacred color
                                           As they go forth on life's journey.

Truly, the god who reddens the sky as he approaches,
    They shall make their sacred color
    As they go forth on life's journey.
When they paint their bodies with the crimson color shed by that God of Day,
Then shall the little ones free themselves from all causes of death,
    As they go forth on life's journey.[10]

Havasuwapay

Earth, my relative, hear us!
Hear us, my relatives, Trees and Rocks,
Water, Wind, and earth, my relatives,
    Hear us!
    Be good for us today!
    We want to prosper.
We want to be like the earth or rock,
    To live to be old.[11]

SINGER: Sinyella.

Ka'igwu

Prairie Dogs, Prairie Dogs,
Wag your tails,
Now dance your best. (2)
Huh! (3)[12]

A Prairie Dog Dance Song. The girl singer played Trickster and "made little slashes in the air with the side of her hand to show that she was Trickster cutting the prairie dogs' heads off." In Trickster stories, prairie dogs often acted as improvidently as humans and provided examples that cured humans of pride and folly.

HEALERS AND SHAMANS

Dakota

My paw is sacred!
Herbs are plentiful!
My paw is sacred!
All things are sacred![13]

SINGER: Eagle Shield. A Curing Dream Song. A bear sang this to the dreamer.

Inuit

> Earth, earth, Great Earth,
> Around on earth
> There are bones, bones, bones,
> Bleached by Great Sila,
> By the weather, the sun, the air,
> So that all flesh disappears,
> He-he-he.
> Spirit, spirit, spirit,
> And the day, the day,
> Go to my limbs
> Without drying them up,
> Without turning them to bones,
> Uvai, uvai, uvai.[14]

ᔓ Angutingmarik won this song, which has great vitalizing powers, after shooting a raven with an arrow, running up to it as it died, and stating aloud his intentions and all that occupied his mind. The dying raven gave power to those words and thoughts.

Kiliwa

> "You moving clouds, you've chased me,
> You've crossed the Great World:
> Twice, thrice you've done it,
> You've done that, Sand Cloud.
> Brave Cloud, Storm Cloud, you've chased me,
> You've chased me, North Cloud.
> Thunder Cloud, you've chased me, I say!
> Western Cloud from the Forked Ocean,
> Oh Cloud Path for the Dew, I say,
> Cloud from the Weak Eastern Ocean,
> Night Walking Cloud, it was you," he said![15]

ᔓ SINGER: Trinidad Ochurte. Scolding the clouds, which invokes their power for the shaman.

Tsistsi'stas

> Thunder gave me black paint;
> He pitied me!
> He gave me black paint;
> He gave me protection from harm.
> The thunder makes a noise high up in the air.[16]

ᒧ   SINGER: Turtle. Cheyenne Healing Song. Turtle bought his songs from
Dragging Otter, who bought them from earlier medicine men. Black paint
marked the successful warrior, who escaped death and was invisible to his
enemies. Red paint marked health and healthy blood.

Inuit

Avaya!
Lovely, to put a bit of song together.
But too often I do it badly.
Avaya!
Lovely, hunting caribou:
But I seldom shine
Like a bright burning wick
On the ice,
Lucky, like a bright flame.
Lovely, getting wishes granted:
But they all slip past me.
It is all too difficult.
Avaya![17]

ᒧ   SINGER: Piuvkaq (Utkuhikjalik). A Holy Person or tutelary sometimes ap-
pears as a flame.

Yaqui

The bush sits under the tree,
Singing![18]

SINGER: Juan Ariwares. Singing here means evoking magic creative power.
The Quileute and Cocopa sang Medicine Songs in which tutelaries rose
from singing bushes. In Haida cradle songs, babies fell from salmonberry
bushes. The creosote bush, the second creation, sang songs that took the
form of Earth Magician's designs.

A'a'tam A'kimult

Black butterflies sing!
Black butterflies sing!
As I go below the ruins,
As I pass before the Houses of Magic.[19]

SINGER: Ki-iwa. Kakau Nyoi (Rattlesnake Song). Southwestern songs often
associated the ruins left by the Hohokam, the Anasazi, and other pre-

historic cultures with preemergence peoples, inimical spirits, magicians, and witches who drew their power in part from the magicians. The Navajo name "Anasazi" means "Enemies of the Ancients," or the enemies the First People encountered after emergence.

Tsimshian

> Fastened together are sea-otter and killer-whale;
> Scattered are the cockles where Tsegu'ksku wanders
> In his great house at Wa-opele'![20]

ॐ SINGER: Chief Mountain. In this shaman's vision, the singer went underground and brought back gifts from the sea people. The song came to him from the sea.

Dene

> They will kill us all,
> Ahead there, in the narrows.
> Only I will be able to run away.[21]

ॐ Otters sang this Montagnais song to a dreamer. It summons otters for either medicine or the hunter.

EVIDENCE OF POWER

Chahiksichahiks

> This I did
> [Threw this fireball]
> When I became angry
> So that in the future,
> The earth might be formed.[22]

ॐ SINGER: Coming Sun. This song, Morningstar's Fireball Song, was so sacred that the singers would not let it be recorded. Shamans, imitating Morningstar, learned to throw fireballs when healing or performing in ceremonies and, when singing this song, added, "And I imitate this power."

Kwagutl

> Old Man, put your hands on the sea
> And press it down!
> Thank you, Old Man,
> That we have passed safely.[23]

ॐ Addressed to an overhanging cliff.

Numa   Our song will enter
                                  That distant land,
                                  That gleaming land, (2)
                                  And roll the lake in waves.[24]

> Native Americans used "Shining" or "Gleaming" mountains as a common name for the Rockies or the Sierra Nevadas, because of the year-round snow cover on the summits.

A'a'tam A'kimult   Moonlight shines here in me and abides.
                                      You men and women will see
                                      The Blue Reed I blow
                                      Sing the distant moon down to meet me.[25]

> SINGER: Juan Thomas.

SHELL AND STONE

A'a'tam A'kimult   Around those standing stones there,
                                      Around those two singing stones,
                                      Around their tops, black wind roars,
                                      Driving birds fluttering, back and forth.
                                          On white Ngiwolik,
                                          Around his top,
                                          Green frogs sing,
                                      Near the blue storm clouds
                                      Lie many (frogs) singing.[26]

> SINGER: Sutatki (Prepare). Tciataki Nyoi (Gila Monster Song). The singers repeated the second to the last line of each stanza and repeated the resulting stanza four times. An Inuit stone[27] washed down in the melt flood, sang in a vision, and brought medicine. These stones also evoke the people whom Elder Brother preserved as stones. Not all stones brought medicine, of course. "A peculiar stone lay at the old man's feet. . . . It was not one of the usual . . . rough and gray. This was smooth and rounded, its white surface striped with green lines. It had been washed down by torrents . . . from some distant hill. . . . 'This is not a stone-stone. . . . I think it may have power. Perhaps it can bring rain.' . . . Holding it in his right hand, he whirled it sunwise. . . . 'If it does not bring rain? . . . I shall throw it away. But I always look for rainbringers. . . .' "[28] Stones struck by lightning or found near lightning strikes worked most dependably.

O'maha

" 'One of these creatures is the greatest,
    Inspiring to all minds,
    The Great White Rock!
    Yes indeed—as high as the heavens':
    As he speaks, my little ones shall speak of me, Wakonda.
    As long as they shall travel in life's path;
    Thus they shall speak of me."
    Such were his words, it has been said![29]

Lines 8–15 of an In'kugthi Athin (Translucent Pebble) (Holders) Pebble Society Song describing the vision of all beings meeting for the Creation. Wakonda, the first spirit, held all things, including spirits, in his mind. When these spirits sought physical being, he created his first earthly creation, the White Rock. "Suddenly, from the middle of the waters, up rose a great rock. It burst into flames"; clouds, dry land, grass, and trees appeared, and spirits descended to fill bodies. The Creation rejoiced.[30] This chant describes the First Born embodied as the original White Rock, from which stone and shell medicine descends to such avatars as the white pebbles and shells that the Pebble and Shell Healing Societies and individual shamans use to heal, perform ceremonies, and display power. If lightning strikes a tree, someone who hurries can sometimes find or dig up a white medicine stone that will help the finder heal, predict events in war, and see soldiers coming from far away.[31]

Dakota

From everywhere they come flying!
From the North, the wind is blowing to earth!
Rattling, flying, they come,
They come from everywhere,
    They come![32]

SINGERS: Bear Necklace, Charging Thunder. A Stone Dream Song, alluding to both white pebbles and hail from the North.

Pomo

Medicine, you will be,
You will be a bead, a medicine bead!
You will be thick beads!
Charms, you will all be, medicine beads!
Charm, a medicine kernel you will be!
You will be a good song![33]

〜   SINGER: Benson. Song for making a stone into a medicine object. A
lightning-struck stone made a powerful medicine object.

Walwarena

I shall tell:
My heart uneasy,
I have none,
No Charmstone!
Sad, I have none.[34]

A'a'tam A'kimult

Powerless! (2)
My magic crystal, powerless!
I must embody them in stones![35]

〜   SINGER: Thin Leather (Ka'mal Tkak). Archaic. During the flood in this
Pima origin myth, South Doctor raised a mountain above the waters four
times. Unable to stop the flood, he held his medicine crystal in his right
hand and sang this song. To save his people from the flood, he petrified
them, thus making them last, like the mountains. The stones still stand on
Crooked Mountain.

Inuit

With leaps, I jump in long leaps;
    Men hear me!
When the ice melts,
When there is plenty of water for me,
    I jump well![36]

〜   A stone, washed down from the hills by the ice melt, sings this Cumber-
land Sound song. The stone will become the supernatural helper of the
one who finds it. The stone is cousin to the medicine stones of the Great
Lakes, the plains, and the Southwest. Jumping here implies luck and spiri-
tual power in gambling and hunting. Leaping may allude to a hunting
party's trick of blanket-tossing a scout into the air, to see an expanded
horizon and prey in the flat North. Modern Inuit hold blanket leaping
contests. Leaping stones carry power in the North, as lightning-struck
stones carried it in the South.

Tsistsi'stas   [Name], the stones alone will last long.[37]

        SINGER: Elk Woman. A War Song. "Stones" alludes to the mountains, Iya Tanka (the great Grandfather Stone) and his avatars, and the medicine stones and shells that help shamans and warriors. Roman Nose sang a version of this song at the fight at Beecher's Island.[38] Many peoples sang a variant of this song, as a War, Death, or Medicine Lodge Song. The Mandan sang, "Earth always endures";[39] the Dakota sang, "The old men say the earth only endures. / You spoke truly, you are right!"[40] A Papago hunting sequence evokes the permanence and endurance of the Rock when the hunter sings that the deer he is about to kill resembles streaks or cracks in the rocks,[41] and suggests that the deer, through the Deer Holy Person, shares that permanence appropriate to Holy People.

A'nish'inabeg   I stand here!
                     Behold, a stone is filled with spirit power!
                     I shoot with it![42]

        SINGER: Na'jobi'tun. Ceremonial Song IV.3 initiation, song 53. When healing or initiating a new member into a medicine lodge, the shamans "shot" fetishes, miniature arrows, medicine shells, or pebbles into the body of the patient or candidate or themselves. These miniature missiles carried healing power, killed disease, and healed. Usually the shooter blew on the missile in the direction of the target. The shooter retrieved the missile from the body of the target, thus demonstrating the cure. Shamans, in their wicked mode, shot disease rather than healing into targets.

A'nish'inabeg   The seething waters cast up
                     The white *mi'gis* shells![43]

        SINGER: Na'jobi'tun. A water spirit, a male beaver, sang this. Hyon-watha found the shells he used to make the first wampum belts in a lake.

Inuna'ina'   I go around the sweathouse.
                     The shell lies on the mound.[44]

        The dancer saw a shell, like the *mi'gis* (medicine shell used in Midé healing rites), on the *thi'aya,* a mound of earth made outside the Sun Dance and Ghost Dance lodges, instead of the usual buffalo skull.

Tsimshian

Now the spring will come,
Now the lake will come,
Now the water will change me.
Now the water will come
That I will drink.
The wind will come,
The wind that will toss me,
The wind will take me now![45]

ᔓ SINGER: Waterseh. From a drinking song. The torrent of water and the
rushing wind that accompany drunkenness resemble the dizziness and
whirling that accompany ceremonial drunkenness among the Papago and
Pima. For instance:

Witches' singing place,
Witches' singing place there arrive,
There dizzied me,
There will dizzy me,
Homeward dance,
All along the tassels
Wave.[46]

Singer: Paul Manuel. Also:

Dizzy women are seizing my heart.
Westward they lead me. I like it.
One on each side, they lead me.[47]

The witches and dizzy (dizzying) women are the Wild Women who, like
the Greek Maenads or Bacchantes, carry dangerous and intoxicating power
with them and sing outside the firelight at ceremonies. Pima poetry relates
dizziness to the Wild Women, Hunting and Scalp Dances, and the visions
induced by *Datura*.[48]

Coos

He'e He'e!
My grandmother,
The wind blew away my grandmother![49]

ᔓ SINGER: Annie Miner Peterson. In a myth, a disobedient young man was
beaten and in rage blew on his toy (medicine, fetish) canoe. A wind rose
and blew away his tipi and grandmother. The toy canoe suggests the medi-
cine or fetish canoes that ancestors and shamans used to call winds and
rain, catch diseases, and extract them from patients.

Tlingit

Ashore the people's canoe drifts
    With my Uncle!
My Uncle is dead.
I don't expect him anymore.
Kacka'lk and his brothers waded out
    Across the Stikine.
Their sister looked at them.
Then they turned to stone.[50]

ᢌ   SINGERS: Kakasguxo, Dekina'ku. Lqaya'k and Kacka'lk, hero-twins, were
crossing the Stikine and appeared to drift downstream. Their sister, during
puberty seclusion, violated taboo and peeked at them. They turned to
stone and sank.

Numa

My curved horns,
Like a necklace stand.[51]

ᢌ   SINGER: Chuar-ru-um-pik. Song of the Mountain Sheep.

TESTS OF POWER

Ontinonsionni

30.   I know why she got sick.
31.   I make her well, I cure her,
        I know.
35.   Songs mix,
        Our songs are confused.
36.   The songs clash,
        Our songs.[52]

ᢌ   Shamans' Round Dance Songs. The songs mix and clash when shamans
stage contests. If a shaman had used a song to inflict sickness, the clash
reflected the clash between healing and harmful medicine.

Walwarena

    Now I begin,
Begin to make my defense.
I have put my plant in this ground.
    I don't know the end.
I barely put my foot on land.
I come from Great clouds!

I am the son of all the dead!
That is why I am hungry.[53]

꙰ SINGER: Librado. Ciqneq, the Son of the Clouds, sang this Medicine Song against a *yowoyow* (devil). Such contests were both common and mythic. For instance, an Omaha Pebble Society member, bathing, saw a hawk. Fearing an enemy, he turned himself into a fish. When the tempted hawk stooped, he turned himself into a rock. The hawk, another shaman, broke its bill and claws on the rock. Many legends and Pebble and Shell Society Songs refer to this sort of shape-shifting shamans' contest. Such contests also infuse a children's and gamblers' game, similar to "Rock, Scissors, Paper," with both power and significance.

Salish

1. Fern roots, grandchild;
   The fog settles, grandchild;
   Fern roots, grandchild;
      It settles.
2. Fog and cloud over the world. (2)
   Fog settles, grandchild.[54]

꙰ SINGER: John Xot. The Crow people sang the first of these fog-bringing Medicine Songs when, trying to kill a monster child, they saw the mother and child digging roots. They sang the second when drowning the monster child.

Tsimshian

Around the foot of the door it seeps!
Fog surrounds, stars surround
The headwaters of the Skeena,
The headwaters of the Nass.
As I walk at the foot
Of a beautiful green mountain,
All the stars of heaven glitter
As the north wind clears the sky.[55]

꙰ SINGER: Henry Tate. Porcupine's lament for power in a mythic version of the shamans' contest. Great Grizzly threw dying Porcupine out of its den. Porcupine lay outside for a long time singing this "crying song," lamenting for power. The wind rose and stars came out and brought cold. The river iced at the fourth song. The ice caught and killed Great Grizzly.

Chehalis

Slice it up, the blue sky, (2)
 Change color to blue. (2)[56]

ᔓ   SINGER: Jonas Secena. Preparing for a shamans' contest, Rabbit calls on his *tamanos* (tutelary) to clear the sky and warm the weather just enough to thin the ice so that he can cheat wildcat at gambling, lure him onto thin ice, and drown him.

Kwagutl

Don't come near me,
You who are flesh only!
I am one whose face brings death,
And who throws power at you,
Who are flesh only.[57]

ᔓ   SINGER: George Hunt. Great Shaman sings this, his Medicine Song. In spite of the power of the song, Trickster turns Great Shaman into a perch.

Tohono Au'autam

A little black turtle sat cross-legged!
The black feathers were like lightning.
Red sparks fell and sprinkled down!
The turtle was afraid and backed away,
Waving his paws round and round.[58]

ᔓ   SINGER: Antonio. Diagnostician's (*siatikum*'s) song. The Black Turtle Medicine Person often failed. He tended to resemble a trickster.

Akume

Over in the East at his home
You think there are
All kinds of blossoms.[59]

ᔓ   Snowbird, gathering medicine, sings this charm to overcome the sisters who helped Beautiful Man.

Akume

Butterfly, fly west.
The women run wild after you,
They call to one another,
"Let's catch him."[60]

ॐ   Snowbird sings this, having shape-shifted into a butterfly, as bait to lure the girls who helped Beautiful Man.

Inuit

In what shape
Shall I wait at the breathing hole?
In the skin of a fox
Will I wait at the breathing hole!
In the skin of the Leaper
Will I wait at the breathing hole!
In the form of a wolf
Will I wait at the breathing hole!
What do I want at the breathing hole?
   To catch seals![61]

ॐ   A hunting charm when game is scarce.

Akume

Western river, western river,
Coming from the west
I sing of you![62]

ॐ   Swallow sings this song and tricks Coyote into breaking his teeth on a stone.

Walwarena

The little Lizard,
In order to find out
What was going on in the world,
   Would play the flute.
And the Coyote,
In order to take it in,
   Would cock his ear.[63]

ॐ   SINGER: Fernando Librado.

Kasogotine

Above Great Trout Lake
I speed my flying song.[64]

ॐ   A Hare Indian shaman sang this in a self-induced convulsion, sending his visible breath and medicine against another shaman.

Treatments

Yokuts

   Do you see me?
See me, Tuushiut! See me, Pamashiut! See me, Yuhahait!
See me, Echepat! See me, Pitsuriut! See me, Tsukit!
  See me, Ukat!
  All of you,
  Help me!
My words are tied in one
  With the great mountains,
  With the great rocks,
  With the great trees!
In one with my body, and my heart!
  All of you,
Help me with supernatural power!
And you, Day, and you, Night,
  All of you, see me,
  One with this world.[65]

  A general prayer for good fortune. The last four names are Serraño, southern Shoshonean; the first three Holy Persons occur in the Jimson Weed Initiation:[66] Tuushiut = maker (in Juaneño myth and Chumash ritual; *tosaut, tushaut,* stone); Yuhahait = Crusher; Ukat = seer (Fernandeño, Luiseño, Iuichepet); Pitsuriut = breath (Juaneño, *piuts, piuch,* breath of life); Tsukit (in the myth, one of five brothers); Ukat (Yokuts, sister of the first six holy persons) Manisar, the wife of Iuchipet, derives her name from *mani-t, Datura.* Jimson weed (loco weed) or perhaps *Datura,* a hallucinogen and poison, provoked visions and sometimes killed.

Creek

Come, White Fox Spirit! (3)
Come, Snake-hater, come,
Snakes who have hurt this man, come,
Come and kill this snake, White Fox![67]

  SINGER: Tuggle. Stanza 1 of a Medicine Song that cures snake sickness or snakebite. Stanzas 2 and 3 substitute "Red" and "Black" for "White." Perhaps a verse referring to a yellow or blue fox has been lost.

Inuit

The gull, it is called,
Who splits the air with its wings,
The one usually above you!
    Qo-qe, aja! Qo-qe, aja!
Gull, you up there,
Steer down toward me, come to me.
Your wings are red
Up there in the coolness.
    Aijija Aijija![68]

SINGER: Nakasuk. A healing charm.

Dakota

"In a sacred manner I am sitting,
At Bear Lodge!
In a sacred manner I am sitting,
At night, roaming about,"
    Is said to me![69]

SINGER: Eagle Shield. This Curing Dream Song, sung when a patient is
healing after treatment with *tao'pi pezhu'ta,* an herb recommended by
Bears, alludes to Bear Lodge, probably Bear Butte, South Dakota, a butte
the people camped on, from which they could see for a hundred miles.

Nanbe

Eat, Old Man,
Make me a bear.
Take my prayers to your heart, Old Man,
Don't throw them away.[70]

Nambe, Healing Song, Shaman (Pofuno) Society. Bear fetishes surround
the medicine bowl. The participants burn ritual objects, pile the ashes
around the Kiva, and offer cornmeal that absorbs the sickness, which they
throw away. The supplicant draws a hand from the fetish to his or her
mouth, inhaling through the fingers, and thus draws in the fetish's breath,
spirit, and power.

Kitksan

1. He will walk around, the grizzly,
    A long way behind the sky.

2. Through fire,
   Underneath the house!
   The fires
   Of the people![71]

ᠵᠣ   SINGER: Isaac Tens. *Gitskan swanassu* or Medicine Songs. In his vision, the *halaait* (shaman) saw from underground the fires of ordinary people. The *halaait* sang nonsense syllables, but kept these words in mind while singing the nonsense syllables, although the words were not secret. In a vision, and when singing while preparing to heal, Tens saw his uncles Tsigwee and Guksawawtu and heard them sing. While his uncles, themselves *halaait*s, sang, the Holy Person Grizzly Bear ran in through the door around the room, circled up into the clouds, and then ran back to the house. His uncles placed rattles in Tens' hands, and he saw many fires burning. Tens usually sang over patients and used objects only in difficult cases. When healing, he put on a bearskin robe and a bear-claw headdress. He wore his charms (*hogwest*) around his neck. The *halaait*s, merging with their songs and tutelaries, become at least semi–Holy People and thus, to missionized or converted people, devils: "all medicine men eventually die a very hard death, because they are not truly human. They are bad spirits."[72]

Tiwame

Headman:	I say, Look, look, look look!
Crystal holders:	We are looking,
	We can see the infectious witch.
	He is far from our land.
	Of course, we will now go after him.
	We may catch him, or he may escape us,
	But we will do our best.
	We, medicine men, are ready to start.
	We wear the bear-paws.[73]

ᠵᠣ   Domingan Healing Song. The witch causing the sickness usually comes from another tribe, but may be anyone. If the healers identify a relative as the witch, they may tell the patient to forgive. The healers find the sickness-bearing objects that the witch shot into the patient's body and suck them out. The healers identify witches by a flickering light that marks them. They pin the witches down with bear-paws or eagle claws to make them speak and reveal the nature of the sickness.

Karuk

Wolf of Inam, where are you?
When you run after deer
You don't go far before you get him.
While he runs, you begin eating him.
When you down him, you eat him,
    Bones and all.
You don't digest his bones.
They come out whole, and don't harm you.
I, Wolf of Inam, eat deer,
    Bones and all.
      They do not harm me.
You can call on me if you know medicine
    And nothing will harm you.[74]

SINGER: Mary Ike. Ivan Charlie, a bone-using shaman, used this formula to cure his aunt, who had had a fish bone in her throat for three days.

Sekani

O Mother Caribou,
    Bring your young.
    Bring them slowly
And feed on the grounds where you will find plenty.
    When you come, come carefully.
The spirit of my patient hovers near.
    Don't crowd your young
Lest they trample down my patient's spirit.
    I need your help, Caribou.
    Come swiftly to me.
See, I have laid my hand on the patient.
Come lay your hooves where I have laid my hands.
    I need your help.
Without your help there is no healing in my hands today.
Come so quickly that your tail stands erect.[75]

A Caribou Medicine Song.

Tohono Au'autam

Then the little sleeping people, the ants, came forth.
Entering my house in ceaseless journeys,

They took the poisoned food
And sent it yonder to the north wind.
Then the moisture that lies above began to fall
And destroyed the sickness altogether.[76]

ɔ   Stanzas 3 and 4 from a chant to cure sickness in a village. In earlier stanzas
a black tarantula magician, red wasp magicians, and eagles or thunderbirds
bring power to attack the disease. The singer learned it from his father.
The chant recalls the power of the shaman who once cured the sickness. In
Paiute creation stories, the Ant People helped the Creator.

Ani'Yun'wiya'

Listen!
Now you have come near to listen, Little Whirlwind,
Adawehi, in the leafy shelter of the lower mountain, you rest.
(Adawehi, you can never fail at anything.)
Now rise up.
A very small portion (of the disease) remains.
You have come to sweep it into the small swamp in the uplands.
You have laid down your path near the swamp.
It is ordained you will bat it into utter disappearance.
By you it must be scattered.
So shall there be healing.[77]

ɔ   SINGER: A'yu'nni. This formula invokes the whirlwind, which dwells in
trees, whose leaves warn of its approach. The charm asks the little whirl-
wind to sweep the disease into mountain meadow swamps and scatter the
disease as it scatters forest leaves, to rifle the disease into the swamp as a
lacrosse player rifles the ball into the net.

Kwagutl

Tohwit:	I went, taken in an oar-driven canoe
	By those beautiful ones who uphold the world,
	Heya!
Hams`hamtsus:	Now push up, with your hands, this, your sky,
	By your magic, good magic.
	Now push with your hands this your sky
	(by) your magic, the good (magic).
	Hammamama!
Winalagylis:	Taken from one canoe to another,
	I, there, ten traveling canoes in a row,

> I, Winalagylis,
> Ye we yewe!

Haiyalikyilahl: Already the food in you gorges everybody,
> Sated by your body, around the world.[78]

ᡖ   A "word passer" composed this Awilotililahl (Embodiment of Great Gain)
Song impromptu. He used songs from four dancers: Tohwit, Hams`hamt-
sus (primitive cannibals, eaters off the ground), Winalagylis (the war spir-
it), and Haiyalikyilahl (the personation of healing). The song refers to a
dancer, a young woman who was spreading disease, and brings the powers
of the songs and dancers to bear to heal.

Tohono Au'autam

> In the great night, my heart will go out.
> Toward me the darkness comes rattling.
> In the great night, my heart will go out.[79]

ᡖ   SINGER: Owl Woman. One of Owl Woman's Healing Songs. The spirit of
José Gomez, a powerful medicine man, gave her this and two other songs
in a dream. "Rattling" evokes the ceremonial rattles of the dance and
thunder on the mountains and in the canyons. Ruth Underhill prints a
similar Healing Song from the Maiden Dance in which darkness resounds
and rolls over the singer.[80]

Hamakhav

> The night halfway to midnight,
> The good night,
> The finished night, here now
> The sound of the night moving.
> Dreams of these night-times
> Will bring luck.[81]

ᡖ   SINGER: Perry Dean. Tortoise Narrative, location 7a. So Matavilye's two
young sons sang, after burning his body.

Paviotso

> Stay here, stay here,
> This is your own country!
> In the morning,
> Talk to the sun.[82]

ℑ   SINGER: Charlie Washoe. A Curing Song, sung to the patient's spirit.

A'a'tam A'kimult

> Here over you (2)
> There is light, it moves about!
>   Here over you
> There is light, tassels downward.[83]

ℑ   This Medicine Song marks healing accomplished. The tips of the light shining down on the patient evoke corn tassels and link healing a specific patient to healing the land.

Diné

> The medicine lies in my hand. (4)
> Now, I being Talking God,
>   It lies in my hand.
> On top of Black Mountain,
>   It lies in my hand,
> The Black medicine, the living medicine,
>   It lies in my hand.
> Unfailingly it is spreading round me,
>   It lies in my hand.
> With Soft Goods it lies,
>   It lies in my hand,
> With Jewels it lies,
>   It lies in my hand.
> Now, I being Long-Life Happiness Young Man,
>   It lies in my hand.
>   Happiness before me,
>   It lies in my hand.
>   Happiness behind me,
>   It lies in my hand. (4)[84]

ℑ   SINGER: Claus Chee Sonny. In this *ajilee* or hunter-derived song, the singer calls Daildilhil (a mountain on the southeast corner of Black Mesa) "Black Mountain." In this ceremony, he calls Depenitsa (Hesperus Peak) "White Mountain." More often ceremonies name Depenitsa, the sacred mountain of the North, the "Black Mountain"; Sis Naajini (Blanca Peak), the eastern sacred mountain, "White Mountain"; Tsoodzil (Mount Taylor), the southern sacred mountain, "Blue Mountain"; and Dook Oosliid (San Francisco

Peaks), the western sacred mountain, "Yellow Mountain." The sacred mountains also include Choolii (Gobernador Knob), where Changing Woman was created, and Dzil Naoodilii (Huerfano Mountain), "Crystal," "Precious Stones Mountain." The reference to this Hunter's Black Mountain (Black Mesa) reflects the hunting journeys the *ajilee* ceremonies and their origin myths recount.

𝔂 VIII *Love*

Hotcangara

> Whoever I stare at becomes thus!
> Whoever I speak to becomes thus!
> Whoever I whisper to becomes thus!
> Friend, whoever wants women,
> One under my power becomes!
> Whoever I touch becomes thus![1]

𝔂 "Thus" means obsessed with desire, like Coyote or Trickster in heat. The singer, a Winnebago girl, heard the song in a dream of a mythical Sioux woman, probably a member of the Double-Woman Cult, who crazed men. Double-Woman taught the Sioux quillwork and conferred Wakan powers that could craze men for love.[2] The Winnebago girl won powerful medicine. The song warns warriors, who must not let lust distract them, but rather concentrate on war. The Deer Women and Flint Women in myths caught young men through their appetites and tried to destroy them.[3] This woman bewitches. Cherokee men aspired to the same power to bewitch.[4]

Kwatsan

> When I play this flute,
> The girls will love me.[5]

𝔂 SINGER: Joe Homer. Kwichana Ata'xamaili' (Flute Origin Legend, song 1). Hero brothers found material for a flute and decreed its power to charm.

Havasuwapay

> Hank Ward (4)
> To Riding Rock, (3)
> To Riding Rock, to the store there,
> That's where he went! (2)
>   He's so proud! (4)
> A string of bullets on his belt, (2)
> Boots, he's so proud wearing spurs! (2)

122

He's so proud, (2)
Hank Ward! (4)[6]

    ॐ   This woman's love song teases a desirable and vain young man.

Havasuwapay

My father and my uncle, those two,
They can't do anything about my vagina!
They can't control it.
They better listen to me.
They seem to be dying over my vagina. (3)
     This is how I am.
     I am what I am. (3)
I can't be like this, just sit around alone (3)
. . . A good woman, a good girl! . . .
They can't make [me] just sit around

. . . .

Until [I] become so old,
[I] use a cane to get around.
     They can't do it.
They better listen to me.
     This is how I am.
     I laugh at them.
     I am what I am. (2)
My father, he told me lies!
It's just a coyote tale that he's telling me here.

. . . .

I don't believe him.
Instead, I believe my own way. (2)
A bird, a large bird,
My body has turned into a large bird. (2)

. . . .

At Wavaho, I perch on top of the cliff,
     I look down, (2)
     I spy on the people.
They are sitting around down there.
I think about marriage there, I do,
But he is not good-looking,
     Not at all!
When I see this, I move on.
I fly to Wii Gl'iiva,

Through the cleft of Wii Gl'iiva, I go through there.
  I go on. (2)
At Ha Sogyavo, at the top, I land. (2)
  I look down. I spy on the people.
  I see them. I spy on the people.
Painted Man, a good-looking man,
  He's sitting down there.
There I settle, my thoughts go there.
  I sit down there,
  There I stay! (4)[7]

꙰   This modern Rebel Girl's Song suggests the Wild Women who circle outside puberty rites and other ceremonies, singing in the dark.

Yaqui

In Cocori lives a young girl,
  Whose name is Hesucita.
  She is a pretty girl.
  Her eyes look like stars.
Her pretty eyes are like stars moving.[8]

꙰   SINGER: Anka Alvarez. A romantic postoccupation, Spanish-influenced love song.

A'a'tam A'kimult

I am playing the flute here,
  Shaking the woman's heart. (2)
When the sun goes down (2)
I am making her heart bloom,
  Shaking her heart.[9]

꙰   From the Flute-lure myth. This song uses medicine to charm and trap.

A'a'tam A'kimult

Coyote starts to sing!
Coyote starts to sing!
The maiden hurries,
Runs to hear Coyote's songs rise.[10]

꙰   SINGER: Virsak Vai-i. Pan Nyoi (Coyote Song). When the First People celebrated the first war and fertility ceremonies, Coyote instituted ceremonial promiscuity and overindulged himself to death.

Numa

Bark aprons
Bounce up and down.[11]

ᘝ SINGER: Tony Tillohash. Badger sisters sing this while luring Coyote to the mountains. Coyote tricks them.

Ta'n-ta'wats

My little jackrabbit apron
Flaps up and down.[12]

ᘝ SINGER: George Laird. Poo'wavi sings this song to keep Coyote chasing her until she can catch him. She wears only this apron, which accentuates her movements. The story is of the *vagina dentata* genre.

Hopitu

Corn plants among rain!
Butterfly girls chasing each other
    Just after rain.
    See how they flit about
    Over and through the corn.
Thus they, singing, enjoy themselves.[13]

ᘝ SINGER: Lahpu. Anga Kachina Kawi (Song). A ceremonial song of the Anga Holy Person, sometimes modified into a courting song. The song associates romance, ceremony, and rain-bringing power. "Butterfly girls" evokes not only butterflies and bees in a cornfield after a rain, but also unmarried girls, with their hair in wheels at each side of their heads, looking like butterfly wings. Papago songs make similar associations:
    On the flat land a rain house stands covered with clouds.
    Very white it stands. Butterfly wings are about it.
        I like it. I saw it all.[14]
From the Maiden's Dance, the ritual purification of a girl after her first mense, four days of ceremonies and fasting. Elder Brother (a Papago Creator and culture hero) may have made this song up. The First People killed him because his songs at the Maiden Dances seduced too efficiently. Later, those songs brought rain.

Isonkuaili

There from the love thoughts,
Longings and love words,
Sprang beautiful trees and flowers.
Little streams gurgled through the forests;
Leaping waterfalls foamed;
Great rivers flowed to the sea;
Fish abounded;
Buffalo roamed the plains
And through the wood-paths
Sped all the wild things
Of a new world.[15]

ᔛ   SINGER: Y-Ail-Mihth. From the Okanagon Creation cycle. The singer checked the translation very carefully and accepted the detail and phrasing in this translation, according to the translators, Mrs. C. L. and E. Streit.

A'nish'inabeg

Oh! I am thinking! Oh! I am thinking,
    I have found my lover!
    Oh! I think it is so![16]

ᔛ   SINGER: Mrs. Julia Warren Spears. Young men sang many love songs like this one in which they mimicked a girl singing, to tease girls within earshot.

Ottawa

They both courted me using the same words.
    We can't believe anything men say![17]

A'nish'inabeg

In the center of the earth,
    Wherever he may be,
    Or under earth.[18]

ᔛ   SINGER: Na'waji'bigo'kwe. This song works as a charm to obsess the singer's target.

Maklaks

The lark flies toward me,
Grazes the ground,
And stops every little while![19]

∼ SINGERS: Chief Johnson, Minnie Froben. This song suggests that courting behavior among shy birds resembles courting behavior among shy humans.

Maklaks

Shaking her body,
The girl broke her camas stick![20]

∼ SINGERS: Chief Johnson, Minnie Froben. Men sang this song, teasing young women who wriggled (the men hoped unnecessarily and provocatively) when using their camas digging stick.

Yokuts

Walk around, promiscuous! Not I!
   Lovers? Not I!
   I am happy!
   Wild? Not I!
Get power and riches for my body?
   Not I![21]

∼ SINGER: Josie Alonzo. The singer dreamt of danger and chanted this to avert the danger.

Maklaks

Insane, the prairie wolf flees me!
   Hallucinating, he runs far away.[22]

∼ SINGERS: Chief Johnson, Minnie Froben. The male, obssessed by love and lust, acts like a rutting or hydrophobic coyote.

Akume

Today I will be lucky.
Here I come, a bird boy.
Girl in the East,
I have come to bring gifts
To stir your passions and heart![23]

∼ SINGER: A Kachina gave Basityamuti (bushy-haired youth) this song to use for wooing a war chief's daughter. It became a popular love charm for both men and women.

Akume   For everyone's sake I start out, (2)
                                         I start out this morning
                                         From my home, seeking women!
                                         For the sake of any girl,
                                             I am traveling![24]

            ᔔ   Beautiful Man sang this song.

Diné   At me on top of Earth you are looking.
                                         Into Marsh-Plant Young Man I have changed
                                             As you are looking.
                                         When Sun's red headplume is my headplume
                                             You are looking at me.
                                         When Sun's halo is my halo
                                             You are looking at me.
                                         As Hopi maidens mate with Traveler-on-Earth
                                             You are looking at me.
                                         As she now gazed at my headplume and thrilled
                                             You are looking at me.
                                         As the pollen of my headplume dizzied her
                                             You are looking at me.
                                         As her mind with her body is given into my hand
                                             You are looking at me.
                                         As I have changed into Jimson-Weed Young Man
                                             You are looking at me.
                                         As Sun's flexible plume is my plume
                                             You are looking at me.
                                         When Sun's halo is my halo
                                             You are looking at me.[25]

            ᔔ   SINGER: Slim Curley. Scrap-Picker Boy's father, the Sun, an inveterate and
                       omnivorous seducer, sent him, a male Cinderella, through an initiation
                       and gave him new names, seductive powers, and magic that allowed him
                       to hunt game and women successfully. Scrap-Picker Boy used these preda-
                       tor's powers to seduce two Hopi virgins ("women untouched by sun-
                       light"). He established power over his prey by using the hunter's trick of
                       empathizing with and imitating the prey: he changed his and their bodies
                       into duplicates, as the hunter wears a disguising skin. The plants whose
                       names and medicine he assumed, jimson weed and marsh plant, produce
                       hallucinations. Overheard women's laughter accompanied his puberty rite
                       at Wide Ruin in Chaco Canyon. The association with women's overheard

laughter, Anasazi ruins, and a puberty ceremony suggests comparison with the Wild Women who initiated Girls' Puberty Rites among the Pima and Papago.

Shis-Inde

> Oh, Mescalero maiden, don't be afraid!
> They are already gossiping about us,
>> But don't be frightened.
>> Gossips chew rocks!
>> Don't be afraid.[26]

∽ A Social Dance Song from the Girls' Puberty Rite. The envious and witches "chew rocks."

O'maha

> Alas, I have revealed myself, ah! (2)
> Last night, when you sang,
> I spoke your name!
> Alas, I have revealed myself, ah!
> When they said, "Who is it singing?"
> I sitting there said,
> "Waguntha, passing by, ah!"
> I uttered your name, ah![27]

∽ A "Woman Song, Wa-u-wan," which men made and sang, pretending to be women. The "ah" reveals the girl's surprise and fear. The girl, naming Waguntha, betrayed her infatuation to her family. She told Waguntha what she had done. Chivalrous Waguntha made this song and bragged about her to his friends.

Karuk

> Oh, Sweetheart, we quarreled!
> Oh, let's live as two again!
> Oh, Sweetheart, I am lonesome.
> You may go to the end of the earth,
> But you will return.
> We will roll together
> Here at the Middle of the world.[28]

∽ SINGER: Nettie Reuben. Evening Star's sweetheart made and sang a song to charm him back. She originated love songs.

Numa

Lying in the sun like gravel,
   She changes color
As the sunbeams wave over her.[29]

꒰   Greyhawk's wife, Lizard, wants to go with her husband, one of the sky and sun emblems, on a mythical journey. The imagery merges light and water.

Ka'igwu

I have but one love, (3)
Gone somewhere, somewhere far.
Time lengthens.
He is lonely and weary.[30]

꒰   SINGER: T'e-ne-t'e (Eagle Chief). A Gomda Daagya (Wind Song, lonely as the prairie wind), which mourns the absence of a loved one.

Tlingit

If one had control of death,
It would be very easy to die
   With a wolf woman.
It would be very pleasant.[31]

꒰   SINGER: Don Cameron. Raven-Skin (Yel-dugu) wrote this love song when his sweetheart left him.

Kwagutl

Would that I might go, dear,
   To sit beside you,
Beside you, my love, my darling!
Would that I might go, dear,
   Sitting inside a cloud,
   Inside a moving cloud,
   Moving in a flying cloud,
To sit beside you, my love, my darling.[32]

A'nish'inabeg

A loon's wing, I thought it. (2)
But it was my love's splashing oar.
To Sault Ste. Marie he has departed,

My love has gone on before me.
Never again can I see him.[33]

꒰   A woman from Madeline Island sang this mourning and love song while
her family was camping on the site that would become Duluth. Later
singers sang lines 1–3 as an independent song. In several versions, it has
become one of the most often reprinted Native American lyrics. Densmore
adapted Mary Warren English's translation. A. Bimboni used it in sheet
music.[34] Frederick Russell Burton rewrote it as a sentimental love song.[35]
Gerald Vizenor translates sparely: "the sound of a loon / I thought / it
was my lover / paddling."[36] The loon is a powerful medicine being, an
earth diver, a symbol of rebirth and a bringer of medicine.

Maidu   I am the wire-grass queen,
I am the water riffle queen.[37]

꒰   SINGER: William Joseph. The Water People's Transforming Song. This
song changed a man so that he could live underwater with a water woman.

Inuit   Toward the south I ever turn my gaze,
For at the point of Isua land,
Near the strand of Isua,
Yonder from the south,
   He will appear!
That way he certainly will come.
Korsarak will surely clear the point!
In his kayak, Korsarak will be equal to it!
But if he still happened not to come,
Not until halibut season,
Not before the halibut fishing begins,
Not until the men haul up the halibut?[38]

꒰   SINGER: Arsut.

Haida   I have taken a fair maid from my Haida friends as my wife.
I hope her relations won't come and take her from me.
   I will be kind to her,
I will give her berries from the hill and roots from the ground.

I will do all I can to please her.
For her I made this song
And for her I sing it.[39]

ᕋ The bear who married a Haida woman sang this song. It took years before
Haida friends would sing this song for an Anglo.

Tlingit

1. The world is rolling around
   With our breath, our life!
   That's why we should prepare
   And cherish each other.
2.   Very happy
   It would make me,
   Ginexqwani-child, wife,
   If I died in front of your land.
      I would smile.[40]

ᕋ Dry Bay George composed the song for his wife, Mary. He drowned in
the Bering River in 1880.

Natinnoh-hoi

If ten times his heart strays from me to other women,
   Finally it will return to me.
   I hope he may be crazy.
However many women he likes, even if they lie in his arms,
   This medicine will reach him.
However many he goes among, my heart will find him.
    It will be thus:
   You will hate the one you used to like!
   Before all others, you will think of me.[41]

ᕋ SINGER: Emma Lewis. The first target of this love charm was the straying
lover Kixunai, the moon.

Tlingit

1. Whenever I see the mountains at the head of Ahrnklin
   I always imagine my dead uncles there.
2. Whenever I see you,
   Tcicquedi Child, my wife,

Strength of mind
You always give me.[42]

SINGER: Olaf Abrahamson. This sad, old-style Antlen River Song merges
the singer's love for his ancestral land and for his wife. The mountain
reminds him of his youth and his forefathers' deeds.

Dakota

Finally I weep, (3)
Weeping I roam!
Among young men, courting,
I was the most enthusiastic.
Weeping I roam![43]

SINGER: Two Shields. Ghost Hill Song. Densmore found it difficult to per-
suade Two Shields to sing this song.

Dakota

As the young men went by
I was looking for him!
It surprises me anew that he has gone!
It is something to which I cannot be reconciled![44]

SINGER: Two Shields. Mourning Song.

Karuk

You are too old.
We are going to dance around the world
And down the Klamath River.[45]

SINGER: Phoebe Maddox. Pleiades Girls sing this to Turtle Old Man, who
has tried to seduce and deceive them.

Walwarena

Who is like me?
My plumes are flying.
They will alight in an unknown land above
Where banners fly!
They will be carried
To the nest of the eagle

And remain there in joy!
Joy fills the world![46]

ᔓ   SINGER: Librado. Rejected Eagle Daughter's Song.

Kwatsan

Such is my life in this wonderful air
And I long to have little children,
    A boy and a girl
To enjoy this wonderful air.[47]

ᔓ   SINGER: Alfred Golding. Kwichana Akwa'k (Deer Dance), song 75.

Bana'kwut

What is This?
Is it *huska,* the groundnut?
Is it *ipha,* the potato?
Is it *iphacoo,* the little potato?
Is it *euma-kaik,* a little baby?
Is it the baby of my children on Snow Mountain?
Did they throw you down for me to keep?[48]

ᔓ   His grandmother, digging for roots, digs up Edoochme, thrown to his
grandmother from Snow Mountain. He cries at each question until the
fifth. It can serve as a tickling song or lullaby.

Lku'ngen

I had a bad dream last night.
I dreamt my husband took a second wife.
Then I packed my little basket
    And said before I left,
"There are plenty of men."
    Thus I dreamt.[49]

ᔓ   A woman shaman sang this song.

Siksika

Where is it? Here?
Wolf Plume and I
Leaned against one another.[50]

   SINGER: Curley Bear. A Sun Dance Song. Wolf Plume and the woman singer were lovers. During a Sun Dance, Wolf Plume leaned against her and left traces of her red paint on the center post. Having profaned the Sun Dance, he died in battle. She saw traces of the red paint on the post later and hung herself. The Piegan liked the song and adapted the words to a popular Sun Dance tune.

Wintu

On the north slope of Baqakilim
   I was deserted.
Some flower made me heedless
   And I was deserted.
A wild orange blossom made me heedless
   And I was deserted.[51]

   SINGER: Jennie Curl. A pregnant woman sang this song.

Akume

First, the baby,
Through the medicine man's prayers,
Has been given life,
Here and there,
With the medicine man's song.
For the baby
He sang these songs.
Next, the baby's mother,
With the songs of the rain gods,
She has cared for the baby!
Here and there the mother,
With the cloud cradle,
Has cared for the little baby.
It was beautiful
That the clouds came up like foam,
As if it was raining
Among those soft little clouds!
With this the baby was cared for.[52]

   SINGER: Philip Sanchez (Ho-ni-ya). A mother's song to a baby.

Hunting

PREHUNT

Ontinonsionni

(62) And now this is what Our Creator did:
He decided, "I shall now establish various animals
To run about on the earth.
Indeed, they will always be a source of amusement
For those who are called warriors, whose bodies are strong."
He decided to provide the warriors, whose bodies are strong,
With the animals running about,
To be a source of amusement for them.
"And they will be available as food
To the people moving about on the earth." . . .
(70) And we are using them as Our Creator intended.
And therefore let there be gratitude
That it all continues as he intended.[1]

ↄ   SINGERS: Chief Corbett Sundown, Chief Ellsworth George. From the
Thanksgiving Ceremony.

Kwagutl

He will rise from the depths,
    The Great Ia'k'im.
He makes the sea boil,
    The Great Ia'k'im of this world.
He will throw out blankets,
    The Great Ia'k'im of this world.
He will throw out blankets from the sea,
    The Great Ia'k'im of this world.
He makes the sea's face frightful, tribes,
    The Great Ia'k'im of this world.
We fear him,
    The Great Ia'k'im.[2]

136

ॐ   In this Ia'k'im (Water Monster) Song, the blankets, given away in the pot-
      latch, symbolize fish and other prey from the sea, as well as wealth.

Karuk   I am going to move to Assewai.
                                 That will be my home.
                                 Deer will like it when I move up there.
                                 Now I am going to move up there.
                                     If you know my song,
                                     You will kill deer.[3]

ॐ   SINGER: Georgia Orcutt. A song that brings good luck in hunting.

Aa'shi'wi   Here, grandfathers, eat!
                                 And whoever had good luck in hunting,
                                 Lend me your hand and your thoughts.[4]

ॐ   The hunter chanted this prayer to famous dead hunters, whom he thus
      treated as Kachinas, Holy Persons. The hunter burned piki bread as an
      offering. The spirits ate the smoke.

Havasuwapay   Sun, my relative,
                                 Look kindly at us.
                                 That is why I am here.
                                 Send us your wild herds,
                                     Your animals!
                                 Let us see them quickly,
                                 We want to kill some![5]

ॐ   SINGER: Sinyella.

A'nish'inabeg   My war-club
                                 Thunders through the sky
                                 To make animals answer my call![6]

ॐ   SINGER: Be'cigwi'wizans. A Hunting Song. The entire song forms a single
      rhythmic unit. Densmore translates "resounds."

Dakota

In the North
The wind blows! They are walking!
The hail beats! They are walking![7]

ᴦ   Sung in the Buffalo Dance. The singer envisions the buffalo moving down
from the North, huntable. The song also suggests the favorable interven-
tion of the Thunder Beings. Such songs often came from visions.

Konhiak

The deer is hungry.
He goes through the bushes
Till he finds an iron wood in flower.
He eats the green leaves
And the flowers and says:
"Now I am not hungry.
I have eaten of the green
And I have eaten of the flowers."

I will go out to hunt.
I will go out to kill a deer.
I will kill him quickly.
The sound of my voice
Does not reach the deer.
I will sing louder and he will come.
He comes closer! Now he is near
And I will kill him quickly.[8]

ᴦ   SINGER: Juan Molino. The Deer Song. Hunters sang this all night to avoid
offending the deer, who might feel slighted when the tribe sang to fish in
the Fish Dance.

Shis-Inde

At the East,
Where the jet ridges of the earth lie.
At the South,
Where the white ridges of the earth lie,
Where all kinds of fruit are ripe,
We two will meet.
From there,
Where the coral ridges of the earth lie,
We two will meet.

> Where the ripe fruits are fragrant,
>> We two will meet.[9]

    SINGER: Antonio. A Deer Ceremony Song, marking the recovery of Panther Boy's wife, who had been turned into a deer by Turquoise Boy because Panther Boy had killed without the Holy People's permission, killing too many deer and endangering the stock.

Inuit

> Beast of the sea,
> Come offer yourself in the lovely early morning!
>> Beast of the plain,
> Come offer yourself in the lovely morning![10]

    SINGERS: Qiqertainaq, Aua.

Iyiniwok

> Pity my children,
> My men and all my camp!
>> Give me buffalo![11]

    Song for the Black Pipe at the Buffalo Ceremony.

Sulatelik

> Please help me. Do not make it rough today.
> Help me along. Make it smooth!
> I know where you were born.
> You were born far in the South.
> I know your father's name. Your father was a shaman.
> They took you up to the Northwest when you were sick.
> When you got to the Northwest, you became well.
> Your father went away to the South and left you in the Northwest.
> You told your father, "I am going to be the waves and breakers
> And I will make the ocean rough."
> Now today please be kind to me and help me
> Because I was born at Tuluwat
> Where you came on your way to the Northwest.
> So please help me today, and keep the ocean smooth.[12]

    SINGER: Jerry James (Humboldt Bay Wiyot). First sung to Tahahalakukkuwiliyawanaq (Shaman's Son), son of Aviluk, who beat and reformed the

Cannibal child-eating shaman Avakirask. Wiyot fishers sang this when planning to fish the open sea outside Humboldt Bay.

Pomo

No shadow will strike this hunter!
Nothing will scare the game![13]

꒰   SINGER: Benson. The hunter or a *yomta* (medicine person) sang this song before the hunt, often while steeping the prey's bones as medicine, to absorb the prey's mana and insert it into weapons.

Aa'shi'wi

Indeed, this day, my Father, my Mother, unexpectedly,
    I have passed you on your road.
For my Fathers, Dance priests, Beast priests, Divine ones,
With whatever plume wands I have prepared,
Bringing plume wands for them,
    I have passed you on your road.
With prayer meal, desiring your children,
Upon my Earth Mother yonder with prayers,
    I will make my road go out.
Over all the land, your children, the deer,
Obeying your breath, go wandering.
Desiring their flesh, their blood,
Yonder with prayers,
    I will make my road go out.
Let it be without fail that you grant me your children,
That you make me happy, that you bless me with light.
    Ah! Thanks! My Father, my Mother.
This day, following your road, yonder with prayers,
    I will make my road go out.[14]

꒰   Midwinter Hunt prayer. The hunter goes to the Deer Medicine Kiva for a fetish from a basket offered by the Keeper. Facing in the chosen fetish's direction, the direction of the hunt, the hunter sprinkles prayer meal over the basket. Then, holding meal in his left hand over his heart, he chants. Predators control prey; the deer's heart obeys the predator's heart. The hunter's breath, from his heart, can stun prey at a distance. Lightning shriveled the "Beast priests," six powerful predatory Holy Persons, into stone fetishes, in which the hearts of the predators still live. The hunter must carry such a fetish while hunting.

Ontinonsionni

3. In the hemlocks,
Owls abound,

Crowd: Hai'yéh.
Singer: Ne'too.
Crowd: Nyoh.

7. I know every one
Of all the wild animals,
I know every one.

8. They come running,
The medicine company,
They come out of the woods.[15]

   Shaman "throwing," or individual, songs. At this point in the ceremony, each medicine singer speaks and sings the song.

Hopitu

Now, Father, Water Bullsnake, pity us.
Father, Water Bullsnake, we are your people.
   Grant them abundance.
   Here there will be plenty!
Now, our Father, calm the rattlesnakes,
So that none anywhere will be angry,
   That good will come.
   Rain will come.
On their account, good will come.
   So be it.[16]

   On the tenth day of the Snake Ceremony, preparing for the snake hunt, the snake-priests pray to snakes at Teveskya Spring to call rain. During the ceremony, the priests may drink only from living springs or falling rain.

Aa'shi'wi

This day, He who holds our roads, Our Sun Father,
   Has come out standing to his sacred place!
Now that he has passed us on our roads,
   Here we pass you on your road.
Divine One, the flesh of the white corn,
   Prayer meal, shell, corn pollen,
     Here I offer you.
With your wisdom, taking the prayer meal,
   The shell, the corn pollen,

This day, my fathers, my mothers,
In some little hollow, in some low brush,
   You will reveal yourselves to me.
Then with your flesh, with your living waters,
   May I sate myself.
That this may be, here I offer you prayer meal.[17]

Takelma

   Drive the elks here,
The elks that dwell in the back of the mountain,
The black-necked ones down in dark places.[18]

SINGER: Francis Johnson. Sung to a heavy fall of snow.

Tewa

From far frozen Buffalo Country
They head here with their little ones,
Walking rapidly, walking rapidly now,
Now they reach Red Bird Pass.
Buffalo Old Man! Buffalo Old Woman,
Come here rapidly with your children!
Come to Cactus Ridge Town with your children!
They bring us long life together!
Even now they reach Tesuque.[19]

Tesuque Summoning Buffalo Magic Song. The summoning song traces the journey the summoned buffalo will take from the Staked Plains and Buffalo Ice Water, over Red Bird Pass at the head of the Pecos to an old Tesuque town.

Maklaks

I am a magic song
   And circle high above the earth.[20]

SINGER: Sergeant Morgan. The Shka bird tutelary sang this song in a vision. The power that fills the bird fills the song and gives a bird's view.

Chahiksichahiks

   "Listen," he said,
"The great buffalo herd comes,"
   He says!

"The great herd comes in a dust-billow,
The great herd comes, (3)
Raising dust, marking the wallow!"[21]

       Buffalo Dance Song. Nara'dudesa'ru dreamt of a cloud of dust rising from a duststorm, which he watched until late afternoon. It seemed to him like a cloud of people, but after the storm passed he saw a great herd of buffalo.

Numa

On the plain (2)
The dust hovers.[22]

       The dust that hovered over a herd of buffalo located them for the hunters. Hunters traveled great distances to find the herd. Buckskin Charley, a chief of the Utes, traveled eight days to find a herd on his first hunt as a boy.[23]

O'maha

The black bird soaring
On wings, to search, he goes, soaring.[24]

       White Buffalo Ritual. "Bird" means "crow." Crows followed the herds and circled them, hunting for carrion. Circling crows showed scouts, hunters, and raptors where to find a herd.

Chahiksichahiks

1 Now I climbed the hill and arrived at the top
    There where the stream of water shortens people's legs,
    From where great herds of buffalo once started,
    Yet I saw nothing yonder but an expanse of land,
       Only the expanse of land. (2)

     . . . .

22 Now I climbed the hill and arrived at the top.
    There where the stream of water separates,
    There on the island's point where stands a tree clump,
    From where great herds of buffalo once started,
       There I stood.
23 I stood surprised and rejoiced, (2)
    For there were the buffalo, like threads covering the earth!
    There they were, there they were.[25]

↭   SINGERS: Thief, Singing Hawk. Buffalo Bundle and Hunt ritual. Two of twenty-three stanzas during which the scout Singing Hawk recounts the topography he passed: the elm grove, the foothill, the hilly island, the slippery hill, the first hill, the swallows' bank, and so forth. The ritual reenacts the myth of the first hunt and the origin of the Buffalo Bundle. Before the first hunt, women built a grass lodge (the first dwelling) for a medicine priest and carried corn mush to him. The priest told buffalo stories and coyote stories telling how coyotes called buffalo. Hawk scouted and came back to report buffalo near the village, to the east.

O'maha

> The village, soaring, I circle!
> " 'May I go,' they [ask,]" I say![26]

↭   White Buffalo Ritual. The herald rides around the camp and announces when the hunters will leave for the herd. The soaring herald evokes and imitates the raptors circling the herd. The herald circled the camp to the left when he announced the time the hunters would start. A Papago Hunting Song also evokes the hunter's trick of attending to birds to locate quarry:

> *Deer:*   Bird children, there by my singing place,
>   They chatter low and sing.
>   Bird children, there by my standing place,
>   They chatter low and run away.[27]

The deer notices the birds who mark him for the hunter; the birds also warn the deer of the hunter's presence.

Diné

> Ah'eh na-ya-ya, ah'eh yeh-eh-na-ya,
> The one who flies in the sky na-ya-ya,
> Above the top of Black Mountain I fly in the sky.
> A bow made of wood, I have in my hand,
>   Na-ya-ya, I fly in the sky,
> A child of Female Wind,
>   I fly in the sky na-ya-ya,
> With sensitive ears,
>   I fly in the sky na-ya-ya,
> I am ready to move anywhere
>   As I fly in the sky na-ya-ya,
> I am the son of Light Feather,
>   I fly in the sky na-ya-ya,

Ah'eh na-ya-ya, ah'eh yeh-eh-na-ya,
The one who flies in the sky na-ya-yeh.[28]

     SINGER: Claus Chee Sonny. A Sweatlodge Song, sung by Black God, who
takes the form of the crow. Hunters sing this song to lure deer close.
Other Holy People sang this song to trap Black God.

Chahiksichahiks

He said, "There it stands!"
He says, "Father was startled.
The crow was flying and cawing.
He was startled, but not frightened.
Father was startled.
The crow was flying and cawing."[29]

     SINGER: Wicita Blain. An old and valuable Buffalo Dance Song. The buf-
falo heard a circling crow caw and were startled, but did not run. This
song describes the reaction the hunter wants when the crows caw, seeing a
scout approach.

O'maha

"After the smoke, as they retreat there,
   I go,"
   I say! (3)
I say, "I go," I say!
"After the smoke as they retreat there,
   I go,"
   I say!
   I say![30]

     White Buffalo Ritual. The herds retreat. Smoke evokes the tobacco smoke
that accompanies prayer and is a metaphor for the dust that rose from the
moving herd. When the herds scented hunters, they scattered, under a
dust cloud.

Chahiksichahiks

1. Pah-o-o-o I bring news,
   But I must have compensation!
2. You people who are camped here,
   Listen! I now say something wonderful:
   The buffalo, the buffalo,

        The buffalo have arrived.

3. These things you have given me,
    I do not want them.

4. I want the chief's daughter. (2)

    . . . .

7. As I climbed the hill yonder
    And sat on the top,
    I looked far over the country.

8. Let the people make an opening
    For I am hot. (2)

9. As I sat upon the hill
    I looked down the valley;
    There, from one end to the other,
    There, the valley was filled,
    Filled, with—with—with—rosebuds![31]

SINGER: Thief. Coyote, traveling, saw rosebuds filling a valley. He falsely reported seeing buffalo and claimed a chief's daughter as a reward. Having successfully cheated, he revealed the trick and mocked his victims.

Tsimshian

1. The mountain goat's heart is saddened
    When it falls below.

2. This is why the large mountain moved;
    Where the Large Spirit Goat of the sky
      Will walk.

3. Nowhere to lay my empty body,
    There is nowhere here at the mountain's foot!
    Raven will pluck out my empty eyes.
    I will swing my hooves at one side
      And kick the mountain aside.

4. Make it walk, my dog,
    My dog, make it stand,
    Stand at the foot of the large falls.
    My dog, make it stand,
      Make it walk,
    Make it stand at the foot of the large falls.
    Make it walk to the foot of the rock slide,
    To the foot of the slide.
    A good place for the bearded goat to lie,
      At the foot of the slide.[32]

꙳   The first three songs accompanied a ceremonial performance. The audience sang the first song while hunters, one disguised as a mountain goat, climbed a stage-mountain built for the ceremony. The performers sang the second as the hunters shot the "goat" and cut off its head, which turned into a mask, which turned into a Thunderbird. The hunters sang the third after the kill, over the body of the "goat." Hunters sang the fourth song on the mountain after they had killed a real mountain goat and over every dead mountain goat before eating it.

Chahiksichahiks

1. The distant line there,
   Drawn thin across the wide land,
   The distant line of trees there,
   Stretched waving across the wide land,
   The distant flashing line of trees there!
2. The distant line there,
   The river, drawn thin across the wide land,
   The distant outstretched river there,
   Stretched flashing across the wide land,
   The distant sparkling river there!
3. The distant line there,
   The river, stretched thin across the wide land,
   The distant outstretched river there,
   Stretched sparkling across the wide land,
   The distant rippling river there![33]

꙳   Hako, Fifth Ritual, II, first song. The officiants in the Hako met this stream in the ceremonial journey to bring a chosen adoptee back to the camp. Mother Corn enjoined and protected this journey, which recalled the sun's movement, the origin journey, and the scouts' report of the buffalo herd. The officiants faced east and passed in front of the congregation, which turned and followed them.

Kwagutl

Many Salmon come ashore with me.
They dance ashore to you,
   The post in the middle of heaven.
They dance from the Salmon's country
   To the shore with me.
They come to dance to you
   At the right side of Heaven.

> The Salmon,
> Overarching, towering, outshining, surpassing,
> The Salmon.[34]

    ᔓ   The Salmon Dancer imitates the motions of the leaping salmon, with legs stiff together and body turning from side to side.

Shis-Inde

> That the buffalo may be near,
>   I make smoke for you!
> There will be many buffalo close to us.
>   You will surround us.
> Right there we will go among them
>   And will kill many.
> There will be much meat not far from us!
>   We will camp among them
> And from there will bring meat home
>   To our own country.[35]

HUNTING

Tewa

> Now the deer comes up to our houses.
> He brings the food we need.
> We offer him food he needs.
> Old Women deer, Old Men deer,
> We love you, so come here
> On the road we have laid!
> Come here to our house
> Where we may love you!
> Eat this little gift now.[36]

    ᔓ   A hunter's wife laid a thread down as a road leading into her house, sat in a corner, and sang this summoning song while her husband was off hunting.

Tlingit

> 1. I feel sad
>   When I leave Yakutat
>   And your mountains
>   Sink behind me,
>   Tluknaxadi-child, Wife!

I weep, I always weep
  About leaving.
2. Raise the banner of feelings
  For Tluknaxadi-child
  So that all their Ravens
    May see it.
    Whoo! Whoo![37]

SINGERS: John Nishka, Annie Johnson. Nishka composed this song for his wife when he was leaving Yakutat to go sea otter hunting off Icy Bay. The song suggests the symbol of visible breath. When he sang this song, which contained his feelings, his breath, visible in the chilly air, trailed up like a banner and carried the song and his feelings.

Diné

Coyote: Snow, Snow, Snow, Snow,
      As high as the grass!
      With that much snow,
      We can kill rabbits!
Badger: Snow, Snow, Snow, Snow,
      As high as groundwort!
      With that much snow,
      We can kill rabbits![38]

SINGER: Late Little Smith's Son. Hunting Coyote sang this to make snow. Observers have seen coyotes, badgers, and hawks cooperating to drive prairie dogs out of their holes and into the teeth of one of the hunters.

Ani'Yun'wiya'

You were conceived in Rabbit Place. Yoho!
You were conceived in Mulberry Place. Yoho!
You were conceived in Uyâ'ye'. Yoho!
You were conceived in the Great Swamp. Yoho!
Now, surely, we and good black things,
The best of all bears, will see each other.[39]

The hunter sang this charm, from the Origin of Bears, on the trail to attract bears. Ani-Tsâ'kahi (people before they turned into bears) taught the Cherokee this song. Tsistuyi', Kuwâhi', Uyâ'ye', and Gâte'kwâhi are four mountains: the first three are in the Smoky Mountains on the

Tennessee line, near Clingman's Dome and Mount Guyot; the fourth may be Fodderstack Mountain, southeast of Franklin, North Carolina. Bears had council houses under these mountains and held a ceremony and dance before hibernating. Bear Chief lives in Kuwâhi, with a medicine bath that resurrects the bears.

A'nish'inabeg

Going with footwear on his feet![40]

SINGER: Na'jobi'tun. Ceremonial Song IV.7 initiation, song 57. This song refers to a bear's paw. In the accompanying pictograph, a hunter with bow and arrow leaves bear tracks. Bears brought powerful medicine for healing and hunting.

Diné

A foot, a foot with toes,
A foot with toes came,
He came as a foot with toes.
Aging as he came with a foot with toes.[41]

Sung by Bear (Shash) when gambling against Giant, son of the Sun, to determine the duration of dark and light. Gamblers in the moccasin game also sang it. The song invokes the power of the bear. It reflects a dream or myth that included a bear's spoor and, by telling how Shash put his moccasins on the wrong feet, explains the pigeon-toed tracks of the bear. Hunters sang it when they found bear-tracks. Shamans sometimes wore bear-paws on their hands when healing or invoking power.

Maklaks

High up in the skies
I draw my magic circles.[42]

SINGER: Sergeant Morgan. The Eagle tutelary in this shaman's song, circling in a thermal, perhaps hunting, traces or creates by singing the magic circle the shaman traces during medicine-making.

Diné

I follow the river
Seeking a young beaver!
Up the river I go,

Through the cut willow path I go,
Seeking a young beaver.[43]

ᢌ   Sung by Beaver when gambling with Giant, son of the Sun, to set the
duration of dark and light. Sung by gamblers in the moccasin game and by
hunters.

Iyiniwok

You who stand sideways
Looking at us!
You who flick your tail up,
You whose fawn is covered
With dew![44]

ᢌ   SINGER: Samuel Grey Sturgeon. From a Swampy Cree hunting ceremony.
Two Loons sings this to make Wesucechak doff his disguise as a deer.
"Her song went on, and it had many deer in it, and the things you always
see deer doing. The deer were listening. They heard that Two Loons knew
many things about them, and they were pleased with this. The deer walked
into the village. 'They're giving themselves up!' someone said." The cere-
mony alluded to a shamans' contest in which the contestants tried to re-
member magical names and make the opponent forget those names. Two
Loons, forgetting Wesucechak's common name as a deer, uses periphrases
that reflect the shaman's medicine vocabulary and turns the trickster's
power against him. Two Loons originally disguised herself as an old wo-
man, teaching others.

Chahiksichahiks

There one comes, one comes standing. (2)
Quietly standing, waiting for the sun![45]

ᢌ   Sung in the Buffalo Dance. The hunter sees a buffalo, and the Holy Per-
son Buffalo, at dawn.

Inuit

By chance I sighted one wearing a bearskin
Out in drifting pack-ice. (3)
It came at me wagging its tail.
Only turning when I dodged,
Hampered it. (3)

It wore itself out against me
And I thrust my lance
    Into its body. (3)
I call this to mind
Because they breathe self-praise,
Our northern and southern neighbors![46]

SINGER: Aua. Aua made this song about a polar bear that attacked him on
the ice. He added the doglike tail-wagging and other details when he ex-
plained the song for Rasmussen.

A'nish'inabeg   Whence does he dawn, the buck?[47]

SINGER: Mec'kawiga'bau. "Dawn," for "spring, jump," suggests the Holy
Deer, rising with and from the sun. Bierhorst translates: "Whence does he
spring, the Deer? / Whence does he spring, / The Deer, the Deer, the
Deer?"[48]

Tua'dhu   If I were a baby seal,
Every time I surfaced
I would go close to the shore.[49]

SINGER: Mary Adams (Skokomish). Crow, Raven's sister, sang this Hunting
Song on the beach.

Nimipu   Buck, come out of the brush to me. (2)[50]

Coyote sang this song to lure and trap a fawn.

Hopitu   The eagles are coming.
Come in. Sit down.
Walk into the house! Enter!
Come into this place! Enter![51]

The Hopi words to this Eagle Catching song are so archaic that the inter-
preter was unable to translate them exactly.

Wazhazhe

> See, my grandfathers rise,
> They of the shaggy manes, rise quickly.
>   See, my grandfathers rise,
> They of the curved horns, rise quickly.
>   See, my grandfathers rise,
> They of the humped shoulders, rise quickly.
>   See, my grandfathers rise,
> They whose tails curl in anger, rise quickly.
>   See, my grandfathers rise,
> They, the four-legged, rise quickly.
>   See, my grandfathers rise,
> They who paw the earth in anger, rise quickly.[52]

ᔣ SINGER: Tsezhin'gawadainga. Waxo'be, Buffalo Song 3. The buffalo move from the spirit or invisible world to the visible world in these songs. They also rise from the earth and become visible.

A'nish'inabeg

> My shining horns![53]

ᔣ SINGER: Mec'kawiga'bau. In a vision, a deer appeared, walking alone, singing proudly to himself.

Inuit

> In our house I sit,
> Constantly huddled up from the cold.
> The people beyond us now,
> They don't sit huddled up.
> In our house I sit,
> Constantly huddled up.
> The people beyond us—
> Let me stand up again—
> With a harpoon—a seal!—No!
> In our house I sit,
> Constantly huddled up.[54]

ᔣ SINGER: Kexulik. A Dance Song.

Aa'shi'wi

> Antelope, (3)
> Like cream is your skin,

Like charcoal, your nose,
Like piñon gum, your eyes,
Like cedar bark, your sinew!
Antelope! (3)[55]

SINGER: Nick. A lame boy and a blind boy, hero-twins, sang this song to lure antelope into range.

Tsimshian

Where did the voice of the spirit chief
    Locate our wealth?
The humming voice, voice of the hummingbird,
Will hum over my head in the spring,
    Hum amidst great plenty.
My spirit has gone where the Nass flows.[56]

SINGER: Hrkwawyem. This song and the vision in which it appeared brought success and wealth in bear hunting. The hummingbird tutelary helped the visionary, who became a wealthy chief.

Ennesen

Because of my feather
Elf hangs by his foot.
    Whoo. (3)[57]

SINGER: Maria Ocarpia. Barn-Owl, hunting with his magic feather, caught Elf in a noose, like a rabbit. Prairie Falcon rescued Elf.

Pomo

Short-nosed, I, a man, run around, a puma!
Short Nose, I run over the long open ground,
    I creep up on the good side,
    The windward side!
I am a deer hunter.[58]

SINGER: William Benson. This Hunting Song calls the Puma Holy Person to fill the singer.

A'nish'inabeg

Come! Behold! Let's compete!
Rattlesnake, let's compete,
Most subtle reptile spirit![59]

꧁   SINGER: Be'cigwi'wizans. Midé power can overcome Rattlesnake, the most subtle, dreaded, and successful of reptiles. In the accompanying pictograph in Schoolcraft's edition are a man and a snake in the middle of the zigzag line that marks Midé power.

Inuit

The walrus, I harpoon it,
     Stroking its cheek.
You have become quiet and meek!
The walrus, I harpoon it,
     Patting its tusks.
You have become quiet and meek![60]

꧁   SINGER: Akernilik. Akernilik made this song to use should he harpoon a walrus and need to keep it from fighting near his kayak. He said, "[The song] was of no use to me. I never succeeded in getting a walrus."

Walwarena

Come out, Salmon,
See your kinsman dance.
Don't you know how to dance
     Like he does?
Why don't you know how to dance?[61]

꧁   SINGER: Juan de Jesús Justo. Coyote sings this Medicine Song to catch salmon. Coyote, who always falls victim to his own desire to steal others' medicines, here tries to make the salmon envy and desire his medicine dance. The song was popular. Maria Solares sang another version:
     Jump, Salmon, Jump!
     So you may see your uncle dance.[62]

Diné

Comes the deer to my singing.
Comes the deer to my song.
Comes the deer to my singing.
He, the blackbird, he am I, bird beloved of the wild deer.
     Comes the deer to my singing.
From the Black Mountain, from the summit, coming down the trail,
     Comes the deer to my singing.
Through the flowers, in beauty coming through now,
     Comes the deer to my singing.

Through the dew drops, coming through now,
    Comes the deer to my singing.
Through the pollen, flower pollen, coming through now,
    Comes the deer to my singing.
Starting with his left forefoot, stamping, turns the frightened deer.
    Comes the deer to my singing.
My quarry, I am blessed in hunting!
    Comes the deer to my singing.
    Comes the deer to my singing.
    Comes the deer to my song.
    Comes the deer to my singing.[63]

ॐ   The first of two verses. The second verse substitutes *baad*, "female," for *bekan*, "male"; and *deshnash*, "right," for *desklashdji*, "left," two ceremonial words not used in ordinary speech. If the hunter sat absolutely still and sang this song exactly (and silently), the deer, charmed, would come within range of the arrow. This song describes the condition it aims to create.

Dakota

At dawn I roam,
    Loping, I roam!
At dawn I roam,
    Trotting, I roam!
At dawn I roam,
    Timidly, I roam!
At dawn I roam,
    Watching cautiously, I roam![64]

ॐ   SINGER: Weasel Bear. A Wolf Dream Song an old wolf sang on a hill.

Chahiksichahiks

The great herd running away,
The buffalo running,
Their drumming hooves
Send dust clouds billowing to the sky
    And promise good hunting.
The buffalo and her child approaching,
Mother and Calf coming,
Turned back from the herd,
    Promise abundance.[65]

꙳   SINGER: Tahirassuwichi. Hako, Fifth Ritual, II. Before the invaders killed
the great herds, the officiants sang this song on their journey to bring back
the adoptee. After the invading buffalo skinners slaughtered the herds, the
officiants sang this inside the lodge, in memory of the herds and the days
of freedom.

Tohono Au'autam   *Deer:*   Lo, surely I shall die.
                                    Over there toward the west,
                                        Here and there I went running.
                                    Over there toward the west
                                    There was a thundering.
                                        It shook me.
                                        Lo, surely I shall die.
                                    Over there toward the east,
                                        Here and there I went running.
                                    Over there toward the east
                                    There was an echoing.
                                        It threw me down.[66]

꙳   This Papago Hunting Song presents the attitude the hunter desired in the
prey.

Diné   Ah'eh na-ya-ya,
                           Early in the morning you can see me na-ya-ya, (3)
                           The Yellow Hawk can see us na-ya-ya,
                           The Male rain can see us na-ya-ya,
                           The Black Bow can see us na-ya-ya,
                           An Eagle Feathered Arrow can see us na-ya-ya,
                           All the arrows that fit your bow can see us na-ya-ya,
                           The Arrow-that-hits-the-heart can see us na-ya-ya,
                           Early in the morning you can see us na-ya-yeh.[67]

꙳   SINGER: Claus Chee Sonny. Deer Huntingway. The deer sing this at
Tloo'haali (Fish Point, the southern tip of Black Mountain, southwest of
Chinle, the emergence site of the Deer People). The Deer Huntingway
traces two life journeys, northern and southern, in which the deer leave
and return to their place of origin at Fish Point, where they reenter Black
God's house. Those whom hunters have killed escape the debilities of old
age. The deer gods instructed the people that they might trap deer in pits,

but could not cook them in pits, only above ground on hot coals. This song makes the hunter who sings it Black God and gives him the power to "hold the deer in his hands."

Chehalis

Come, Come, E-e-e-lk!
Let's play, and run back and forth
This side of the prairie,
That side of the prairie.[68]

SINGER: Peter Heck. Little Wren sang this to attract prey. He lured Tiny Mouse, then Mouse, then Deer, and finally, on the fourth attempt, Elk.

Noam-Kekhl

Water goers, go in a circle?
Eyes pop out, pop out, pop out.[69]

Fishers, drugging fish, chanted this song until the poison killed the fish in the pool.

A'nish'inabeg

Like a star (3)
I shine!
My light fascinates the animal.[70]

SINGER: Be'cigwi'wizans. Hunting Song. The accompanying pictograph in Schoolcraft's edition shows a man connected to a star. The song may allude to jacklighting with torches, as well as to the Midé power derived from vision, song, and the Holy People.

Nuxalk

Let your children look at me, father.[71]

Sung while hunting mountain goat.

Maklaks

Ripples in the water-sheet
I spread far and wide.[72]

SINGERS: Chief Johnson, Dave Hill. This shaman's song asks the tutelary Mink to hunt as fiercely for the disease as mink hunt other prey.

Inuit
Cold and mosquitoes,
Those two pests never come together.
I lie down on the ice,
Lie down on the snow and ice,
Till my teeth fall chattering.
 It is I.
 Aja-aja-ja.
Memories from those days,
From those days,
Mosquitoes swarming
From those days,
The cold is bitter,
The mind grows dizzy
As I stretch my limbs
Out on the ice.
 It is I.
 Aja-aja-ja.
Ai, but songs call for strength
And I seek after words,
 I.
 Aja-aja-ja.
Ai, I seek and spy
Something to sing of,
The caribou with the spreading antlers!
And strongly I threw
The spear with my throwing stick,
And my weapon fixed the bull
In the hollow of the groin
And it quivered with the wound
Till it dropped and was still.
Ai, but songs
Call for strength
And I seek after words,
 It is I,
Aja, aja-haja-haja.[73]

SINGER: Ivaluardjuk (Iglulik). The throwing stick (atlatl) has a notched end into which the spear-butt fits. The stick nearly doubles the velocity of the spear by doubling the leverage exerted when throwing, since it doubles the length of the hunter's arm.

Chahiksichahiks

"Listen," he said, " 'There she comes,'
They say, 'There she comes, the buffalo woman,
There she comes, imitating a buffalo,
Walking, stopping, walking again!' "[74]

A'nish'inabeg

The Buffalo, as they stand in a circle,
    I join them![75]

SINGER: E'niwub'e. The singer dreamt he heard human sounds, topped a rise, and saw buffalo circling in mud, with heads swaying and tails flicking. He joined them, became a buffalo, and learned this song.

Chahiksichahiks

He said, " 'The man was coming along the line,'
They say, 'He was riding along the line,
    Driving along the line. (2)
Along the line, smoke was standing above it,
He came riding along the line, driving the herd.' "[76]

SINGER: Wicita Blain. Buffalo Dance Song. Blain's grandfather rode along a line of buffalo, driving them to other hunters. The "smoke," the dust above the herd, located it for scouts and hunters. The ceremony associated tobacco smoke, from the pipe White Buffalo Calf Woman brought to the Siouan nations, with successful and decorous hunting.

Tlingit

1. From inside the fishtrap's wings
   At the head of the river
   The frogs begin to come out.
   Inside the wings,
   They make a noise.
   Because of the visitors, the salmon,
   They make a noise.
2. Within my reach almost,
   To the beach they come.
   My last uncle
   By accident fell in.
   Already I give up.[77]

SINGERS: Dry Bay Chief George, Frank Dick. This Frog Screen Song describes the effect the salmon run produces when the salmon enter the fish trap. The second stanza refers to the composer's uncle, who drowned near the beach.

Diné

> I came as Hastceyalti.
> On the trail to Black Mountain summit,
> On the trail among the flowers,
>> Male deer are there.
> Herb pollen I will put in his mouth!
> The buck steps along in the dew on the plants.
>> I kill him, but he likes me.[78]

ჯ A man who went on a journey to Whirling Log junction in a tree, recapitulating some incidents from the emergence myth, learned Hunting Songs and decorum from Talking God and sang this song while successfully killing deer.

A'a'tam A'kimult

> 1. Down from the windy ruins,
>   Down from the houses of magic,
>> In their shade,
>> In their shadow,
>   The winds blow around my large antlers,
>   The winds blow around my ears.
> 2. Over there I ran trembling,
>   Many arrows ran after me,
>   Many magic bows and arrows
>> Reach me here![79]

ჯ SINGER: Ki-iwa. Hovi Nyoi (Black-Tailed Deer Song).

Wazhazhe

> It is stricken, it still lives and flees. (2)
> I shall pursue and find it, wherever it goes. (2)
> It is stricken, it still lives and flees. (2)
> Though it has gone afar, I have found it. (2)[80]

ჯ SINGER: Waxthi'zhi. Deer Songs 4, Rite of Vigil. In both the Waxo'be and Vigil Ceremonies, these Calling the Deer Songs invoked the power that brought the deer to feed the people and directed that power toward successful war, which, like food, saved the people. Only the Nonhonzhin'ga had the right to sing this song to help a hunter.

O'maha

One I have wounded, he moves there,
　　He gets there, mouth bleeding.
One I have wounded, he moves there,
　　He gets there, staggering.
One I have wounded, there he moves,
　　He gets there, falling!
One I have wounded, he lies there,
　　There he lies, lies still![81]

A'a'tam A'kimult

In the White Dawn
I rose to go!
As Blue Evening fell,
As Blue Evening fell,
In the Blue Evening, I rose to go!
2. Thornapple leaves,
Thornapple leaves,
I who eat them
Stagger dizzily as I run!
Thornapple flowers,
Thornapple flowers,
I drank that drink,
And, drunk, staggered as I ran!
3. Great Bow Remaining hunted,
Here overtook and killed me,
Left my horns here,
Cut off, thrown away!
Great Reed Remaining hunted,
Here overtook and killed me,
Left my hooves here,
Cut off, thrown away!
4. Crazy flies,
Crazy flies,
Drop here and there with flapping wings.
Drunken Butterflies
Drop here and there with opening and shutting wings![82]

SINGER: Virsak Vai-i. Hunting Song: Katotapi Nyoi (*Datura* Song). A man at Blackwater ate an undivided *Datura* root. Locked in the house at noon, he ran through a mesquite thicket in the evening. Scratched and bruised, he acknowledged no pain until he recovered his sanity.

Inuit

Down, down inside,
One can get cold with fear.
The big black bears and the big musk-oxen,
The beasts down there,
Those that usually flee,
Down there, the game flees,
   I wonder where?
Those down there,
The beasts down there,
Those that flee at nothing,
The big caribou cows and bulls,
The beasts down there,
Those that flee at nothing.[83]

SINGER: Netsit (Copper Eskimo). Part of a contest song.

Inuit

Grandmother: Get ready for the hunt.
              Where will you go?
              Distance you will cover.
   Mouse: When I go to the right,
              Evil spirits will get me.
              When I go to the left,
              Evil spirits will get me.
              Everywhere evil spirits will get me.
                I'll go home![84]

Mouse didn't hunt diligently. His grandmother stopped making kayaks, and Mouse could only hunt on land thenceforward.

Yokuts

Do not think I shall harm you!
You shall have a new body!
Now turn your head to the north and lie flat![85]

꙳ The hunter captures the eagle in a noose rigged to a stuffed skin bait. The hunter stepped on the eagle to kill it. He promised it a new body, perhaps embodiment as a Thunder Being.

POSTHUNT

Sanpoil

1. Make the other animals do as you have done!
    Even you, Bear, you have lain down for me;
        Now make the bucks lie down.
2. You have given up to me!
    Now make good-looking women
        Give up to me.[86]

꙳ SINGERS: Song 1, John Tom; Song 2, Bear. Sanpoil hunters sang these songs after killing a bear.

Konhiak

The air was cold,
A man sat on his balsa.
He had paddled long
And was very tired.

The tide ran swiftly
Away from his home.
He was tired and cold
And could paddle no more.

    He fell asleep
With his paddle across his knee.
    When he awoke
His balsa had brought him home.

His wife came out
With all her neighbors.
They took his hand
And led him into the house.

    Each one said:
    "You will not die,
Though you are so tired and cold
    You will not die."

And the balsa sang to him:
   "You will not die.
You were cold and tired,
But I brought you home."[87]

SINGER: Santo Blanco.

Shis-Inde

I came there.
Where the Sun and the Dipper look at each other,
   I came there!
Where two male deer, docile, came down,
   I came there![88]

SINGER: Antonio. A Deer Ceremony Song, sung by Panther Boy, who killed many of the prehunting docile deer.

Inuit

Fear surrounded me.
Intolerable, staying in my igloo.
   Hungry, starving,
I staggered inland, stumbling,
   Tripping.
At Little Musk Ox Lake
Trout mocked me; I got no bite.
   On I toiled,
To Young Man's Reach.
I caught salmon there once.
I wished to see swimming caribou or fish
   In the lake.
My thought ended in nothingness,
   Like a line all run out.
Would I ever, I wondered,
Have firm ground to stand on?
   I staggered on,
Mumbling magic words all the way.[89]

SINGER: Kimerut (Copper Eskimo).

Shis-Inde

Make a smoke for her!
The girl who became a deer is far away, where she is better pleased.

When you make a smoke for her with a pipe of jet
   She is pleased.
She is far away, where the Dipper descends.
   There she likes it better.[90]

    SINGER: Antonio. A Deer Ceremony Song, sung about Panther Boy's wife, whom Turquoise Boy turned into a deer. Panther Boy's Wife, She Who Walks on Water, returned to the North with the deer after Panther Boy, an immoderate hunter, killed her fawn-children by mistake.

Tsimshian

I came from the headwaters
   In the mountain caves
Where the small streams
   Have all dried up.[91]

    SINGER: Laelt. This Arteeh family dirge also served as a Hunter's Song. According to legend, Arteeh's family sang this over dead bears. The song derived from a trapped bear-husband's Death Song.

Inuna'ina'

It is dark, but the moon is shining!
I carry home my game.[92]

    SINGER: Yellow Horse. An Arapaho Hunting Song.

Dakota

Father, somewhere, heads home howling!
Mother, somewhere, heads home howling!
Father brings a young calf home and
Mother, somewhere, heads home howling!
Now she returns in a sacred manner, comes home![93]

    SINGER: Charging Thunder. A Wolf Dream Song. The cubs sing joyfully of a successful hunt.

A'a'tam A'kimult

1. Young Hare Magician, running in blackness,
   Brings in black-tailed deer meat!
      I will bring in Dawn!
   Young Badger Magician, running in blackness,

           Brings in black-tailed deer feet!
              I will bring in Dawn!
        2. Had I no wind? (3)
           Had I no clouds? (3)
           In the distant dawn, under Yellow Ikol,
           That was standing there, calling me,
              I had no wind, I had no wind.
           Far in the east, under Yellow Ikol,
           That was standing there, calling me,
              I had no wind, I had no wind.
           Far in the dawn, under Yellow Ikol,
           That was standing there, calling me,
              I had no clouds, I had no clouds.[94]

SINGER: Virsak Vai-i. A Pihol Song (Pihol Nyoi). The pihol flower, when mixed with tobacco and smoked, cures *komotan* sickness and attracts deer.[95]

Nimipu

This Bear was my friend, living in the great woods!
I did not kill him, too-na-a-na-ta-hoe!
He committed self-death by coming before the arrow!
Gus-nee-whey, oh-ta-hee-na-go gus-kee!
Perhaps he knew a hunter in my camp
And came that our lives might be strengthened!
I did not kill this bear, my friend of the woods! (2)[96]

From a manuscript in the Library (Los Angeles) of Nipo Strongheart (Yakima).

Dakota

The poor are many
So meat and food
I give away now.[97]

SINGER: John Good. This Giveaway Song reflects *wouncage* (Sioux customs). A successful hunter might sing so after a successful hunt.

War

PREWAR

Wazhazhe

Dry is my tongue from marching,
Oh my elder brother, (2)
Dry is my tongue from marching,
And lo, my death draws near.
Dry is my tongue from marching,
Oh my elder brother, (2)
Dry is my tongue from marching![1]

～ SINGER: Waxthi'zhi. The Charcoal Carrying Ceremony. Crying and Broken
Song 3. Young men who had not yet fought sang this song in the cere-
mony to accustom themselves to the hardships of war.

Ka'igwu

Idlers and cowards stay home now. (2)
Whenever they wish, they see their loved ones.
  Somewhere the warrior I love,
  Gone to war, is sick, alone![2]

～ SINGER: Apiatan (Wooden Lance). Gomda Daagya (Wind Song). Women
sang these songs when their warriors went raiding. They also sang them to
encourage reluctant warriors to volunteer. A Papago preraid song shows
the effect such songs were designed to provoke:
  Is it for me to eat what food I have, and all day sit idle?
  Is it for me to drink the sweet water poured out, and all day sit idle?
  Is it for me to gaze upon my wife, and all day sit idle?
  Is it for me to hold my child in my arms, and all day sit idle?[3]

Diné

Now this warrior kills them for me,
His enemies he kills for me!

168

If you continue to kill them for me
I shall despise my husband for your sake!
I get restless to prostitute myself!
As my skirt rustles "Swish, swish,"
I tiptoe along, I tiptoe along,
Ya ra ai! His tail, tail, tail.[4]

SINGER: Slim Curley. Such Tail Songs follow the Enemyway Ceremony.
Tail Songs accompany ordering the now ineffectual enemy ghosts into the
ground. The tailed people (coyotes) originally sang these songs and
swayed their tails (*bi'ce*) at the chorus.[5] Any warrior could pay to have this
song sung with his name inserted in the appropriate place. Nearly all lan-
guage groups contain songs that attribute immoderate admiration for war-
riors to the women of the nation. Such songs may reveal more about the
warriors' hopes than about the women's psychology. The songs presum-
ably inspired enthusiasm in warriors. During World War I, English music
hall singers sang similar songs, for similar reasons, and English ladies
passed out white feathers. "Prostitute" suggests the ritual promiscuity of
the "Wild Women" rather than the commercial exchange Anglo culture
associates with the word.

Tsistsi'stas   Old Age is hard to bear![6]

SINGER: W. Goodsell. A Weasel Society Song. Old warriors made this song,
which resembles the Pawnee White Lance Society Song:
    "He comes. It hurts to use a cane.
    It is becoming painful to pick it up."[7]
Such songs encouraged warriors to fight, even to death, since old age can
be more painful than death.

Suquamish   I am quick tempered, (2)
    I eat men fast;
    You cannot hold me. (2)[8]

SINGER: Jacob Wahelchu. A war-spear, transforming into a war-club,
danced and sang this song in a vision. The song brought Wahelchu power
in war.

Dakota

I am a Fox.
I am supposed to die.
If there is anything difficult,
If there is anything dangerous,
That is mine to do.[9]

꒰ Henry Crow Dog sang a version of this song in 1969:
I am a Fox.
I am supposed to die.
I already threw my life away.
Something daring, something dangerous,
I wish to do![10]

Pestamokatiyak

I will arise with my tomahawk in my hand
And I must have revenge on that nation that has slain my poor people.
I arise with war-club in my hand,
And follow the bloody track of that nation that has killed my people.
I will sacrifice my own life and the lives of my warriors.
I arise with war-club in my hand and follow the track of my enemy.
When I overtake him I will take his scalp and string it on a long pole,
And I will stick it in the ground, and my warriors will dance around it for many days;
Then I will sing my song for the victory over my enemy.[11]

A'nish'inabeg

I am rising to seek the war-path.
The earth and sky are before me.
I walk by day and by night
And the Evening Star guides me.[12]

꒰ Schoolcraft regularized a song made up of several lines, each of which
could work as an independent song: (1) I am rising; (2) I take the earth, I
take the sky, I take; (3) I walk, through the night sky, I walk; (4) The
Eastern Woman calls. George Belden says that his guide and companion,
Washtello, sang her "Indian songs," including this one, while leading their
horses.[13] She added verse 3, which Schoolcraft prints, as another indepen-
dent song.[14]

Konhiak

Let's go and fight!
We are brave.
Let's go and fight! (2)[15]

ꜱ   SINGER: Santo Blanco.

Numakaki

No one lives forever.
Whatever may happen, I will go.[16]

ꜱ   SINGER: Black Chest. A Bravery Song sung at the final investiture of those
who have bought initiation into the Little Dog Society.

Siksika

I care for nothing! (6)[17]

ꜱ   SINGER: Eagle Head. A Defiance Song. Spear Woman told Eagle Head to
stop singing that bad luck song. Little Otter sang it just before he went
out against the Cutthroat White Dog and never returned. Eagle Head
thought it a good song that made the singer brave.

Snohomish

I belong to the Snohomish.
    I have no friends.
I am a Snohomish.[18]

ꜱ   This War Dance Song means, "I have killed all the people around here."

Ontinonsionni

Now I am greatly surprised
And therefore I shall use it,
The power of my War Song.
I am of the Five Nations and I shall appeal
To the Mighty Creator.
He gave this army.
My warriors shall be mighty
In the strength of the Creator!
Between him and my song they stand,
For it was he who gave the song,
This War Song that I sing.[19]

ꜱ   A War Song, for a formal declaration of war.

Tiwame

I, the Sun,
Move back to the south.

My weapon, I take that back with me!
   With this I go!
My shield, I take that back with me!
   With this I go.[20]

๛   This Opi Dance Song protected warriors. It belonged to the Society of
Scalp Takers, who blackened their faces and wore buckskin kilts with black
horned snakes painted on them. They wore eagle down on their heads.
Masewi and Oyoyewi, hero-twins, protected the warriors, who usually
fought in winter, when the sun went south.

Diné

I am the Turquoise Woman's son.
On top of Belted Mountain
Beautiful horses, slim like a weasel!
My horse has a hoof like striped agate!
His fetlock is like a fine eagle plume!
His legs are like quick lightning.
My horse's body is like an eagle-plumed arrow!
My horse has a tail like a trailing black cloud!
I put flexible goods on my horse's back!
The Little Holy Wind blows through his hair!
His mane is made of short rainbows!
My horse's ears are made of round corn!
My horse's eyes are made of big stars!
My horse's head is made of mixed waters
(From the holy waters—he never thirsts.)
My horse's teeth are made of white shell!
The long rainbow is in his mouth for a bridle!
With it I guide him!
When my horse neighs, different colored horses follow.
When my horse neighs, different colored sheep follow.
I am wealthy because of him!
   Peaceful before me!
   Peaceful behind me!
   Peaceful below me!
   Peaceful above me!
   Peaceful around me!
   Peaceful voice when he neighs!
   Peaceful I am, and everlasting!
   I stand for my horse![21]

∿   SINGER: Tall Kiaah'ni. The War God's Horse Song. David McAllester ana-
lyzes, explicates, and reproduces this song in its original length and sets it
in its cultural and ceremonial context.[22]

Kwagutl

You had your wish
When you attacked my tribe,
You, called a chief of supernatural power.
But my power surpasses yours:
I am the Doubleheaded Eagle,
Protecting my tribe.[23]

A'nish'inabeg

Strike ye our land
With curved horns![24]

∿   SINGER: Main'gans. Densmore "unpacked" Main'gans's original:[25]
Strike ye now our land with your great curved horns!
In your mighty rage toss the turf in the air!
Strike ye now our land with your great curved horns!
We will hear the sound and our hearts will be strong
    When we go to war.
Give us of your strength in the time of our need!
King of all the plain—buffalo, buffalo.
Strike ye now our land with your great curved horns!
    Lead us forth to the fight!
Densmore explicitly stated the sounds and images that the ceremonial, and
brief, form of the song evoked in those listening and singing it: rumbling
thunder, the rumbling of the running herd, the clash and crack of buffalo
horns when the bulls fight, the crack of lightning striking earth and bring-
ing power to the warriors.

Wazhazhe

I rise, I rise,
I, whose tread makes the earth rumble.
    I rise, I rise,
I, in whose thighs there is strength.
    I rise, I rise,
I, who whips his back with his tail when in rage.
    I rise, I rise,
I, in whose humped shoulders there is power.

I rise, I rise,
I, who shakes his mane when angered.
I rise, I rise,
I, whose horns are sharp and curved.[26]

ဢ   SINGER: Waxthi'zhi. Vigil Ceremony, Rising of Buffalo Bull Men, song 1.
Ghost Dance buffalo songs and "Strike ye our land" also invoke the thun-
derlike buffalo for power in war.

Pahodja

I—I am a War Eagle.
The wind is strong, but I am an Eagle!
I am not ashamed—no,
The twisting Eagle's quill is on my head.
I see my enemy below me!
I am an Eagle, a War Eagle.[27]

ဢ   The dancers imitate eagles.

Kwagutl

Let them call your name, Great Bear!
Great Bear, you will go
To the highest copper, the highest chief.
You will enslave the tribes, the Great Bear.
Then we will have battle!
Then we will have woe![28]

ဢ   A Bear Dancer's Song.

Cowichan

Wa! Yi! We Spirits, we are Stlalukum,
Wa! Yi! We Dragons, we are Stsinqa,
We Thunder-fighters.[29]

ဢ   Cowichan warriors sang this during the War Dance.

Potawatomi

A man standing in the door holds blades of grass.
Grass of all kinds.
Enter!
Take a blade to stick in your hair.

When the enemy shoots at you, they cannot hit.
No more than they can hit the wind,
    Tossed grasses in the wind.[30]

    Stanza 2 of Wounded Bundle Chant.

Choctaw

I am going.
My face is painted.
They cannot see me.
I am going. (repeat *ad lib.*)[31]

    SINGER: Lysander Tubby.

Kwagutl

Don't cut!
Shoot![32]

Hopitu

Houses will be wrapped in a red cloud!
    Coming from the South,
Enveloping first one place and then another,
    Here it will arrive at last.[33]

    The song calls for purgation and help from *yayaponcha* (wizards who control wind, storm, and lightning) to destroy Pivanhonkapi, a village infested by *pawaka* (witches). A red cloud, fire, will settle on the village like a destroying storm.

Aa'shi'wi

Now! This day, my Fathers, Holy Ones!
Here in this enemy-filled land make me precious,
That in any way, even unexpectedly,
No enemy may dare to strike me,
This day, make a shield for me.
That none may pass through, no enemy, none whatsoever,
Make me a shield.
    Mountain Lion! Knife Wing!
    May you shield my heart![34]

    Sung while raiding or passing through enemy land. The singer took the fetish of the appropriate Hunter-God from his medicine bundle, scattered prayer meal to four quarters, held the fetish over his heart in his left hand, knelt, and prayed. With the edge of the arrowhead lashed to the back of the fetish, he scratched the first of four six-inch lines on the ground. He invoked the Lion Hunter Holy Person as he drew the second line. He invoked the Hawk or Eagle Hunter Holy Person as he drew the third line. He breathed on the fetish and replaced it in the medicine pouch as he drew the last line.

Fighting

Dakota

Clear the way!
In a sacred manner I come!
The earth is mine!
Hence in a sacred manner I come!
Clear the way!
In a sacred manner I come![35]

SINGER: Little Buffalo. This Ozu'ye Olo'wa-n Wolf Song was sung by Little Buffalo on a raid, as the raiders painted their horses before a fight.

Dakota

Friend, my horse flies like a bird
As it runs![36]

SINGER: Brave Buffalo. A Horse Society Song. These songs made horses swift and sure in war and hunting.

O'maha

Wolves don't fear strange lands,
Nor do I![37]

Sanish

I fear nothing except the Heavens.[38]

SINGER: Bear's Teeth. Singing this song, a young warrior, a *sakhuu'nu* (a contrary, who did everything backward as a result of a vision of Thunder Beings), shot an arrow into the midst of the Sioux, rode in, retrieved it, and was shot while riding back.

O'maha

I hear distant voices speak, send me words! (2)
They send words where I lie,
The owl speaks!
With morning comes a shout to me![39]

ᕀ   A Hethu'shka Society Memorial Song. An Omaha warrior, awakened by an
owl-hoot, heard answering hoots. The hoots sounded false. He scouted,
found enemies, and warned his fellows, who ambushed the attackers when
they charged at dawn. The Owl Holy Person, owls, and owl medicine men
often warned war parties of their enemies. On raids, the Papago sang:
    Gray owl medicine man, come with me!
    Find my enemy there and make him helpless.
    Blue hummingbird medicine man, come with me!
    Find my enemy over there and make him helpless.[40]
An owl medicine man can talk to owls. Dead Papago warriors take the
shape of owls to visit the living. Such a dead warrior can tell the medicine
man accompanying the Papago war-party all about the enemy.

Dakota

This is my land!
I will not give it up![41]

ᕀ   SINGER: Sitting Bull. A War Song. Sitting Bull rode a black horse into
battle at Scarf Creek in 1870, singing this song.

O'maha

There they come who seek for me! (2)
They come there who seek for me!
"The Omaha, where is he?" they say!
    There they come,
    Here I stand!
    Come here![42]

ᕀ   A Hethu'shka Society Memorial Song. The warrior singing this song per-
sonified the Hethu'shka warriors, who personified the Omaha. He dares
the enemy to attack: the Omaha, who do not fear death, shout defiance.

Absaroke

Crows in danger, your protector is here.
Behold him well! Double Face!
In swift water, a big branched tree

Lies, roots facing upstream, branches downstream.
Very heavy, it doesn't float away.
The rapids swirl small driftwood and debris
To the sheltered side, where it circles!
It doesn't float away! It becomes entangled!
Like that driftwood, Crows, you seek shelter.
We all run to Double Face.
Tomorrow whenever they chase us, he'll dismount.
We'll swirl to shelter behind him.
There we will be entangled.
He will shield you.[43]

ᢞ   SINGER: Plays with His Face. The singer sang this to hearten the warriors to fight. Double Face pledged to stake himself out as a rallying point if the Crow had to retreat. The singer then told the young women and young men to enjoy each other, cook lots of food, feast, and make a square on a hillock. He donned a Buffalo Dancer costume and sang in front of a buffalo chip pile, telling people to join. He cast a shield as an omen and predicted many dead enemies and no Crow casualties. "The Crows said nothing but did not believe him. 'A great many we are going to meet. How is it possible that none of us be killed?' they thought. Then they went away."

Absaroke

Sky and earth are everlasting.
    Men must die.
Old age brings evil.
    Charge and die![44]

ᢞ   Wants-to-Die owned this song. Iron Hawk heard Lakota warriors sing or shout a similar song ("Take courage! This is a good day to die!") at Little Big Horn.[45] He may have heard Good Fox, Lame Deer's grandfather, singing a version there.[46] Cante Witko (Crazy Heart), Lame Deer's other grandfather, fought so well that he became a Shirt Wearer.[47] Howling Wolf sang a similar song as his Death Song at the Bear Creek Massacre.[48] Crazy Horse (Tshunke Witko) shouted his famous war cry ("A good day to die and a good day to fight!") at the Battle of the Rosebud.[49]

O'maha

I shall vanish and be no more.
The land over which I wander shall remain!
    And change not.[50]

～ A Hethu'shka Society Song. It could be sung as a Death Song. The Hava-
supai morning song "Make me always as I am" draws the same assurance
based on the enduring land, not from fighting for it, but from planting
and irrigating it.

Tewa

So we have bad luck, for we are men!
You have good luck now, for you are women!
To Navajo camps we go now, ready for war!
　　Good-bye![51]

Tohono Au'autam

Night coming down!
Sitting in the night!
Seeking my enemy![52]

～ SINGER: Sivariano Garcia. Warriors sang this to help shamans accompany-
ing the war-party locate the enemy.

A'a'tam A'kimult

There stands the doomed pueblo!
There the chief scampers about
In his yellow robe,
Decorated with hand-prints.[53]

～ SINGER: Thin Leather (Ka'mal Tkak). Elder Brother's army attacked Casa
Grande, singing this song. Hand-prints often decorated the walls of Ana-
sazi and Hohokam ruins.

Ta'n-ta'wats

People's blood
I am drinking, drinking.
I will rise up. (2)[54]

～ SINGER: George Laird. Mosquito's War Song on a raid Coyote led.

A'nish'inabeg

They will take me home, the spirits![55]

～ SINGER: Gi'wita'bines. Mary Austin expanded Densmore's version (proba-
bly her best expansion):

> If I die here in a foreign land,
> If I die in a land not my own,
> Nevertheless the thunder, the rolling thunder,
> > Will take me home.
> If I die here in a strange land,
> The wind, the wind rushing over the prairie, the wind
> > Will take me home.
> The wind and the thunder are the same everywhere.
> > What does it matter then
> > If I die here in a strange land![56]

Informants said the song meant, "The Thunders will take me home, whenever I wish, and the winds will too!" A man condemned to hang sang this song. When the invaders were about to hang him, thunder and lightning struck the tree, and rain drove everyone home. The authorities freed the man. This song suggests and invokes the medicine of the eagle and Thunder Being.

Ka'igwu

> I live, but I will not live forever.
> Sacred Moon, you alone remain,
> Powerful Sun, you alone remain,
> Wondrous Earth, you remain forever.
> All of us soldiers must die.[57]

A song of the Crazy Dog Society. Marriott also prints Sitting Bear's version.[58] Setanka sang a version as his Death Song in 1871, just before he attacked a guard, knowing he would die:

> Sun, you remain forever, but we Kaitsenko must die!
> Earth, you remain forever, but we Kaitsenko must die![59]

It recurs across the continent in many variants:

> I live, but I cannot live forever!
> Only the Earth lives forever!
> Only the Sun lives![60]

Mildred Mayhall prints another version.[61]

Numa

> In that ancient land of the Ai-ats
> My bowstring was wet
> > While I slept.[62]

    SINGER: Chuar-ru-um-pik. The Paiute lost the battle against the Mohave that this song recalls. The dream of a wet bowstring warned a brave.

Oma'nomeni'wuk

It causes fog.[63]

    SINGER: Pigeon. The war bundle, placed on the ground on a raid, calls up a concealing fog that protects the raiders. The bundle shares the power Maheo used to protect a Cheyenne scout in hostile territory: "Wolf I am. / In darkness, in light, / Wherever I search, / Wherever I run, / Wherever I stand, / Everything will be good / Because Maheo protects us."[64]

Tohono Au'autam

Morning began to run upon us. Then, leaping, in we went.
Out came a lone enemy, and, looking about in surprise,
He broke a tree and went down rolling.
Then Rattlesnake, who kills with his mouth,
Took his body and went dragging it along.
Out came another lone enemy. Looking about in surprise,
He slipped on the grass and down he went rolling.
Then Hawk, who kills with his claws,
Took his body and went dragging it along.
Then the sun reached the rising point.
Then, no more, we wrestled.
    An end of them we made.[65]

    This narrative of a successful attack carried so much power that some warriors refused to sing or discuss it.

A'nish'inabeg

Greatly she, defending her children,
She, defending her children, the old woman,
Defending her children, fought for us all![66]

    SINGER: Odjib'we. This song honors Bica'ganab, who fought Sioux raiders.

Tohono Au'autam

Apache: "Near sunset, I fall down!
    Near sunset, I fall down!
    I am going like a drunken man!"

Papago: Toward evening, he falls! [Yell!]
Toward evening, he falls! [Yell!]
He falls, [Yell!]
Staggers [Yell!] like a drunken man.[67]

SINGER: Mendez. A Papago warrior chased a wounded Apache and killed him when he fell. Every time the wounded Apache staggered, the Papago shouted a war cry.

A'nish'inabeg

The prairie land
Whence I rise![68]

SINGER: Niski'gwun. Odjib'we fought without medicine and sank exhausted. A comrade, Niski'gwun, sprayed medicine on him. He recovered, fought, and counted coup. This War Song cures exhaustion.

Tsimshian

Don't pass me by,
Don't you pass
When a Grizzly lies eating!
I am the Grizzly.[69]

Hlabeqs sang this Wolf Clan War Song in 1869.

A'nish'inabeg

The noise of passing feet on the prairie,
They are playing a game as they come,
   Those men.[70]

SINGER: Odjib'we. A War Song. The Chippewa, retreating from a costly raid, remembering the pursuing Sioux's footfalls, sang of war as of a ball game, perhaps lacrosse. Black Elk explains the ceremonial and sacred significance of such games when he discusses the *tapa wanka yap* (throwing the ball game).[71] Ceremonies such as Black Elk describes lie behind many of the games mentioned in these songs. Stewart Culin, *Games,* describes many games.

Nimipu

Eagle banks on tilting wings, circling! (2)
Elk's feet planted deep in the ground!

       Eagle circles, banking! (3)
       Eagle swoops, dives, swoops! (3)
  Elk's antler tips brush the ground!
  Eagle banks on tilting wings, circling![72]

᧥   SINGER: Waptipas. Elk's Medicine Song. Eagle and other Holy People predators wounded and cornered Elk, who backed against a cliff to fight. Elk
sang this song in his defense posture, antlers lowered, feet planted, facing
wolves, the hovering Eagle, and other predators.

Wailaki

    That arrow must hurt you badly!
    You killed old men and women
    And never thought how it hurt them.[73]

᧥   SINGER: Nahlse. A War Chant. Nahlse went on a retaliatory raid in a party
that killed three warriors. The enemy, Chumichekechun, escaped and
wounded two Wailuki. Nahlse shot Chumichekechun as he stood adjusting
his quiver. As Chumichekechun lay moaning, Nahlse "exclaimed" this
song, which became popular as a War Song.

Tlingit

    1. I chose to do this.
      I would not let pass what my conscience said.
      Before his death, I saw his ghost.
    2. As soon as he stabbed Cadasi'ktc,
        Cadasi'ktc died.[74]

᧥   SINGERS: Lqena', Dekina'ku. Lqena', the sole survivor of his party, composed this when his enemies wanted to make peace with him. He danced
as a deer, feigning a Peace Dance, sang this song, and cut the man standing next to him in two. It became a Deer Song later, with a different last
line.

Tsistsi'stas

    Nothing lives long
  Except the Earth and the mountains.[75]

᧥   White Antelope sang this Death Song at the Sand Creek Massacre,
Colorado, in 1864, looking west. The Arapaho placed the spirit world in
the West, higher than this world and separated from it by a body of water.

Ghost Dancers believed that the New Earth would descend from the West.[76]

Diné

    Now, Slayer of Alien Gods, among men am I,
Now among the enemy's gods with weapons of magic am I!
    Rubbed with the summits of mountains,
Now among alien gods with weapons of magic am I!
    Now upon the beautiful trail of old age,
Now among alien gods with weapons of magic am I![77]

SINGER: Hataali Natloi. The first of four stanzas sung on going into battle. The medicine bags the Diné made and warriors carried contained various items, including earth, from the sacred mountains.

BACK HOME

Dakota

Soldiers, you fled.
Even the Eagle dies.[78]

SINGER: Eagle Shield. Members of the Warrior Society on the Rosebud still sing:
    Soldiers, you deserted [name],
    So he lies there![79]

Pahodja

    O-ta-pa, Why do you flee us
When you are the most powerful?
    But it was not you, O-ta-pa,
It was your body that ran!
It was your body, O-ta-pa!
It was your body that ran.[80]

Taunting the enemy at a Victory Dance.

Konhiak

I sing this song to the rattlesnake.
I sing it to the Big Mountain.
I have fought with the Papagos
    And killed many.[81]

SINGER: Santo Blanco.

Tohono Au'autam   At the foot of the East I got drunk, my younger brothers!
                      The white wind met me and drove me mad:
                      "Kill the Apache! Kill the Apache!
                      Dry the skin! Dry the skin!
                      Soften it! Soften it!"
                      I am happy with it! Aaah!
                      But there are still some Apache left.[82]

Kwagutl   I began at the upper end of the tribes.
                          (Who asked for it!) (2)
                      I came downstream setting fire to the tribes,
                      Everywhere, with my fire-bringer.
                          (They asked for it!) (2)
                      My name, just my name, killed them,
                      I, the great Mover of the World.
                          (Serves them right!) (2)[83]

        ೫   SINGER: Neqap'enk'em. A War Song against the Sanetch.

Tana   Down there at their village
                      The Navajo youths lie scalped.
                      The young men of Santa Clara
                      Stripped off those bluebird skins.[84]

        ೫   A Santa Clara Scalp Dance Song.

A'a'tam A'kimult   1. We begin the Scalp Song.
                         We begin the Scalp Song there!
                             I try to begin,
                         But I don't know the words.
                         In the darkness, the song grows very loud.
                      2. The Scalp Song rises!
                         Hearing it, they run toward it,
                         The women going wild.
                      3. Pitiful me,
                         Strip my disease from all over me.
                         Strip my disease from all over me, singing.

4. I am going to the night singing!
   It leads me to Sivat Mountain,
      I, that go there running![85]

SINGER: Virsak Vai-i. Kokpu Nyoi (Fetish Song). The fetish, an Apache scalp, placed in a medicine basket with bird down, developed into a spirit that would help the Pima if they propitiated it properly and set food out for it. If they neglected these rituals, the spirit would cause a disease, which this song cures. The women dancers rush from the edge of the firelight to the scalp and the singers, as the Wild Women rush toward the Puberty Ceremonies.

Ivitem

There stands the whirlwind (2)
Where they burned him, (2)
Puchueulchalmalmia.[86]

An Enemy Song, sung during fiestas to tease visiting friends and rivals. The songs derive from Scalp and War Songs and use the secret (war) name of the visitor and, at one time, the war name of the enemy. The whirlwind arises from the hot ashes of a ritual cremation and also embodies the spirit of the dead, which travels as a whirlwind or dustdevil, the thermal common in the desert.

Chehalis

Snake was looking cross-eyed.
That's why he was left behind.[87]

SINGER: Peter Heck. A Victory Song. After the people beat Snow, Snake got lost on his way home. When he got home, Frog was singing this Victory Song, mocking him as an inept warrior. This mockery explains the enmity between snakes and frogs.

A'nish'inabeg

Here on my chest have I bled!
See—See! my battle scars!
You mountains, tremble at my shout!
I strike for life.[88]

SINGER: Wabojeeg. Stanza 2 of a five-stanza song, first sung after a victory at St. Croix Falls over a Sioux, Sauk, and Fox alliance in the late seventeenth century. These scars resemble the scars of the Sun Dancer. Thunder makes mountains tremble. This song evokes characteristics of the Sun Dance, including the suggestion of a vision brought by the Thunder Beings. A Papago rain-bringing song similarly describes thunder making the mountains tremble:

> Where on Quijotoa Mountain a cloud stands,
>> There my heart stands with it.
> Where the mountain trembles with the thunder,
>> My heart trembles with it.[89]

This song, or a very similar version probably sung to the same tune, can work for an individual, for a group in a ceremony, for a warrior, for a hunter, for a vision seeker, and for a medicine singer.

A'nish'inabeg

Across the river,
They speak of me as being.[90]

SINGER: Odjib'we. Sung about the fight at Ca'goben's village. The Sioux across the river lament because the Ojibwa singer collected a Sioux scalp.

Inuna'ina'

Way out there on my enemy's ground
I have cooked my meals.[91]

SINGER: Yellow Horse. Only a very brave, successful warrior, protected by very powerful medicine, would cook meals while raiding in enemy territory, since fire could always make betraying smoke.

A'nish'inabeg

In the coming heat of the day,
    I stood there.[92]

Mec'kawiga'bau recorded this song. Butterfly (Memen'gwa) sang this song commemorating a victory or coup at a Dog Feast in his honor.

A'nish'inabeg

Some will envy
Up there in the sky!
I dance around
A man's scalp![93]

꒰   SINGER: O'deni'gun. Sung returning with Sioux scalps: the raiders danced around a scalp on a pole stuck in the grave of someone killed by the Sioux. The victor left the scalp on the pole. This song inspired two modern poets: Gerald Vizenor translates it as "thoughts of revenge / soaring / across the sky / when we are dancing / around a Dakota scalp";[94] Lew Sarett as "I am dancing in the sky (2) / With the scalp of a cutthroat."[95]

Diné

A Warrior has killed the Ute enemy man.
He killed the Ute at Dolores.
Your young warrior from Lukachukai killed him!
    To the people at Lukachukai,
    To Lukachukai itself,
The trail leads home with the Ute.
To a distant place, the trail leads home with him.
At a distant place, the trail ends with him.
    Here, much rejoicing sounded,
    Much flute playing!
    Ya rah ya! His tail, tail, tail.[96]

꒰   SINGER: Slim Curley. A Tail Song. The second stanza substitutes "Ute enemy woman."

Aa'shi'wi

Indeed it is so. We started out.
    We went.
At Rock Cave we arrived.
There we spent the night.
Early next day we arose.
    We went on.
At Ox-Eye-Place we arrived.
There we spent the night.
    Next day we went on.
At Cattail Spring we arrived.
There, when we arrived at their camp site,
    We attacked them.
There this Aa'shi'wi warrior
And one of the Navajo enemy
    Fought together.
Under a shower of arrows,
A shower of war-clubs,

With bloody head, this enemy
Reached the end of his life.
Our fathers, Beast Bow Priests,
Took from the enemy his water-filled covering,
    His scalp.[97]

ᷰ   From the Scalp Dance.

Diné

Into the ground with it, and then
Everywhere in Enemy Country,
I wish that the enemy shall die.
Into the ground with him, and then
In all Dinetah joy has returned,
    Flute playing has returned,
    Peace has returned!
    Down into the ground with him,
    Into the ground with him.[98]

ᷰ   SINGER: Slim Curley. A Blackening Song, in the Enemyway Ceremony.
Monster Slayer ceremonially rubbed the earth, Mountain Woman, and
himself after he returned from war,[99] and instituted blackening. A Black-
ener rubs a mixture of tallow and ash on the patient. The tallow represents
moisture, the ash vegetation, in the myth that the ceremony evokes. The
Ash Bearer also sprinkles ash around a scalp to kill it and memorialize the
death of the enemy warrior. The symbolism, complex enough for the most
metaphysical of poetry, converts the death, scalping, and burial of an
enemy into a ceremonial planting that revives or revegetates the earth.

Tsimshian

Red skies mean the blood of my people flows,
    Among the Haida.[100]

ᷰ   SINGER: Tralahaet. This Eagle War and Victory Song celebrated a raid in
the 1820s against the Haida. After a clash on the bar outside the Haida
village, the Niskae won, took scalps, and, on the way home, remembered
the ten Niskae warriors who had died. They sang this song.

Takelma

Hoot Owl,
Do you bring me news?

Look there to the North.
Who has been killed?
There are many people far away there.
Did you see them there?
Did our people die there?
Did you bring me news for that reason?[101]

૪   SINGER: Francis Johnson. The owl often brought news from the spirit
world or presaged death. The singer wonders whether an enemy has killed
raiding warriors.

Coos

I am ugly, I alone left!
Red prickly heat spots on my belly.
I am ugly, I alone, left alive!
They killed my people.[102]

૪   SINGER: Annie Miner Peterson. Robin laments the deaths in the war be-
tween the birds that left only him alive.

Inuit

Why won't people pity me?
I can't wake from a bad dream
Since Qaitaq killed Maula
    And showed no pity.
    Ijaja.
I pity my dead brother
Because he shed tears
Above his breathing hole.
    Ijaja.
Why, I wonder, pity him now!
Why, I wonder, did I dream
That I should take my husband's brother?
He sat in a house with bowed head,
And as Itqilertaoq sat in his house,
Head drooping, I pitied him.
    Ijaja.
It is not strange
That I pitied my husband
When he sat on the naked earth,
Head bowed, murdered by Qaitaq.

Then I pitied him!
    Ijaja.
It is not strange
That I loved my little boy!
Then to the shadows
I was to follow him.
    Ijaja.
It isn't strange
That I feel trapped in my house
Since Quaitaq took my refuge from me,
That I feel caught in a trap,
My refuge taken from me.
    Ijaja.
It isn't strange
That my path on earth seems long.
The road of sorrows I have walked
I cannot leave.
    Ijaja.
It isn't strange
That I loved my husband,
But now maggots have taken
His homecoming.
    Ijaja.
I have only my amulets:
While the northern lights play,
Scattering sparks across the sky.[103]

ᠵ   SINGER: Qernertoq (a Copper Eskimo woman). Qaitaq killed Maula.

Kasogotine

Little brother, the caribou tricked you,
    And marched you too far away!
Little brother, I came back,
    Came back alone from that land.[104]

ᠵ   A Hare Indian sang this mourning song for his younger brother, killed on a raid.

Dakota

"That Fox leader did not return,"
    You said!

White Butterfly you mean.
But then he went looking for this
   And it has happened![105]

∾ SINGER: Mrs. Laurence. Mourning Song for White Butterfly.

Tewa

Today, a little while ago, you lived.
But now you are neither man nor woman.
You are breathless, for the Navajo killed you!
   Forget us,
For here and now we bring your food.
Take and keep your earth-walled place!
Once! Twice! Three times! Four times!
   Leave us now![106]

∾ This song helped a warrior, killed while raiding, on his journey to the spirit world. War parties buried casualties as soon as possible after death.

Tlingit

Where is that Crane Canoe?
All smashed up, that Crane Canoe!
Below the waves there it was paddled!
   There it remains.
Behind the mountains, the warriors went away.
The Crane Canoe remains there.[107]

∾ SINGER: Charley White. This lament for the Crane Canoe mourns warriors killed in a raid.

Kasogotine

The fogs of the Northern Ocean
Settle on the waves.
The sea mourns and wails!
Enemy-of-Barren-Coast-People
Will no more return whole and safe
As he was when he left.[108]

Death

OMENS

Sanish   The Earth will be left behind![1]

ə   SINGER: Dan Howling Wolf. An Arikara war party heard this song and dis-
covered the singer, a toothless coyote dying of old age.

Havasuwapay   Dripping Spring,
Land I used to roam, there,
Listen to what I say,
        Don't mourn me.
I thought I would live forever,
I thought I would roam forever,
        But I can't continue.
        I am too weak. (2)
Land I used to roam, there,
Listen to what I say,
        Don't mourn me.[2]

ə   SINGER: Heart Horn. From Henry Hanna and Kit Jones. Old men, prepar-
ing to die, visited familiar places and sang this good-bye to the land. The
song containing this stanza has survived from ca. 1800. For the complete
song, which journeys through Havasupai homeland, see Leanne Hinton
and Lucille J. Watahomagie, *Spirit Mountain,* 147–53.

Dakota   This land is beautiful.
        Sun, now, for the last time,
        Come and greet me again![3]

ə   SINGER: Unknown singer in the Rosebud Reservation Hospital.

193

Hotcangara

> I am ready.
> I do not want to be put in chains.
>   Let me be free.
> I have given away my life.
> It is gone like that dust!
> I would not take it back.
>   It is gone![4]

↦ Red Bird, surrendering to American troops, picked up some dust, let it drift into the wind, and sang this. He surrendered to the government to prevent another massacre, after he and other warriors ambushed some keel-boaters in 1827 to rescue Winnebago women the keelers, or soldiers, had kidnapped and raped near Prairie du Chien. He chanted this song on the way to the cell where he died awaiting trial.

Neshnabek

> Charcoal, Charcoal! Charcoal
> Taught me how to follow the Great Spirit.
> Power lies in the Charcoal!
> The Charcoal lies in the fire,
> And ashes come from the fire.
> So my body will be, so will we all be!
>   We go down the same path.
>   We go down the Charcoal Way.
>   We go down to dust.[5]

↦ Stanzas 1 and 2 of Bear Bundle Chant 7.

Shis-Inde

> When I was young,
> I took no heed;
> Old, old I have become![6]

↦ An old man sang this song. "Because I knew that age would come to me, I took no heed."

Dakota

> In war, thought mighty!
> Now no longer.[7]

↦ SINGER: Tashunke-Ciqala (Little Horse). Sitting Bull sang a similar Death Song.

Lenape

I go to torture and death!
I will defy my enemies' torments!
I will die like a brave,
And join warriors who have died like warriors.[8]

∿   A Death Song. Sometimes captors compelled prisoners to sing such a song. George Henry Loskiel, *History*, translates: "I go to death and shall suffer great torment, / But I will endure the greatest torments inflicted by my enemies with becoming courage. / I will die like a man, and go to those heroes who have died in the same manner."

Dakota

I wish to encourage the children of the other flower nations,
Which are now appearing all over the land;
    So, while they wake from sleep
And rise from the bosom of Mother Earth,
I stand here, old and gray-headed.[9]

∿   The pasque flower (*Pulsatilla patens*) blossoms through the snow; by the time other prairie flowers bloom, it has developed a white seed head, looking like an old man. Old men sought the flower to sit beside, smoke, meditate, and seek a vision. Hartley Alexander discusses the ceremony at greater length.[10]

Inuit

    Eye-aya,
I call to mind and think of the early spring
As I knew it in my youth.
Was I such a hunter! Was it I?
For I see in memory a man in a kayak;
Slowly he pulls toward the shores of the lake,
Towing in many speared caribou.
Happiest am I in my memories of hunting in a kayak.
On land, I never won much admiration among the herds of caribou.
And an old man, seeking strength in his youth,
Loves most to think of the deeds that brought him fame.[11]

∿   SINGER: Ulivfak (a Caribou Eskimo).

A'nish'inabeg   The odor of death,
                                 I sense the odor of death
                                 In the front of my body.[12]

ᘒ   Odjib'we recorded this, the Death Song of Name'bines' (Little Carp), a
      great warrior. During the retreat from Gaye'dawuna'miwun, mortally
      wounded in the abdomen, Name'bines' shot a pursuing Sioux, claimed the
      kill, and then sang this song.

Ka'igwu   I envy young men.
                                   They miss you at home.
                                 Me nobody misses, nor thinks of it.
                                 Why not sit around and sing for joy![13]

ᘒ   SINGER: Sah-mount. Kiowa Gomda Daagya (a Wind Song). An old man
      envies young men, off to war.

A'nish'inabeg   I feel no fear
                                 When a Great River Man
                                 Speaks of Death![14]

ᘒ   SINGER: Odjib'we. A prewar song, sung by the Mississippi (Great River)
      band of the Chippewa at the first formation of a war party.

Maklaks   *Shaman:*   The smallpox I, the otter, brought
                                     Is upon you.
                       Chorus: The otter's tread
                                     Has whirled up the dust![15]

ᘒ   SINGER: Sergeant Morgan. The disease-bringing tutelary whirls up dust and
      evokes the little whirlwind or dustdevil that clothes the spirit of the dead.

Maklaks   I hear the owl's cry
                                 And it seems very near![16]

Shis-Inde   He made the black staff of old age for me.
                                 He made the road of the sun for me.

These holy things he made for me, saying,
   "With these you will grow old."
Now when I have become old,
You will remember me by means of them.[17]

From the Life-Stages Song in the Girls' Puberty Rite.

Tsulu-la

A little while I will endure.
For a short while I will live again.[18]

SINGER: Molasses. Molasses's wife, a powerful medicine woman, "died" and found herself enclosed in clouds. She heard Feather Ornament sing this song.

Tohono Au'autam

No talking! No talking!
The snow is falling.
The wind seems to be blowing backward.[19]

SINGER: Leonardo Rios. Sung by an old woman. She received the song during a hard winter, when the old people sat around the fires, silent.

Numa

Aiai. (3)
Here long enough I have walked the earth.
   Enough. (2)
   I will die. (2)[20]

SINGER: Chuar-ru-um-pik. An Old Woman's Death Song. The singer mimed the story of three old women leaving the line of march to die.

Takelma

I shall prosper, Moon! I shall live,
Even if people say of me, "Would that he had died!"
Just like you shall I do, again I shall arise!
Even if all sorts of evil beings devour you,
When frogs eat you up, many evil beings, lizards,
Even when those eat you up, still you rise again.
Just like you I will do in time to come![21]

SINGER: Francis Johnson. Sung to the rising new moon.

DYING

Pomo

> I will go down in peace,
> But when I sink,
> I will take something with me.[22]

> ♪ SINGER: Benson. A sunset song. The sun takes a spirit at every sunset.

Tlingit

> Your grandfathers were watching the paddlers' mountain.
>   Close by it, your hands miss the waves,
>   My brother.
>   Your uncles were watching the paddlers' mountain.
>   Close by it, your hands miss the waves,
>   My brother.[23]

> ♪ SINGERS: Wuckika, Mrs. Frank Dick. Paddler's Mountain, Mount Fairweather, supposed to predict weather, did not warn this expedition of the storm. When the canoe overturned, their hands missed the stroke.

Tsimshian

> I am almost dead, almost done now.
>   What happened?
> The people have left me aside.
> I walk about among the tall trees
> Where lies something glad for my heart!
> I will hold on to both sides
> Of the sun's offspring.
> If you speak to me now
> Your voice will settle my heart,
>   It will be like riches![24]

> ♪ SINGER: Watserh. This Gitksan song was a favorite of the elders. "Side" refers to the two divisions of the people and to the side of the living and the side of the spirits.

Tlingit

> Help me with your believing,
>   Kagwantan's children.
> It is as if my grandfather's house

Were capsizing with me.
Who will save me?[25]

ᔥ   SINGERS: Here-Is-a-Feather (Taoya't), Dekina'ku.

Kasogotine   Flowing around Grand Isle,
The black water bears sorrow
In its treacherous current.
My unlucky sister has drunk her death
From the wave that swallowed her,
My sister, whom Little Sparrowhawk scorned![26]

ᔥ   A Hare Indian sang this dirge for his sister.

Tlingit   My younger brother brought me
A great joy of laughter.
If I knew the way the spirits go,
I would go with him.[27]

ᔥ   Other-Water's Song.

Wintu   Above there the summons
Perhaps he heard.
At the earthlodge of the flowers, the summons
Perhaps he heard.[28]

ᔥ   SINGER: Fanny Brown.

Diné   Farewell, Younger Brother!
For me they have come, the Ye'ii, from the Holy Place.
You will never see me again!
Whenever the rain passes, whenever it thunders,
"In that, my Elder Brother's voice is," you will think!
Whenever crops ripen, of small birds of all kinds,
Grasshoppers,
"In that, my Elder Brother's Plan is," you will think![29]

꙳   Dsilyi'-Neyani's last words to his younger brother.

Tlingit

>   Where does he paddle? (2)
>   Perhaps here, my son,
>   Into the mouth of Ahrnklin River?
>   Alas! (8)
>   Where does he paddle? (2)
>   Perhaps here, my son,
>   Into the mouth of Yakutat Bay?
>   Alas! (8)
>   Already another dawn, (2)
>   Another night spent longing,
>   Wishing very much.
>   Alas.[30]

꙳   SINGER: Maggie Henry. A mother mourns her son, lost in a snowslide.

DISPATCHING THE SPIRIT

Cowichan

>   Red Sun, look at us, Blood-Red Sun,
>   You have taken the blood,
>   Red glowing sun, red dawning sun![31]

꙳   Singing this funeral song precedes washing the body.

Yokuts

>   You are going to another land.
>   You will like that land.
>   You will not stay here.[32]

꙳   This song and the ceremony it suggests dispatch the ghost on its journey
        to the spirit world.

Tewa

>   We have muddied the water for you!
>   We have cast shadows between us!
>   We have made deep gullies between us!
>   Do not, therefore, reach for even a hair on our heads.
>   Rather, help us attain that which we are always seeking,
>   Long life, that our children may grow;

Abundant game, the raising of crops;
And in all the works of man
Ask for these things for all,
Do no more.
Now you must go,
Now you are free![33]

ॐ   Releasing the Spirit Ceremony. The mourners offer food and tobacco
smoke at an outdoor shrine. Returning, the party stops four times; at each
stop, each mourner spits out a bit of charcoal and draws four lines in the
ground.

O'maha

Fly over the four hills,
Spiraling in the wind.
Fly straight and land on the fourth hill,
Land on the tree-tops!
The Buffalo will direct you.
The breath goes on;
The body stays.
Do not be sorry![34]

ॐ   The medicine society, burying a member, sang this over the body. The
spirit, like the eagle, will fly over the four hills, light, and follow the path
the Buffalo points out. The last three lines were a powerful secret chant to
send the spirit on the night road of the spirits.

Wintu

You are dead.
You will go above there to the trail.
That is the spirit trail.
Go there to the beautiful trail.
May it please you not to walk about where I am.
You are dead.
Go there to the beautiful trail above.
That is your way.
Look at the place where you used to wander.
The North Trail,
The mountains where you used to wander,
You are leaving.
Listen to me: go there.[35]

ᴧ   The spirit, the *les,* clothes itself in a dustdevil and wanders for three or four days, visiting the trails and places it frequented in life. Then the spirit goes north to Mount Shasta. The whirlwind rises to the Milky Way, the spirit trail. It travels the spirit trail south to the fork in the trail. There a Holy Person identifies the spirit as truly the spirit of the dead person and tells it that the west fork is the wrong fork. The east fork leads straight to wide plains covered with green grass and myriad flowers, where many Indians live, perpetually rejoicing.

Karuk

Then you reached the forks of the road
Where the old man was sitting.
The old man said, "Take the right hand road.
Do not go over to the other side."
There was a bull pine
Standing right at the forks of the road,
Without branches or limbs.
    You ran down the road.
As you were going down,
You heard people shouting and shooting arrows
Because they were glad,
Glad to have one more person with them.
    You looked up the road
And saw the place where you were going,
Where you were going to live.
Halfway there, you heard all your children
Shouting behind you.
    They all fell down.[36]

ᴧ   SINGER: Mary Ike. This death formula, appeasing a ghost, formed part of a formula story, in which a mother died outside, and her ghost stood there.

Meshkwakihugi

Now this day you have ceased to see daylight.
    Think only of what is good.
Do not think anything uselessly.
You must think all the time of what is good.
You will go and live with our nephew.
And do not think evil toward these your relatives.
When you start to leave them this day,
You must not think backward of them with regret.

And do not feel badly
Because you have lost sight of this daylight.
This does not happen to you alone,
So that you thus be alone when you die.
Bless the people so that they may not be sick.
    This is what you will do.
You must not merely bless them
So that they may live as mortals here.
    You must always think kindly.
Today is the last time I shall speak to you.
Now I shall cease speaking to you, my relative.[37]

ॐ   A Fox chant to the spirit of the dead, to urge it to move amiably, and
      quickly, to the spirit world. The Tewa emphasize this departure with topo-
      graphical symbolism.[38]

Wintu   It is above that you and I shall go;
                                Along the Milky Way you and I shall go.
                                It is above that you and I shall go;
                                Along the flower trail you and I shall go;
                                It is above that you and I shall go;
                                Picking flowers on our way you and I shall go.[39]

ॐ   SINGER: Harry Marsh. The singer acquired this Dream Dance Song, from
      the Southland Dance cult, in a dream. He sings of the Milky Way (the
      path of spirits), the land of the dead, the mythical Earthlodge of Flowers
      above in the West.

THE SPIRITS SPEAK

Luiseño   At the time of death,
                                  When I found there was to be death,
                                  I was very surprised. All was failing.
                                  I was very sad to leave my home.
                                I have been looking far,
                                  Sending my spirit north,
                                  South, east, and west,
                                  Trying to escape from death,
                                  But could find nothing,
                                  No escape.[40]

～   The Eagle tried to escape death. He flew to all four sacred directions and finally to Temecula, where he heard a spirit singing, telling him the futility of trying to escape: Death comes to everyone.

Tlingit

I am going to go up there
   Above Yakutat Bay.
There I turned my face down,
   Above Eagle Fort.
There I looked down through a hole,
   Above Eagle Fort.
There I will go,
   Above Yakutat Bay.[41]

～   SINGER: Charley White. The spirit of the shaman Lucwaq sang this song. When the Tluknaxadi mortally wounded Lucwaq, he said he would become a spirit working against them. In Swanton's version, the spirit vows to go to Chilkat and cry through Lxodet, since it has no shaman to speak through at Yakutat.[42]

Tiwame

1. All you white cloud eagles,
   Lift me up with your wings and take me to Shipap.
   And also you other eagles,
   Come and lift me up with your wings,
   High over the world;
   No one can see the place you take me.
   Down in the Southwest
   Where our fathers and mothers have gone,
   Put me there with your wings.
2. Thanks to Mother Earth, the whole world,
   And to Mother Eagle.
   Bless my people.
   I am the spirit;
   I am leaving for my own place
   Where I shall be happy all my life.
   I shall remember you people all the time.
      I thank you all.[43]

～   The officiants sang this song for the dead four days after death. Shipap, the village or Kiva of the dead, alludes to a vent or tunnel behind the fire

in the Kiva, which leads to the Spirit World, and to the world under-
ground, from which the First People emerged. In the Kiva, the Sipapu
brings in outside air and, in the Great Kivas of the Anasazi, offered a tun-
nel through which Holy Persons could enter the ceremonies. Mourners
could send the spirit of a warrior to accompany the dead person's spirit.
The funeral dancers held eagle wings and pantomimed lifting the depart-
ing spirit.

Inuit

1. Joy fills me
    When the great sky dawns!
        Ajaijaija.
    Joy fills me
    When the big sun up there
    Rises over the vault of the sky!
        Ajaijaija.
    Otherwise horror fills me
    When little maggots,
    In the hollows at my collarbone
    And in my eyes, crunch—
    Then I feel horror!
        Ajaijaija.
    I became afraid at Angmalortaq,
    I became afraid
    When, with the Kayak ferry,
    I drifted out to sea.
    At Angmalortaq
    I drifted over to the other side!
        Ajaijaija.
    I was afraid,
    On the ferry.
    I was afraid
    Of the snow block
    That interred me in my snowhut.
    I was stuck fast
    And my way out blocked.
        Ajaijaija.
    I felt horror
    On the fresh-water ice
    In the igloo
    And I felt horror

When the great sky out there
Sent back loud noises
When the cold split the ice.
    Ajaijaija.
2. Glorious, in winter here.
But I only felt terror
At the lack of sole-skins,
The lack of kamik-skins.
I felt fear always.
Always I feared.
    Ajaijaija.
Glorious, in summer here.
But I always feared
A lack of sleeping skins
And skins for clothing.
I felt fear always.
Always I feared.
    Ajaijaija.
Glorious, standing
At my fishing hole on the ice.
But I was sad
Because my little fish-hook got no bite
To tighten the line!
Always I was sad!
    Ajaijaija.
Glorious, in the dance house down there.
But I always worried
Because I forgot the song
I was to sing.
Always I felt fear
In the dance house down there
Because I tired
And could no longer manage the drum!
    Ajaijaija.
Glorious was Life!
Now joy fills me
For every time a dawn
Whitens the night sky,
For every time the sun goes up
Over the heavens.
    Ajaijaija.[44]

SINGER: Netsit. Paulinaq heard Aijak sing the first song in a dream after Aijak died. The Inuit interred the dead in an igloo on the ice and blocked the entrance with a block of snow. Netsit sang these two songs of the departed (Ingulrait Pise) during a feast at which the participants sang spirit hymns.

Tiwame

I am on the way, traveling the road
To where the spirits live at Shipap.
I look at the road, down that way.
Nothing happens to me, as I am a spirit.
I am a spirit, of course I am,
As I go on the beautiful clean road to Shipap.
My spirit meets the others, who come toward me.
I am glad to see them and be with them,
I have a right to be there.
I cannot help it;
I must leave because the spirit has called me back.
I must go! I must obey!
So I am going direct to my spirit.
There are places down there
Where all the people live whom you have seen.
They have gone when the time has come.
Now I cannot say what they will make of me.
I may take the form of a cloud;
I wish I could be a cloud!
I take the chance of whatever is offered to me.
When a cloud comes this way,
You will say, "That is he!"
When I get to the place of the spirits
I will hear everything you ask.
You must always remember me.
You have talked about me,
And in Shipap I can hear everything you say.
I am a spirit and I bless you.
I thank you for everything you have done for me
In past years.
I hope to see you someday.
We send you many good wishes,
    Many good things.
    Thank you![45]

꙳   The priests chant this song in the persona of the departing spirit.

Maklaks   I am now wrapped
                   In garments of fire-flame.[46]

꙳   SINGER: Sergeant Morgan. The spirit of the cremated dead person sings
    this funeral song through the shaman.

Wintu   From the old camping place comes a flash of flowers.
                       I love flowers.
                       Give me flowers.
                   Flowers flutter as the wind lifts them above.
                       I love flowers.
                       Give me flowers.[47]

꙳   SINGER: Mary Kenyon. A song from the Dream Dance, similar in some
    ways to Ghost Dance Songs. The spirit who sang this song in the dream
    felt nostalgia for golden life in the sun. Usually the spirit of a friend or rel-
    ative gave the dreamer such a song. The dreamer sang it in the morning.

A'nish'inabeg   Whenever I pause, (3)
                       The noise of the village.
                   Whenever I pause! (2)[48]

꙳   SINGER: Ki'miwun. Dream-Vision Song 154. Sung in a funeral ceremony
    for a dead Midé lodge member. The song helps direct the spirit on its
    journey. C. H. Beaulieu identified it as sung by a spirit, leaving his village
    and hearing the voices of his Midé friends in the spirit village.[49]

Oma'nomeni'wuk   The little whirlwind says,
                   " 'One who whirls with the wind!'
                   They call me, the spirits!"[50]

꙳   SINGER: Cawunipinas. In this very old Vision Song the name means, liter-
    ally, "whirling air." Whirlwinds clothed spirits. The song alludes to a little
    bug that gathers dust and spins it inside the dustdevil. Such small but
    fierce thermals often precede a cold front and thunderheads.

Kwagutl

Farewell, friends! I am leaving you, my friends.
Farewell, brothers! I am leaving you, my brothers.
Friends, do not grieve too much at my leaving, O friends!
Brothers, do not grieve too much at my leaving, O brothers!
Sisters, do not mourn at my leaving, O sisters!
My guardian told me that I shall not stay away long,
That I shall come back to you, O friends!
I mean, O friends, do not mourn when I leave you, O friends![51]

SINGER: Ts'esqwane. A Parting or Death Song.

Humptulip

There is a fog
Over the Land of the Dead.[52]

SINGER: Lucy Heck. Bluejay's sister, Yoi, whom he sends to the land of the dead and then follows, sings this song warning of peril.

Chehalis

Sister Yoi,
This is the burning prairie
She told me about![53]

SINGER: Peter Heck. A shaman sang this as a Medicine Song. The mythical singer Bluejay visited the land of the dead and, to return, had to pass through four blazing prairies.

Ontinonsionni

I go home now!
I step on another world.
I turn and extend my arms
For a friend to lead me.
I pray all may go where I go.
Now the earth is smoky.
None but I can see the other world.[54]

Midwinter Ceremony, sixth day. A dog sacrifice and tobacco offering precede the Adon'we' or Thanksgiving. This song recapitulates the last words of Handsome Lake (Ganio`dai'io): "Soon I will step into the new world, for there is a plain pathway before me leading there. Whoever follows my teachings will follow in my footsteps and I will look back upon him with outstretched arms inviting him into the new world of our Creator. Alas, I fear that a pall of smoke will obscure the eyes of many from the truth of Gai'wiio` but I pray that when I am gone, all may do what I have taught."

MOURNING

Kwagutl

> Yo he he ya!
> It took my mind when the moon went down
>> At the edge of the waters.
>>> Yo he he ya!
>>> Yo he he ya!
> It took my breath when the Mouse-dancer began to gnaw
>> On the water.
>>> Yo he he ya!
>>> Yo he he ya!
> It took my mind when Modana began to utter
>> The cannibal-cry on the water.
>>> Yo he he ya![55]

ᣟ Officiants sang this song returning from a burial house on an island. Kahetasu became Modana (Four-Man-Eater) when he became a Ha'mats'a, a member of the powerful Cannibal Society.[56] Modana, his sister, and some Bella Coola companions drowned off Virgin Rock in 1908. Kitemat killed them.[57]

Tsimshian

> The chiefs mourn the last man
>> From Gitanraet.
> Now the great chief has died.
> Now it is as if the sun eclipsed![58]

ᣟ SINGER: Semedeek. A woman composed this Eagle Clan dirge when the people abandoned Gitanraet in the 1820s. When the last chief at Gitenraet died, the last surviving woman climbed the house pole with a large wooden drum and sang. The song also served as the first stanza in a potlatch mocking song.

O'maha

> This warrior died a warrior's death!
>> There was joy in his voice![59]

꙳ A war party, at night, heard a ghost sing. The party eventually surrounded a tree and found the bones of the singer. The leader sang or chanted these words. In this incident, the Mawa'dani Society originated.

Hamakhav

Kumatsomo, whirlwind, spirit wind.
The wind wanders, wanders. (8)[60]

꙳ SINGER: Homer. The people mistook this whirlwind for Kwuikumat's spirit.

Kwatsan

The water bug is drawing the shadows of the evening.
    Toward him on the water.[61]

꙳ SINGER: Alfred Golding.

Hamakhav

He has gone.
Perhaps he has become the wind
    Or the rock.
I don't know which.[62]

꙳ SINGER: Perry Dean. Matavilye's two young sons sang this, after burning his body. The chanted narratives, such as this Tortoise narrative, amplify the Emergence and First People narratives and link them to features in the landscape.

Hamakhav

See the White clouds, our father's ghost!
Smoke from his pyre, White Smoke,
White clouds in the East, lying there.
White clouds blown, with the wind gone away,
    Cloud ghost, Wind ghost![63]

꙳ SINGER: Perry Dean. Tortoise narrative, location 8. Matavilye's two young sons sang this, after burning his body. Other stanzas substitute "yellow," "red," and "black" for "white."

Numa

The mountain crest remains forever,
    Remains forever,
Though rocks slide down continually![64]

৵   A version of "Only mountains last!" This song plays on the convention that only mountains endure.

Shis-Inde

> White Painted Woman's power emerges,
>> Her power for sleep.
> White Painted Woman carries this girl,
>> Carries her through long life,
>> Carries her to good fortune,
>> Carries her to old age.
> She carries her to peaceful sleep.[65]

Kumarik

> As the moon dies and comes to light again,
> So we, fated to die, will live again.[66]

৵   Old men sang this song, according to Boscana.

Hopi

> Your beautiful rays, may they color our faces;
> Being dyed in them, somewhere at an old age,
>> We shall fall asleep,
>> Old women.[67]

৵   The singers sang this song, acting for the girls whom the ceremony introduced to holy power. The song invokes the sun's power, which will saturate the girls, as the song or the winds fill the singer in other songs, and bring them happily to long life and fruition.

Rain

CALLING FOR RAIN

Konhiak

    I am sad because it has not rained.
All my trees and brush are dying.
    Because it does not rain
Many of my trees are dead.[1]

ↄ   SINGER: Santo Blanco. A Big Mountain Song. Big Mountain contains a sacred cave leading to the underworld.

Diné

    Rainbow Boy!
Today we humbly come.
Asking for rain, we come.
Corn and the other crops we planted
    Are drying up,
Therefore we come to you for rain.[2]

ↄ   SINGER: Pinetree.

Inuit

    The sea, the sea, the sea, the sea,
To the sea, the salty,
The rain making them sink into the soft snow,
Making them sink into the soft snow.[3]

ↄ   A hunter's weather incantation, for rain to make the snow soft and slow down quarry.

Aa'shi'wi

    Our children, all the different kinds of corn,
    All over their Earth Mother

213

Stand poor at the borders of our land.
With their hands a little burnt,
With their heads a little brown,
They stand at the borders of our land.
So that these may be watered with fresh water,
We keep your days,
That all our children may nourish themselves with fresh water.
Carefully they will rear their young.
And when our daylight children
Have nourished themselves with fresh water
We shall live happily all our days.[4]

Shis-Inde

I wish I might drink water again on top,
Where the black rain stands up.
I wish I might drink water again on top,
Where the water stands up.[5]

SINGER: Frank Crockett's father. An unlucky gambler, Boy-Who-Became-Water, made a shaman's journey underground, met the Holy People, and brought back the Water Ceremony.

Tohono Au'autam

1. I am going to sit here and sing. (2)
   On top of our ground, you will see green scum drying up!
2. I am going to stand here and sing. (2)
   On top of our ground, you will see foam drying up![6]

SINGER: José Panco. A Deer Medicine Song. After a storm, or irrigation, floods the fields, the receding water leaves green foam and scum.

Hopitu

Hevebeta, come,
Hevebeta, Hevebeta-Cloud, come,
   Pour! (6)
The Cloud Persons move in the Sky! (3)
Clouds, Cloud Persons, (3)
Pour, pour, come bathe me!
Make me a cluster of flowers,
Make me a cluster of showers.[7]

꙳ SINGER: Kuwanyisnim. A Hopi Hevebe (an archaic word, probably Cloud) Tawi (Song). The song contains several archaic ceremonial words, one from Laguna. Little girls sang this when they ran through the plaza to get water poured on them ceremonially and when they ran out into rain. The sequence of images here accompanies water from clouds to earth, into flowers, and back into clouds.

Diné

May it be beautiful!
May it rain for me today
So I may raise a big crop,
Corn of all colors,
White, yellow, blue, gray.
May I enjoy the beautiful flowers
Rain will bring!
May my animals grow fat.[8]

꙳ A Pollen Prayer from a Rain Ceremony. Sam Gill identifies the ceremony as a form of Blessingway and discusses the various appearances and significance of the Earth Prayer, of which he makes this a part.[9]

Tohono Au'autam

Poor old Doctor, poor Doctor,
Stringing web over the ground!
Above us, clouds begin to string along
Like the web on the ground.[10]

꙳ SINGER: Sivariano Garcia. A Tiswin Song to locate rain. The spider, like the turtle something of a trickster, makes a web that catches morning dewdrops. Tiswin produced ceremonial drunkenness, staggering, and dizziness. Such dizziness, and the accompanying sensation of whirling or seeing whirling, helped produce visions. Staggering, drunkenness, and dizziness suggest the whirlwind, the spirits that wore the whirlwind, and the whirling within the Tiswin bowl that led to visions. The Lakota pilgrims who visited Wovoka to learn of the Ghost Dance saw whirling when they looked into his hat.

Hopitu

Hail, hail, hail, Fathers,
Gray Flute Chiefs!

At the four world points you call clouds, Fathers!
From the four world points rain will come!
    Here Thunder Rain will move!
    Here Drifting Rain will come!
Among the plants everywhere near and far,
Among the plants the soaked earth will glisten![11]

    Hopi Lene (Flute) Tawi (Song). Flute Societies hold rain ceremonies in August, alternately with Snake Dance Societies.

Neshnabek

Keep turning until you get to the East,
Like the buffalo turning the dirt
Until the dust rings touch the sky.
It makes the buffalo rings soar skyward.
Men, bend to the earth, blow earth.
Blow your whistles while the women turn.
That makes buffalo rings rise to the sky,
Calling for water, for water from above.[12]

    Stanzas 4 and 5 of a Buffalo Bundle Clan Song. The song evokes the dancers raising a dust cloud, buffalo wallowing in the dust in a dry buffalo-ring or wallow, and the herd raising a cloud of dust.

Tsiyame

    White floating clouds,
(Masking the playing Cloud People)
Long clouds like the plains,
(Masking the rain-bearing Long Cloud People)
    Lightning,
    Thunder,
    Rainbow,
    Rain,
Come and water the earth!
Come, White Cloud People,
(Masked in white floating clouds)
Come, Long Cloud People, carrying rain,
(Masked in long clouds like the plains)
Come, Lightning People, lightning-masked,
Come, Thunder People, masked in thunder,
Come, Rainbow People, masked in rainbows,

Come, Rain People, veiled in rain,
    Come work with us
    And water the earth![13]

∾   Matilda Cox Stevenson expanded the original eight-line Rain Song of the
Snake Society by including in the text the explanations the singer offered.

Tewa

At Big Morning Lake, high up,
    Surrounded by Clouds,
    The Cloud Boys come.
They are here,
    We rejoice greatly, and dance.
At Big Morning Lake,
    We have Cloud Boys and Cloud Girls.
Beautiful, at Big Morning Lake,
    We have Clouds at the beautiful Lake.[14]

∾   The Seed Power Ceremony is associated with the Cloud Cult. During this
fertility ceremony, chosen unmarried girls and the boys or men they chose
as partners danced and then stayed alone in the Kiva overnight. On the
afternoon of the dance, the girls ground corn for the men, while censed
with juniper smoke.

Chahiksichahiks

The smoke passes by us
To the Holy Guardians of the Rain.
The smoke climbs above us now.
The fragrant smoke has passed us,
Risen to the Holy Guardians of the Rain.
The fragrant smoke has arrived above us now.[15]

SINGER: Tahirassuwichi. Hako, Seventh Ritual, III, song 2. The adoptee
smokes and sends the smoke and prayers aloft as the officiants sing this
song to the Guardians of the Rain.

Tohono Au'autam

1. Sandy Loam Fields, on top of these lands,
    Elder Brother stands and sings!
    Over our heads the clouds are seen,
    Downy white feathers gathered in a bunch!

2. After hearing these songs,
   The women gather on Sandy Loam Fields,
   Their heads decorated with clouds of feathers.[16]

꙳ SINGER: José Panco. A Deer Medicine Song. This song originated in Sandy
Loam Fields ("Ye'ogam") village. The feather fillets that appear in many of
these songs allude to and resemble rain-bearing clouds.

Nukhstlhayum

What am I carrying on my back?
Nothing but the guts of a seal
Full of water.[17]

꙳ SINGER: Jennie Talicus. Beaver sings this song to call rain.

Walwarena

I am traveling, I, I, I,
I go around the world—I, I,
I cause the mist—I, I,
When I climb the mountaintops,
   I cause clouds,
   I cause rain.
   Long live Coyote!
   He will always be.[18]

꙳ SINGERS: Victorio of Santa Barbara, Librado. Coyote's Traveling Song.
Coyote's Seduction Song exults similarly: "It will continue indefinitely (4) /
Hurray (4)."

Aa'shi'wi

That our earth mother may wrap herself in a fourfold robe of white meal;
That she may be covered with frost flowers;
That there on all the mossy mountains the forests may huddle with cold;
That their arms may be broken by the snow,
In order that the land may be thus,
I have made my prayer sticks into living beings.[19]

꙳ The dedicated prayer sticks become living beings, thus obviating human
sacrifice. Merging frost and pollen, this Zuni song sends the earth into
hibernation, from which, like the bear, it will emerge in the spring.

Salish   Uncle, I am washing my face.
                                Rain in long drops. (2)[20]

            ᔥ   SINGER: Ann Jack. Spetx, the groundsparrow, sang this while washing his
                   face and evoked a heavy, flood-bringing rain. Singers sang the song to
                   bring rain.

Siuslaw   Raccoon, Raccoon,
                            Cause your rain to flow.
                                Speak to Coyote!
                            You two, cause your rain to flow.
                                We are in straits,
                                We are very cold.
                            Raccoon, Raccoon,
                            Cause your rain to flow.
                                Speak to Coyote!
                            You two, cause your rain to flow.[21]

            ᔥ   A formula for invoking rain.

Maklaks   Water snail am I,
                            And call rain![22]

            ᔥ   SINGER: Nancy. This song summoned a tutelary Water Snail, who made it
                   rain immediately.

A'nish'inabeg   "First to come" I am called among birds!
                                I bring rain!
                                Crow is my name![23]

                   SINGER: H. Selkirk. A boy heard south-migrating crows in an autumn
                   grove and made this song. Crows come north before other birds and bring
                   spring rains. This was sung as a War Song.

RAIN APPROACHING

Ani'Yun'wiya'

Yuhahi'. (10)
Listen!
Now you come rutting.
Ha! I fear you exceedingly.
But you only track your wife.
Her footprints show there,
Directed up to the heavens.
I have pointed them out for you.
Let your paths stretch out along the treetops on the mountains
And you shall have them lying down undisturbed.
Let your path as you go along
Be where the waving branches meet.
Listen![24]

SINGER: A'yu'nni. A charm to frighten a storm: Hia'unale (Atesti'yi). It drives away a storm that threatens growing corn. The shaman's song convinces the storm it is in rut, chasing its mate. Mooney collected no other agricultural formula.

Wazhazhe

Come in ranks, you tall hills,
Come, you towering clouds,
Come, come, come,
You tall hills, come here,
Come in scattered bands, you tall hills,
Come, you towering clouds,
Come, come, come,
You tall hills, come here.[25]

SINGER: Shon'gemonin. High Hills Song 1, Rite of the Vigil. The clouds in a front tower over the horizon as does a line of hills or the front range of the Rockies over the plain.

A'nish'inabeg

The sound comes pleasingly across the sky!
The sound, filling the air across the sky![26]

SINGER: E'niwub'e. The singer of this Vision Song saw a thunderbird in his vision. When he heard Thunder, he took tobacco, held it to the sky, told

Thunder, "Go that way," and sang this song. The song directed the destructive storm away from his village. It became popular in drum dances.

Maidu

From up above water is coming.
Give me rain to drink from up above.[27]

☞ SINGER: Amanda Wilson. A Social Dance Song.

Salish

Dry, dry the land
All the nations endure!
There shall come much rain, and salmon.[28]

☞ SINGER: Big John. Grandmother Bullhead, a powerful spirit helper, calls back rain and salmon.

Aa'shi'wi

At the rainbow spring, the dragonflies rise
And fly over the Rain Priests' houses
To bring rain to the village!
Blue, red, yellow dragonflies,
White, black, and spotted dragonflies![29]

☞ SINGER: Falling Star. This Zuni Rain Dance Song evokes the dragonflies that precede and accompany rain, the butterflies that accompany growth, and the dancers in the fertility ceremonies.

A'nish'inabeg

Circling above me,
    A cloud,
Circling above me![30]

SINGER: Odjib'we. The leader on a raid had had a vision of a cloud. He sang this Vision Song when pursued by Sioux. Rain came and covered the A'nish'inabeg escape.

Oma'nomeni'wuk

I am standing on a cloud.[31]

☞ SINGER: Cawunipinas. The vision seeker dreamt of eagles.

Dakota

In darting flight
I have sent a Swallow Nation!
The erratic flight I caused!
Ahead of the gathering clouds
The darting flight I caused!
   My horse, like a swallow,
   Was flying, running!
   My horse, like a swallow,
   Was flying, running![32]

ᛞ SINGER: Lone Man. Heyo'ka Ka'ga (Fool Impersonation). Swallows, relatives of Thunder Beings, fly ahead of thunderheads. The singer wants his horse to move like a swallow, darting, swift, dodging missiles. He also wants it to derive power from the Thunder Beings. This song came to its first singer in a dream of Thunder Beings.

Tewa

1. Fog, Cloud, Rain, and Dew have a lake.
   Fog, Cloud, Rain, and Dew have a pueblo.
2. There in the North, clouds arise.
   There in the West, clouds approach.
   There in the South, there in the East,
      Clouds bloom like flowers.[33]

ᛞ San Ildefonso Summer Solstice Ceremony, Summer Party Songs. The Summer Society also sings these songs at the Beginning of Summer Ceremony in March. Here Fog, Cloud, Rain, and Dew wear their Holy Person Masks and, like or as Kachinas, live under a lake in their Holy Person Village.

Aa'shi'wi

Then, from wherever the rain-makers stay quietly,
They will send forth their misty breath;
Their massed clouds filled with water will come out
   To sit down with us.
   Far from their homes,
With outstretched hands of water they will embrace the corn shoots,
Stepping down to caress them with their fresh waters,
With their fine rain caressing the earth,
With their heavy rain caressing the earth.
And there, wherever the roads of the rain-makers come forth,

> Torrents will rush forth,
> Silt will rush forth,
> Mountains will be washed out,
> Logs will be washed down.
> There, all the mossy mountains will drip with water.
> The clay-lined hollows of our earth mother
> Will overflow with water.
> From all the lakes
> Will rise the cries of the children of the rain-makers.
> In all the lakes
> There will be joyous dancing—
> Desiring that it should be thus, I send forth my prayer.[34]

Diné

> From that peak there,
> A peal of Thunder!
> Over the earth,
> Turtle and the Stubby Rainbow,
> The sound of Thunder!
> From that sky there,
> Mountain Lion and the long Rainbow,
> The sound of Thunder!
> From Badger, badger tail,
> And the nearby lightning strike,
> The sound of Thunder!
> Rain is close, with the Bear,
> With the water creature.[35]

[35] SINGER: Hosteen Hataali (Master Singer). The younger of abducted maidens heard thunder and found water when fleeing the Old Man of Wide Rock. Escaping, she and her older sister learned the ritual of Beautyway. The myth includes war against the Pueblo Indians (the ones the sun never shone on).

RAIN

Tohono Au'autam

> Hicia. By the sandy water I breathe in the odor of the sea.
> From there the wind comes and blows over the world.
> By the sandy water I breathe in the odor of the sea.
> From there the clouds come and rain falls over the world. Hicia![36]

℞ SINGER: Matthias Hendricks. A Salt Expedition Song. The singer did not translate the archaic word "Hicia."

O'maha

My friends, they speak! (2)
The Thunder-villagers, they speak!
The Holy People, they speak! (2)[37]

℞ In a vision of thunder, the thunders taught this song. The song helps make rain, call lightning as a weapon, quiet storms, sanctify sweatlodges, or stop death.

Wazhazhe

There! See the black clouds moving in beauty,
 The beautiful black sky.
There! See the gray clouds moving in beauty,
 The beautiful gray sky.
There! See the white clouds moving in beauty,
 The beautiful white sky.
There! See the beautiful clouds
Moving in beauty, through the blue sky.[38]

℞ SINGER: Shon'gemonin. Rain Song 3, Rite of Vigil.

Numa

It rains on the mountains. (2)
A white feather crown circles the mountains.[39]

℞ SINGER: Chuar-ru-um-pik.

Hidatsa

The rain is coming;
It is here. (4)[40]

℞ Midhahakidutiku (Taking Up the Bowl Ceremony). This ceremony appealed for rain, a bountiful harvest, and healing power.

Akume

Butterfly! (4)
Look, see it hovering among the flowers
Like a baby trying to walk,

Not knowing how to go.
The clouds sprinkle down rain.[41]

ꙅ SINGER: Philip Sanchez (Ho-ni-ya). A song from the social Flower Dance, held in February or March.

Moatakni

Cloudbursts pour down on the house.[42]

ꙅ SINGER: Usee George. After the Modoc war, the singer dreamt that an approaching Great Hailstorm would destroy everything. The Modoc built a large dance house and sang the dreamer's song.

A'a'tam A'kimult

I am Black Bear.
Stretched above me, clouds,
Circling me, light rain, aee!
 Waving dew falling![43]

ꙅ SINGER: Virsak Vai-i. Tcotom Nyoi (Bear Song). This song brought rain.

Siehwib-ag

Rain, people, rain!
The rain is all around us.
Rain will come pouring down
And the summer will be fair to see.
The Mockingbird has said so.[44]

ꙅ Isleta Pueblo. First printed by John C. Fillmore.

Neshnabek

This is my work,
To keep this world green,
Keep it all green.
I begin in the East, to help my friends
I keep this world green,
Keep it beautiful.
I begin to fill the creeks,
To wet everything,
Keep it beautiful and green.
I begin in the East,

Make everything beautiful!
That is my work.[45]

꙳   Thunder Clan Chant (1). A Thunder Being speaks and comes, like the
dawn, from the East.

Tewa

The clouds come,
The rains come.
The rains put a bridge,
The clouds put a rainbow,
From mountain to mountain.[46]

꙳   San Ildefonso, the Kosa (Clown) Society's Koshare Ceremony, the
Rainbow Dance.

Tohono Au'autam

Here I am sitting and with my power,
I draw the south wind toward me.
After the wind, I draw the clouds,
And after the clouds, I draw the rain
That makes wild flowers grow on our home ground
And look beautiful.[47]

꙳   SINGER: José Antoin. A Rain Ceremony Song.

Hopitu

1. Blossoming corn, Corn Blossom girls,
    Blossoming beans, bean blossom clusters,
       Will shine wet,
    The earth will shine after the rain,
       Under blue clouds.
2.   Look!
    Through yellow flowers
    Yellow butterflies chase one another!
    Through blossoming beans
    Blue butterflies chase one another![48]

SINGER: Masahongva. Hopi He-hea Kachina Tawi (Song).

Akume   In beauty, while it is raining,
                                           Corn plant, I sing for you!
                                           In beauty, while the water is streaming,
                                           Vine plant, I sing for you![49]

                       ᔑ   SINGER: Philip Sanchez (Ho-ni-ya). A Corn Dance (Ya'kahu'na) Song.

Numa   Rainwater at the foot of the mountain,
                                               Rainwater singing.[50]

                       ᔑ   SINGER: Chuar-ru-um-pik.

Diné   Far as man can see,
                                           Comes the rain, comes the rain with me.
                                               From Rain-Mountain,
                                               From far Rain-Mountain,
                                           Comes the rain, comes the rain with me.
                                               Over the corn,
                                               Between [the stalks]
                                           Comes the rain, comes the rain with me,
                                               Between the zigzag lightning now,
                                               Now the lightning flashes,
                                           Comes the rain, comes the rain with me.
                                               Between the blue swallows now,
                                               Now chirping together,
                                           Comes the rain, comes the rain with me.
                                               Through the blessed pollen,
                                               Hidden as blessed pollen,
                                           Comes the rain, comes the rain with me.
                                               Far as man can see,
                                           Comes the rain, comes the rain with me.[51]

                       ᔑ   Rain Mountain, the home of the Rain-Boy, lies west of Zuni.

Akume   Perhaps, somewhere in an eastern village,
                                           A new chief has arisen for the year,
                                               This is what I said. (2)
                                           From the north it has rained.

From the west the water comes in streams.
In front of the streams of water,
Down toward the east,
The lightnings strike down to the earth.
    All of us receive life.
Now chief for this life-giving rain,
You must love the earth and the sky.
    Rain blesses us all.
The chief should look after his people.
This is what I ask you to do.
From the south it is raining.
From the east the water comes down in streams,
In front of the streams of water
Toward the west,
From there, westward,
The lightning strikes the earth.
    All of us receive crops.
Now here, Chief, are crops.
With this you may cherish your people.
    This I ask of you.[52]

SINGER: Philip Sanchez (Ho-ni-ya). The Situi Dance from which this song comes resembles the Rain Dance.

AFTER RAIN

Shis-inde

Water Boys all came here where they were dancing!
    With their downy feathers of water,
        They came here.
    They came to the dance ground
    Holding lightning in their hands.
From House Made of Fog, Fog Girls came, where they danced
    With their downy feathers of fog.
    They held lightning in their hands.
Water Boys came behind them in beauty,
    They danced behind them,
    Holding their downy feathers of water,
        They were behind them!
    Holding lightning in their hands,
        They were behind them!

The Fog Girls came from the House Made of Fog
    Carrying downy feathers of fog,
      They danced with fog.
    All holding lightning in their hands,
The dance being made of fog, they started to dance with him.
    They danced with the Boy Who Became Water.[53]

SINGER: Frank Crockett's father. An unlucky gambler met the Holy People and secured the Water Ceremony through a shaman's vision journey to the Holy People's world.

Takelma

How long before you skies will stop?
So long you have been raining!
Do you burn cattail rushes
In the house toward the west?[54]

SINGER: Francis Johnson. Sung when it has rained long and heavily.

Maklaks

    My Crow,
Cross-eyed, cleared the sky.[55]

SINGER: Nancy. This song came from a vision and evoked the Crow tutelary, who cleared the sky and stopped the snow.

Neshnabek

Now I go back. (4)
When I leave, you'll see them come up,
You'll see them sunning themselves.
You'll see earth smoke!
In the mornings and evenings you'll see me.
In the morning you'll see me,
I'll have wet the earth again. You will see me!
    I make no noise. (2)
    I make the dew![56]

Thunder sings. People and plants both flourish with thunder and rain.

Yaqui

> In the summer the rains come
> > And the grass comes up.
> Then the deer has velvet horns.[57]

꩜ SINGER: Juan Ariwares. Hunters call the deer's new horns "velvet" horns. Their surface resembles the velvetlike new grass.

Numa

> On the sand in the canyon,
> > The mountain stream,
> > The feathery mountain stream.[58]

Havasuwapay

> From the mountains,
> From the far mountains and pines I come,
> My rushing water singing for joy.[59]

꩜ The flood sings this Flood Song, which contains only three words, repeated to evoke this meaning, according to the singer.

Numa

> As feathers drift,
> The foam drifts on the Colorado
> Where the creeks run in.[60]

꩜ Feathers often evoke clouds. After a heavy rainfall, foam and drift mark streams and fields after flooding or irrigation.

Nuxalk

> Wipe your face, father,
> That it may be fair weather.[61]

꩜ This is sung to the sun after a long rain.

Planting and Harvesting

Wazhazhe

Footprints I make!
Smoke rises from their midst.
Footprints I make!
The soil lies mellowed.
Footprints I make!
The little hills stand in rows.
Footprints I make!
See! The little hills have turned gray.
Footprints I make!
See! The hills are in the light of day.
Footprints I make!
See! I come to the sacred act.
Footprints I make!
Give me one, two, three, four grains.
Footprints I make!
Give me five, six, the final number.
Footprints I make!
See! The tender stalk breaks the soil.
Footprints I make!
See! The stalk stands amidst the day.
Footprints I make!
See! The blades spread in the winds.
Footprints I make!
See! The stalks stand firm and upright.
Footprints I make!
See! The blades sway in the winds.
Footprints I make!
See! The stalk stands jointed.
Footprints I make!
See! The plant has blossomed.
Footprints I make!
See! The blades sigh in the wind.

231

> Footprints I make!
>   See! The ears branch from the stalk.
> Footprints I make!
>   See! I pluck the ears.
> Footprints I make!
>   See! There is joy in my house.
> Footprints I make!
>   See! The day of fulfillment.[1]

ॐ   SINGER: Tsezhin'gawadainga. The tenth Corn Song. The woman sings of growing corn, from planting to harvest. The smoke that arises from burning last season's stalks, like the mist that rises from the field at dawn, is the earth's visible breath.

PLANTING

Chahiksichahiks

> I like, coming yonder, (2)
> The blizzard and snow drifts,
> Yonder coming, coming yonder,
>   Far away.
> I like, coming yonder, (2)
> The stormy clouds,
> Yonder coming, coming yonder,
>   Far away.
> I like, coming yonder, (2)
> The stormy black clouds,
> Yonder coming, coming yonder,
>   Far away.
> I like, coming yonder, (2)
> The boiling heat,
> Yonder coming, coming yonder,
>   Far away.
> I like, coming yonder, (2)
> The swarming grasshoppers,
> Yonder coming, coming yonder,
>   Far away.
> I like, coming yonder, (2)
> The swarming grasshoppers,
> Coming here now, coming here now,
>   Far away.
> I like, coming yonder, (2)

The swarming grasshoppers,
Flying upward, upward flying,
Far away.[2]

     ဢ   SINGER: Fox. Sung in the basket game, to strengthen seeds. Spider Woman and her daughters gardened; the people wanted seeds to make gardens. Spider Woman enticed them into playing a jumping game for the seeds. Spider Woman called storms, froze them, and surrounded her tipi with their skulls. Two brothers went to steal seeds. They blundered into, then rejected, cannibalism. The boys, ceremonially painted white with black streaks, controlling lightning, then played the jumping game. Spider Woman sang up storms, as before. The boys, as in a shamans' contest, turned into snow birds, then larks. Older Brother sang this song, overcame Spider Woman, and banished her into the sky and the moon, with the locusts.

Aa'shi'wi

When our earth mother is replete with living waters,
   When spring comes,
The source of our flesh,
All the different kinds of corn,
We shall lay to rest in the ground.
With their earth mother's living waters,
They will be made into new beings.
Coming out standing into the daylight
   Of their sun father,
   Calling for rain,
To all sides they will stretch out their hands.[3]

Maidu

The acorns come down from heaven!
I plant short acorns in the valley.
I plant the long acorns in the valley!
   I sprout,
I, the black-oak-acorn, sprout,
   I sprout.[4]

     ဢ   SINGER: Amanda Wilson. An Acorn Song.

Kutiti

1. They go on, on, on, on,
   In the early morning,
   Speaking, singing!

There they come by the sacred spring
With the rain boy
While the rain spirits sing.
We hear this, listen,
And our hearts are happy!
Out in the great open,
The people and the crops rejoice!
For our sake they have come,
And their coming makes us sing!
2. Early this morning,
The happy rain boy came forth
To greet the chief warrior,
To beckon him to this happy gathering,
While the girls join them,
Happily dancing as the others look on.
Then the rain spirits come!
They form above,
And the earth sign appears in the clouds,
In the skies,
And comes down to alight.
3. They descend and then go onward.[5]

SINGER: Evergreen Tree (Ho'cuke). The people of Cochiti dance the Ouwe before planting, to ensure good crops. The "earth sign" appears as clouds in a series of steps down, then up. The ambiguous pronouns refer to both the masked dancers and the rain spirits who live in the masks and in the clouds that form.

Havasuwapay

Corn planting!
Corn growing beautifully!
I do it![6]

SINGER: Garces. Sung while planting. "Grow good; when your stalk grows, grow tall; Grow like the First Corn."

Nanbe

Yellow Flower Girl,
Blue Flower Girl,
Speckled Corn Girl,
Blue Corn Girl,

Thus on the plain (2)
They revive everything
And return here.[7]

᰾   Nambe Turtle Dance or Children's Magic Song. In this Winter Fertility
Ceremony, the Ok Huwa (Cloud People) bring seeds and promise many
children.

Wazhazhe

The buffalo bull, Tho'xe, threw himself to the ground
And a red ear of corn he tossed in the air as he exclaimed:
"The little ones shall make of this their bodies!
Then shall they always live to see old age."
Again Tho'xe threw himself to the ground,
And a blue ear of corn, together with a blue squash,
He tossed in the air, as he said:
"These plants also shall be food for the little ones!
Then they shall live to see old age."
A third time he threw himself to the ground,
And a white ear of corn, together with a white squash,
He tossed in the air, as he exclaimed:
"These plants also shall be food for the little ones!
Then shall they be difficult for death to overcome
And they shall always live to see old age!"
A fourth time he threw himself to the ground
And a speckled ear of corn, together with a speckled squash,
He tossed in the air as he exclaimed:
"What creature is there that would be without a mate!"
And he wedded together the corn and the squash then exclaimed:
"These also shall be food for the little ones!
And they shall be difficult for death to overcome!"[8]

᰾   SINGER: Waxthithe. Stanzas 10–14 of the origin *wigie* of the Tho'xe gens.
This (and an accompanying planting ritual) ends the Child Naming rite of
the Puma gens. Corn, squash, beans, and tobacco appeared as the Four
Sisters in many ceremonies and creation myths.

Hopitu

Thus we, the night long,
With happy hearts, bless each other!
They plant, my fathers there, and Muywinga,

Chiefs in the Kiva, the double ear,
   The perfect ear!
If they plant that
The fields with tassels will shine.
Here to them, here to them
Straight down rain will fall,
Rushing clouds, thunderheads![9]

ᨠ   SINGER: Lololomai. A Hopi Wuwuchim (Kiva Corn Planting Ceremony)
Tawi (Chant).

Akume

You call me skinny boy,
All the women call me that.[10]

ᨠ   Greasy Boy sings this Cornfield Song as he plans to overcome Rainbow.
This and a companion song reputedly carried great power.

GROWING

Karuk

Kupannakanakana,
Shine early, Spring Salmon,
Hither up the river.
   My back is straight.
Grow early, Spring Potatoes.[11]

ᨠ   Storytellers and singers regularly and ceremonially ended myths with "Ku-
pannakanakana" and a prayer for an early salmon run and early spring In-
dian potatoes. If they neglected this ending, their backs would twist, and
the salmon and spring potatoes would arrive late.

Tewa

Thanks, beloved Poseyemo,
That you ripen crops!
Bring rain, Beloved,
Make the corn drink!
Cause the Cloud Boys to bring rain
To ripen wheat for my little ones!
Make the snow bring springtime!
Then, when we plant, make the crops grow.[12]

꙳ San Ildefonso, Buffalo Dance in late January.

Tohono Au'autam

A cloud on top of Evergreen Trees Mountain is singing!
A cloud on top of Evergreen Trees Mountain is standing still!
It is raining and thundering up there.
It is raining here.
Under the mountain the corn tassels are shaking!
Under the mountain, the horns of the child corn are glistening.[13]

꙳ SINGER: Mattias Encinas. A Harvest (Viikita) Song heard in a dream. Conductors of the Viikita Ceremony swung bullroarers (fourteen-inch wooden blades on three-foot ropes) to make a sound like thunder and assemble dancers.

Akume

Beautifully, tenderly,
There in the east
The rain clouds care for the corn shoots
As a mother cares for her baby.[14]

꙳ SINGER: Philip Sanchez (Ho-ni-ya).

Tewa

The rain passes,
Fog cloaks the mountain
And drips moisture.
Our crops grow,
Our crops ripen,
We are happy.[15]

꙳ San Ildefonso, the Kosa (Clown) Society's Koshare Ceremony, the Rainbow Dance.

Tsistsi'stas

"Dear, our sweetheart got married!"
"So I heard.
I am going to fix myself up!"[16]

꙳ SINGER: Elk Woman. A Cheyenne Gardening Song. While gardening, girls sang such songs to their best friends.

Tohono Au'autam

> The wind smoothes the ground well.
> There the wind runs upon our fields.
> The corn leaves tremble.
> On Tecolote field the corn grows green.
> I came there, saw the tassels waving in the breeze,
> And I whistled softly for joy.[17]

 ↋   Singing up the corn.

Aa'shi'wi

> Yellow Butterflies,
> Over the blossoming maiden corn
> With pollen spotted faces chase one another in brilliant clouds.
> Blue Butterflies,
> Over the blossoming maiden corn
> With pollen spotted faces chase one another in brilliant clouds.
> Over the blossoming corn,
> Over the virgin corn,
> Wild bees hum! (2)
> Over your field of growing corn
> All day shall the thundercloud hang.
> Over your field of growing beans
> All day shall the wakening rain come![18]

 ↋   Curtis translates "throng" rather than "cloud." The Papago also sang of bees in the new corn;[19] the Navajo, of grasshoppers.

Ontinonsionni

> That's where I've gone,
> To our life as it is named,
> Our life is beautiful![20]

 ↋   SINGER: Black. In this Yeidos (Holy Power) Throwing Song, the Magic Cornstalks sing.

Hidatsa

> "My *eekupa,* what do you wish to see?" you asked me!
> I wish to see the corn silk peeping out of the growing ear;
> But you wish to see that naughty young man coming there![21]

 ↋   In their cornfields, the Hidatsa built platforms on which girls and women sat to watch the field and discourage horses, crows, skunks, and small boys from stealing green or ripe ears. The watchers sat in shade, looking over the field, and sang. They so enjoyed watching that even married women went out to watch the corn and sing. Two twelve-year-old girls, Red Bird Woman and her sister, Cold Medicine, sang this song, teasing each other. *Eekupa* means "kindred spirit," almost a sister.

Konhiak   All the trees and flowers of the plains
                                                Sing as they dance toward us.[22]

ᔛ   SINGER: Santo Blanco.

Hopitu   1. Yellow Butterflies;
                                                   Corn Blossom girls,
                                                   Pollen painted faces,
                                                   Bright, chasing each other.
                                                2. Blue Butterflies;
                                                   Bean Blossom girls,
                                                   Pollen painted faces,
                                                   Bright, chasing each other.
                                                3. Corn Blossom girls,
                                                   Over wild bees humming.
                                                4. Bean Blossom girls,
                                                   Over wild bees humming.
                                                5. Over your fields
                                                   Thunder-rain all day,
                                                   Thunder-rain all day.
                                                6. Over your fields
                                                   Drifting rain all day,
                                                   Drifting rain all day.[23]

ᔛ   SINGER: Koianimptiwa. A Hopi Korosta Kachina Tawi (Song). It contains several archaic ceremonial words and uses some words appropriate to hunting as well as planting and growing.

Hidatsa   You bad boys, you are all alike!
                                                Your bow is like a bent basket hoop;
                                                Your arrows are fit only to shoot into the air;

You poor boys, you must run on the prairie barefoot
    Because you have no moccasins![24]

       SINGER: Red Bird Woman. Members of the Skunk Society, which included
girls from eight to thirteen, sang this Teasing Song from the watchers'
stage in their cornfield at boys who went bird hunting in nearby woods.
The boys used bird hunting as a cover for stealing ripe corn from the
fields.

Ontinonsionni

    3. In fair fields I walk, (4)
      Along the meadow edge, I walk.
      A pleasant garden is planted,
      It shows pleasing ears of corn.
    4. From beyond the sky we come, (4)
      In beautiful fields I stand.
      From the fields, I came back.
      I returned here!
        It is ended.[25]

       A song of the Society of Woman Planters.

Tewa

    Pretty, we wear flowers.
  We wear the little flowers of the muskmelon,
  We wear the little flowers of the watermelon,
    Now we wear flowers.[26]

       A Children's Song. "Pretty" suggests "In Beauty," "Harmoniously."

HARVESTING

Tsimshian

She will pick wild roses, this little girl,
    That is why she was born!
She will dig wild bitter-rice with her finger, this little girl,
    That is why she was born!
      In early spring
She will gather sap from young hemlocks, this little girl,
    That is why she was born!
She will gather wild strawberries, this little girl,
    That is why she was born!

She will pick baskets of blueberries, this little girl,
   That is why she was born!
She will gather soapberries, this little girl,
   That is why she was born!
She will gather elderberries, this little girl,
   That is why she was born!
She will gather wild roses, this little girl,
   That is why she was born![27]

∿   SINGER: Weerae. This is a lullaby.

Noam-Kekhl

Well, we don't have much help,
   But perhaps one branch
Will bear a load of acorns, anyway.[28]

∿   An Acorn Dance Song.

Ipay

23.   The brothers are talking
      Of how they gather seeds
      When the plants are ripe.
      The plants are growing fast in the rain,
      But they have no wives to gather seeds.
24.   When the wind blows,
      The plants look like waves on the sea.
      It is a fine sight.[29]

Kwagutl

When I am grown
I shall go and stoop, digging clams,
I shall go and splash in the water, digging clams.
I shall go and stoop down, digging clams.
I shall go picking berries.[30]

∿   A Girl's Song.

Numakaki

My daughter, this corn
I can never use up.[31]

〰   SINGER: Scattered Corn. A Goose Woman Society Song. In the old days, women went into a trance when singing it; corn, little ducks, and even singing birds came from their mouths. Such medicine produced bountiful harvests.

Tua'dhu
     Become foggy!
We're going out to dig buttercup roots.[32]

〰   SINGER: Mary Adams. This Skokomish Medicine Song recalls the story in which the people try to get rid of Taboo Breaking Girl, who has become Sharp-Nailed Girl. The crows paddle her out to an island, maroon her, and invoke fog to confuse her.

Choctaw
     Go grind some corn,
We will go camping!
     Go and sew,
We will go camping!
I passed on and you sat there crying.
You were lazy and your hoe is rusty.[33]

〰   SINGER: Lysander Tubby. This is a very old Hunting Song.

Shis-Inde
     He took her away, where the land is beautiful with corn.
Fog Maiden: Where the land is beautiful with pumpkins,
Bil'olisn: Where the land is beautiful with large corn,
     They, two, went.
Fog Maiden: Where the land is beautiful with large pumpkins,
     They, two, went.
Bil'olisn: Where the land is beautiful with large corn,
     They, two, sat down.
Fog Maiden: Where the land is beautiful with large pumpkins,
     They, two, sat down.
Bil'olisn: Where the land is beautiful with large corn,
     They, two, lay down.
Fog Maiden: Where the land is beautiful with large pumpkins,
     They, two, lay down.[34]

〰   SINGER: Frank Crockett's father. The Gambling Boy, the One-Who-

Became-Water, journeyed to the edge of the Ocean, visited the Water and Fog People, and brought back the Water Ceremony, which cures those afflicted by flood and thunderstorm illnesses.

Shis-Inde

At the East, where the black water lies,
Stands the large corn with staying roots,
Its large stalk, its red silk, its long leaves,
Its tassel dark and spreading, on which there is dew!
At the sunset, where the yellow water lies,
Stands the large pumpkin with its tendrils,
Its long stem, its wide leaves,
Its yellow top, on which there is pollen.[35]

SINGER: Frank Crockett's father. Usually sunrise and the East suggest life, birth, and growth; sunset and the West, death and ending; however, here and in the Ghost Dance Songs life and rebirth, or spirit life, can come from the West and the sunset.

Diné

(13) 1. The sacred blue corn seed I plant,
    In one night it will grow and flourish,
    In one night the corn increases,
    In the garden of Hastcehogan!
  2. The sacred white corn seed I plant,
    In one day it will grow and ripen,
    In one day the corn increases,
      In beauty it increases.[36]

This (song 13) and the following songs come from a sequence of forty Hastcehogan (Home Holy Person) Bigin (Songs) sung during the fourth and later nights of the Nightway (the Yei-be-chei). Songs 11–40 follow the myth Hastcehogan-thaike-gisin (In the Garden of the Home God). The Hastcehogan who lives at Tseintyel (Broad Rock) in Cañon de Chelly went out to plant at Agojod. After approaching, and singing song 11, the Approach (Yoohania) Song, he cut a planting stick and sang the Kisaa (Planting Stick) Song. As he and his family planted, they sang this song. Songs 14–17 resemble 13, but change refrains.

    (18) 1.   Because of this it grows, (2)
        The dark cloud, because of this it grows,
        The dew thereof, because of this it grows,

The blue corn, because of this it grows.
2.   Because of this it grows, (2)
       The dark mist, because of this it grows,
       The dew thereof, because of this it grows,
       The white corn, because of this it grows.

Hastcehogan and his family went into the field with Hastceyalthi (Talking God) and found ripe corn, the bluebird (*sialia*), blooming tassels, and harmony. The boy asked the father, the girl, and the mother, "What makes it grow so fast?" The father answered, "Water of the dark cloud"; the mother, "Water of the dark mist." The father then sang this song, with the refrain *benathakala*, "because of this it grows." Song 19 resembles 18, with a different refrain. Hastceyalthi, like the bluebird, brings sounds that mark sunrise.

(26) 1. Truly in the East the white bean and the great corn plant
        Are tied with the white lightning.
        Listen! Rain approaches!
        The voice of the bluebird is heard.
2. Truly in the East the white bean and the great squash
   Are tied with the rainbow.
   Listen! It approaches!
   The voice of the bluebird is heard.

Before singing song 25, the children tied a bundle of mature beans with white lightning; the parents, a handful of corn with a rainbow. When a storm approached, Hastcehogan sent the children on and sang this song.

(27) From the top of the great corn plant the water gurgles. I hear it.
     Around the roots the water foams. I hear it!
     Around the roots of the plants the water foams. I hear it!
     From their tops the water foams. I hear it!

One of the older songs in the myth, this song begins with archaic syllables, probably from an early shaman's vocabulary.

(31)   The corn grows up.
     The waters of the dark clouds drop, drop!
        The rain descends.
     The waters from the corn leaves drop, drop!
        The rain descends.
     The waters from the plants drop, drop!
        The corn grows up.
     The waters of the dark mists drop, drop!

This song contains two archaic or ceremonial words: *ha'huijani,* "corn grows up," and *cihiwani,* "rain pours down," words also contained in Hopi ritual. Hastcehogan's children asked to see rain. He took them to a point overlooking his farm and showed them rain. As it diminished, thunder sounded, and the children asked about the noise. Hastcehogan sang song 32, which resembles 31, but added *yailtho'naga,* "he [the Thunderer] beats the sky, traveling."

(34) 1. Since the ancient days, I have planted.
    Since the time of emergence, I have planted.
        The great corn plant, I have planted.
        Its roots, I have planted.
        The tips of its leaves, I have planted.
        Its dew, I have planted.
        Its tassel, I have planted.
        Its pollen, I have planted.
        Its silk, I have planted.
        Its seed, I have planted.

2. Since the ancient days, I have planted.
    Since the time of emergence, I have planted.
        The great squash vine, I have planted.
        Its seed, I have planted.
        Its silk, I have planted.
        Its pollen, I have planted.
        Its tassel, I have planted.
        Its dew, I have planted.
        The tips of its leaves, I have planted.
        Its roots, I have planted.

After the shower, the boy said, *hui i',* "I rejoice." Hastcehogan sang song 33, which resembles this song. The refrain, *nitha sila,* means "laid side by side" (in a row, planted). Notice that the second stanza reverses the order of plant parts, as does the second stanza in 22. Hastcehogan sent Gaaskidi (Harvest God) and Thonenili (Water God) to the field and sang song 35, which resembles 34. When Thonenili said, "All is ripe," he sang song 36, like 34, with a different tune and archaic vocables. When Gaaskidi's Bighorn Sheep got into the corn and bleated, he sang song 37, like 34, with a different tune, a bleating refrain.

(40) I pulled it with my hand.
    The great corn stalks lie scattered.
    I pulled it with my hand.
    The great standing plants lie scattered.

The harvesters piled only the ripest ears and left the immature corn on the stalks. When they loaded the corn to take it home, Hastcehogan sang song 40. He told them to carry the corn on their backs and to sing the next song, which his wife began since the others could not.

From the East, through the middle of your field,
    Your corn moves. It walks.
From the West, through the middle of your field,
    Your plants move. They walk!

This song, which Hastcehogan's wife and children sang as they carried the harvest home, belongs to the myth, but not to the Hastcehogan-bigin since his wife and children (not he) sing it.

Dawn

Wazhazhe

1. The Sun is not the great god they had in mind,
   Although the Sun also is a god, they have said.
2. The Moon is not the great god they had in mind,
   The god spoken of as of the night,
   Although the Moon also is a god, they have said.
3. They had in mind a god ever spoken of as of the night,
   The god that comes and lies outstretched in yellow light,
   A god that lies in yellow.
4. The Moon is not the great god they had in mind,
   Ever spoken of as of the night,
   Although the Moon also is a god, they have said.
5. They had in mind a god ever spoken of as of the night,
   The god that comes and lies outstretched in pale light,
   That lies outstretched in pale light.
   That also is a god, they have said.
6. It is a god ever spoken of as of the night,
   Not that great god, the Sun, they had in mind,
   But the god that comes and lies outstretched in crimson.
   For that is also a god, they have said.
7. They had in mind that great god, the Sun,
   That is also a god, they have said.
   They had in mind the god that appears in deep red
   And sits on the horizon.
   For that also is a god, they have said.
8. They had in mind the god that lies stretched out in the blue,
   Whose border is like that of a flower.
9. It is not the afterglow of the evening they had in mind,
   But a god ever spoken of as of the night,
   A god who comes and lies outstretched in blue-black light.
10. Truly, here lies a new shrine, they cried,
    A new shrine wherein the sacred emblem shall lie unharmed, they cried.[1]

꙳   SINGER: Tsezhin'gawadainga. The Ca'wi'gie, the Shrine for the Hawk em-
blem. The chant distinguishes between the Universe-Filling Holy Power
and its avatars, the Sun and the Moon (vv. 1–6). It then describes the pro-
gress of that power, lying outstretched in or suffusing the Sun's progress
from the first yellow line on the eastern horizon, through pale predawn,
the crimson line that precedes the sunrise, the Sun itself on the horizon,
and the blue sky over which the Sun will travel, to the blue-black line that
appears after the Sun has set (vv. 7–9). After this journey, the chant ends in
the completed shrine, which covers and guards the Waxo'be, the symbolic
Hawk, and represents the universe as a house for life. The chant praises the
vehicles, the Sun and the Moon, that the Holy Power suffuses. The an-
cient wise men speak in the chant.

APPROACH

Inuit

    I rise from my couch
    With the gray gull's morning song,
    I rise from my couch
    With the morning song
    To look toward the dark,
    I turn my glance toward the day.[2]

꙳   SINGERS: Qiqertainaq, Aua. This aubade wards off sickness when there is
sickness in the village, but not in the house.

Kwagutl

    Slowly we race each other through the world.
    Slowly we race, walking through this world.
    Ha, I make the clouds!
       I come to you
    From the north end of the world.
    Ha, I bring the fog!
       I come to you
    From the north end of the world.
    Ha, I bring the red sky in the morning.
       When I come to you
    From the Great Copper Bringer,
    Ha, I bring the warmth.
       When I come to you
    From the Great World Brightener.
    Ha, and he will dance the Tongass Dance,

Your Chief's son,
Whom we praise.[3]

꒰   Speaking Masks' Dance Song.

Kwatsan

The owl was requested to do as much as he knew how.
He only hooted and told of the morning star,
And hooted again and told of the dawn.[4]

꒰   SINGER: Alfred Golding. The Holy Person Deer asked each animal to do
what it could. He then told each, "It is good. You have done what you
can!" in a series of Deer Dance Songs. The owl warns of both dawn and
death.

Nimipu

Dawn comes; Dawn keeps coming!
Dawn, comes, keeps coming; Dawn keeps coming!
Dawn comes, keeps coming; keeps coming, coming!
And over the mountains the sun shines,
    Lighting the earth.
Coming, keeps coming, Dawn; Dawn keeps coming!
Dawn comes, keeps coming; Dawn keeps coming![5]

꒰   The sun sings this Medicine Song continuously from dawn until dusk. All
beings feel this song and feathers drifting in the ocean or lying on shore
come to life.

O'maha

At Dawn, I seek you![6]

꒰   A respected man sang this to greet the renewal of life every morning.
People listened and eventually sang it as a love song. The original singer
agreed to that use.

A'a'tam a'kimalt

1. At the magician's house, we sing first. (2)
    The round sun arose,
    The sun, with its rays.
2. A band of Wild Women came running. (2)
    Wild Women with crowns,

With flower crowns, came running.

3. Black Lizard found Elder Brother's trail,
      Where he ran!
   He came out of white clouds
   With white pools on his arms.

4. On that great stony mountain's summit,
      Darkness settles!
      Circling, it settles,
      Retreating, scattering!

5. The reddish snakes
   Like spider lines drifted down!
   From the West they stretched,
   Spider threads, the sunset rays,
      Touching opposite sides![7]

SINGER: Ha-ata (Finished Olla). Tcoso-okal Nyoi (Black Lizard Songs). This song balances dawn and sunset around Black Lizard, who follows Elder Brother's path, the sun's path across the sky. The Wild, Darkness, or Spirit Women in stanza 2 usually come to ceremonies after sunset, not at sunrise. Tom Hoskinson retranslates many of these phrases and identifies the Wild Women as the Pleiades.[8] The magicians' houses not only recall the houses of the ancients, but also houses of magic located at the solstitial and equinoctial points along the sunrise's annual path along the horizon.

O'maha

Night, moving, going,
   Day comes![9]

This Honorary Chiefs' Society Song is sung while tattooing a star on a child. The star symbolizes night, the mother force, and has four points, the life-giving winds that surround the child in the Turning Child Ceremony.

Havasuwapay

   The icy ground,
Trees icy, the world icy.
We dance in good order and spin,
Spread our dance over the world,
Dance pain and sickness
   And ice away.[10]

    ɔ   This is the last song in the round. The song contains vocables, not intelligible words. The vocables evoke the meaning given here, according to the singer.

Maidu   Dawn appears on the manzanita hill.[11]

    ɔ   This song, at dawn, ends the Girls' Puberty Ceremony.

Siehwib-ag   Over there in the East,
In the Lake of the Rising Sun,
Over straight in the East,
The sun and the yellow corn come to us.[12]

    ɔ   SINGER: Anthony Lucero. The women at Isleta Pueblo sang this song while grinding corn.

Natinnoh-hoi   West, it will retreat.
North too, it will retreat.
East too, it will retreat.
South, it will retreat!
There will be sunshine,
Good weather in the world!
It will be wet.
The frost will melt!
It will settle down!
I brought it down.[13]

    ɔ   SINGER: Emma Lewis. This Rain Rock Medicine prayer calls and greets the sun, warmth, spring, and health.

Havasuwapay   Sky girls, dawn girls,
Sky girls coming up over the hill.[14]

    ɔ   The Sun-up Song at the end of a dance.

Chahiksichahiks

I am like a Bear.
I hold up my hands
Waiting for the sun to rise.[15]

SINGER: Dog Chief. A Bear Dance Song. The bear, facing the rising sun and holding his paws palms up to the sun, renews his medicine, which comes from the sun and centers in his palms.

Aa'shi'wi

On the flower-mountains,
We will see the clouds at sunrise!
By noon they will cover our crops,
    Says the sun-priest![16]

SINGER: Falling Star. A Zuni Rain Dance Song.

Numa

At sunrise the eagle will cry
Where the sea meets the sky
And the rainbow will be in the sky.[17]

SINGER: Chuar-ru-um-pik.

SUNRISE

Konhiak

All night while I feed in the valley
    I hear people singing.
When I am full and go to the hillside
    They are still singing.[18]

SINGER: Santo Blanco. The Mule Deer's Song from the Women's Ceremonies.

Tohono Au'autam

Come all! Stand up!
Just over there the dawn is coming.
    Now I hear soft laughter.[19]

Maiden Ceremony Song, Dawn Song 4. During this puberty-related ceremony, the participants enjoyed a certain amount of sexual license. The soft laughter at dawn balances the laughter of the mythical Wild Women who laugh and sing in the darkness outside the firelight at many ceremonies.

Achomawi

I am in this world.
I travel in the air.
I was not born on the earth.
I was born in the sky.
My father is the North Cloud.
My mother the South Cloud.
I have come to call you from the ocean.
You will be needed in this world.
When trees come, you will quicken them.
When people come, you will comfort them.
You will make the life of the people.
Don't refuse me; I am not deceiving you.[20]

☙ Cloud Maiden, Ah'mahl, brings the first dawn. She sings the Great Sun Woman and Great Moon Man from the sea to light the world, as Anni-kadel ordered.

Diné

The magpie! the magpie!
Here, underneath,
In the white of his wings,
Are the footsteps of morning!
    It dawns! It dawns![21]

☙ The magpie, the southwestern desert and plateau equivalent of the crow, wears elegant white patches on its wings. Gamblers sang a version of the song at the moccasin game:
    The magpie, the magpie!
    The white feather is for dawn!
    The ball is right down in here!
    Now it is dawn, now it is dawn.[22]

Shish-Inde

The black turkey-gobbler, under the East, the middle of his tail;
        Toward us it is about to dawn.
    The black turkey-gobbler, the tips of his beautiful tail;

Above us the dawn whitens.
The black turkey-gobbler, the tips of his beautiful tail;
Above us the dawn becomes yellow,
The sunbeams stream forward.
Dawn boys, with shimmering shoes and yellow shirts, dance over us.
The sunbeams stream forward!
Dawn boys, with shimmering yellow shoes, dance over us.
On top of the sunbeams that stream toward us,
They dance.
At the east the rainbow moves forward.
Dawn maidens, with shimmering shoes and yellow shirts, dance over us.
Beautifully over us it is dawning!
Above us among the mountains, the herbs become green!
Above us among the mountains, the herbs become yellow!
With shoes of yellow I go around the fruits and herbs that shimmer.
Above us among the mountains
The shimmering fruits with shoes and shirts of yellow are bent toward him.
On the beautiful mountains above
It is daylight![23]

ᠵ   This is the fifty-third song in a ceremonial sequence. At dawn, light moves
from the mountain-tops down and parallels the movement of holiness in
the ceremony. The turkey symbolizes creation.

Aa'shi'wi   "The beautiful world germinates.
The sun, the yellow dawn, germinates."
    Thus the corn plants say to one another.
    They are covered with dew.

"The beautiful world germinates.
The sun, the yellow dawn, germinates."
    Thus the corn plants say to one another.
    They bring forth their young.
    Aha ehe, Aha, ehe.[24]

ᠵ   A Kachina Song. Zuñis call the statuettes carved from cottonwood roots,
the masks used in ceremonials, the dancers who wear those masks and sing
songs such as this, and the spirits of the dead turned into rain-bringing
Holy Persons "Kachinas." Kachinas, clothed in clouds, masks, or ceremo-

nial dancers, visit and aid their living relatives. They live in Itawana, beneath a lake in northeastern Arizona.

No-ochi

As the sun comes up
It raises a dust.[25]

ↄ∽   SINGER: So'nawav. Ute Bear Dance Song 9. The sun raises mist at dawn, the buffalo herd raises dust at dawn, and the dancers raise dust at dawn.

Yaqui

The sun rises!
It is time to go out, see the clouds![26]

ↄ∽   SINGER: Juan Ariwares. Yaqui Deer Dance (90), a closing song.

Hopitu

From the East, the white dawn has risen!
From the East, the yellow dawn has risen!
    So now, please, wake up!
    Come look at us!
Empty your water vessel on us,
    Cold, cold, cold, cold!
A cloud burst,
    Pour, pour, pour, pour!
    The white dawn Youth,
    The yellow dawn Youth,
We surprise others, we surprise ourselves!
Here dwell the Corn Maidens, the Rain Maidens.
    Cold, cold, cold, cold![27]

ↄ∽   SINGER: Masahongva. An old Hopi Hevebe (an archaic word, possibly Cloud) Tawi (Song). The men, at dawn, ran through the pueblo, calling on maidens to pour water on them. This dawn ceremony and game invokes rain.

Ta'n-ta'wats

The sun is emerging! Look!
There are many ants.[28]

ം SINGERS: Pete Chile, George Laird. This is a Chemehuevi Salt Song fragment composed of Mohave words arranged to be unintelligible to the Mohave. This song roams into Mohave (enemy) territory and tells of the wandering of birds, who in the course of the journey recognize their homes. The song travels all night. The Creator rolled a ball of the first substance under his feet, sang the world into being, and let ants help him.

Yaqui

The wind is moving the yellow flowers.[29]

ം SINGER: Juan Ariwares. This Yaqui Deer Dance Song suggests the wind that precedes a rain-bringing front, as well as the breeze that rises at dawn. "Flowers" refers to the yellow blossom *ai'aiya*. A song that invokes the deer uses the same tune that this song uses.

Salish

The sun rises.
I think of my love, (2)
    My love.[30]

ം SINGER: James Percival. A popular love song.

Hum'a'luh

When the sun rises in the morning
These two women begin to sing!
    These two women.[31]

ം The two lady spirits, who bring wealth, in this Skagit potlatch song recall the women (Q'o'minoqa, the Rich Woman, and Ki'nqalalala) who help tame the Hamats'a, the cannibal spirits of the Kwakiutl Winter Ceremony.

Nuchalnulth

You whose day it is,
    Make it beautiful!
Get out your rainbow colors
    So it will be beautiful.[32]

ം SINGER: Sarah Guy (Clayoquot). Her aunt dreamed this Nootka weather control song addressed to the sun. A rainbow in the morning assures a beautiful day.

Nimipu   Dawn, Dawn moves and passes me, going. (2)
                        Dawn, Dawn is moving![33]

            ⌇   A Bear Medicine Song. A wounded grizzly, back to a tree, facing east and
                dying, first sang this old song about sunrise, when wounds become most
                dangerous. The bear feared the sun would stop "bad" blood from running
                out of his wounds. The sun's rays would descend from the summit behind
                him, hit his tree, and take some of his blood, part of his life, every day.
                The song brought medicine by invoking the bear who daily renewed the
                sun.

Dakota   Friend, dawn has come!
                        I live then![34]

            ⌇   Shunkmanitu Wan (Coyote Song). Long ago, living in the old way, a war
                party heard singing on a hill to the east. They surrounded the hill and saw
                Coyote facing east, singing. This very old Medicine Song, last heard about
                1938, resembles Densmore, *Pawnee,* 57 (kit fox singing), and *Teton Sioux,*
                190 (an old wolf singing on a hill).

A'nish'inabeg   On the front rim of the earth,
                    The light strikes first!
                    Manitou, your power,
                    Give it to me.[35]

            ⌇   SINGER: Bwonais (1842). A warrior's song, appealing for power in scouting
                and battle.

Diné   E-e-e-ya-a-a-a-a,
                    Beauty settles everywhere!
                    Beauty settles, Beauty settles,
                    Settles everywhere!
                    Now at dawn, Beauty settles,
                    Now, Dawn Boy, Beauty settles!
                    Before it when night passes,
                        Beauty settles!
                    Before it as it brings happiness,

> Beauty settles!
> Behind it as it brings happiness,
>   Beauty settles!
> Beauty settles, Beauty,
> Beauty settles everywhere!
> Now at dawn, Beauty settles!
> Now, Dawn Girl, Beauty settles!
> Behind it when night passes,
>   Beauty settles!
> Behind it as it brings happiness,
>   Beauty settles!
> Before it as it brings happiness,
>   Beauty settles![36]

ᣟ   This is the eighth Dawn Song in Red Antway.

MORNING

Tsistsi'stas

> I see my grandfather, the Sun!
> He has medicine power![37]

ᣟ   SINGER: Bob-Tailed Wolf. A Shaking Tipi Medicine Song. The medicine singer made a Houdini-like escape. Bound, sealed in a small tipi, the singer evoked the voices of spirits and dead medicine men and a medicine wind that shook the tipi. In a vision, Bob-Tailed Wolf saw persons on each side of the sun. A dog came, and the men and dog gave him this song, after looking in the four directions.

Nuxalk

> Cry now as though you had left me!
> I shall tie up my hair, warriors,
>   Like the Bear of Heaven.[38]

ᣟ   Bear of Heaven's Mask's Song. The Bear of Heaven, a fierce warrior, guards the sunrise and the sun moving across the sky.

Ipay

> It was only the night we feared,
>   Only the dark night.[39]

ᣟ   Sisters, seeking the hero-twin boys, sing this song describing their journey.

Maklaks   At dawn the earth resounded.
                       Incensed at us was the earth.
                       The earth wanted to kill us![40]

          ﱠ   Girls sang this song when haze or fog at sunrise commemorated the earth's
                 anger and suggested an earthquake.

Tlingit   Your point has beaten me, Kagwantan Children.
                          Pity me.
                       I wonder what I always look for
                       When I wake up in the morning!
                       Some morning, I might see my brothers.[41]

          ﱠ   SINGERS: Pressing Down (Kasta'k), Dekina'ku. Her brothers drowned off
                 the coast.

Numa   Over the land (2)
                       I walked at dawn,
                       Singing, and trembling with the cold.[42]

          ﱠ   SINGER: Chuar-ru-um-pik.

Tlingit   1. Storm bound, here on Kayak,
                          Where sorrow struck,
                          What Raven will pity this Wolf?
                              Alas!
                       2. There it is—I look at it—
                          Your fathers' land, Teqwedi-child,
                              Just at dawn!
                          Seeking it, I look around.
                              Sadly.[43]

          ﱠ   SINGERS: Billy James, Minnie Johnson. Billy James composed this when
                 stuck on Kayak island, very lonely, thinking of his wife, Jenny Abraham.

Akume   The Mockingbird, (2)
                       In the morning he speaks,

In the morning he sings!
For the people's sake
In the morning he speaks,
In the morning he sings.[44]

〜   SINGER: Philip Sanchez (Ho-ni-ya). The Corn Clan members composed new songs every year for the Corn Dance (Ya'kahu'na). Other versions of this song substitute other birds for the mockingbird.

Shish-Inde

The day broke with slender rain.
On the place called "Lightning's Water Stands,"
The place called "Where Dawn Strikes,"
The four places called "It Dawns with Life,"
    I land there!
I go among the Sky Boys.
He came to me with long life.
When he talked over my body
With Longest Life,
The Voice of the Thunder spoke well,
    Four times!
He spoke four times to me with life!
Holy Sky Boy spoke to me four times!
When he spoke to me,
    My breath became![45]

〜   The dancers impersonating Gans (Holy People) sang this during ceremonies to heal, to initiate, or in puberty ceremonies.

Akume

There in the eastern turquoise chamber,
    There this morning,
A golden eagle was born.[46]

〜   SINGER: Philip Sanchez (Ho-ni-ya). A Winter Dance Song.

Tsimshian

I look up toward the sky
Where daylight comes down early
From the east.[47]

〜   SINGER: Semedeek.

Tewa

1. There in your fields you have
   Muskmelon flowers in the morning!
   There in your fields you have
   Corn-tassel flowers in the morning!
2. In your fields now, the water bird sings
   And here in your village the fogs
   And the black clouds come massing.
   They come here to see! (2)
   Mbe'e a-ha we-o-'e.[48]

∽ A War Chief's Song. The war chief superintended work outside the village.

Kwatsan

Now the sun is up
And the nighthawk is enjoying the light,
Going from one place to another.[49]

∽ SINGER: Alfred Golding. Kwichana Akwa'k (Deer Dance) Song 82, Night Hawk's Dream Song.

Tohono Au'autam

In the east is the dwelling place of the sun.
On top of this dwelling place,
The sun comes up and travels over our heads!
   Below we travel.
I raise my right hand to the sun
And then stroke my body
In the ceremonial manner![50]

∽ SINGER: Leonardo Rios. "Ceremonial" carries the force of "sacred." Sung in a ceremonial dance to the sun.

A'nish'inabeg

As my eyes search the prairie
I feel the summer in the spring![51]

∽ SINGER: A'jide'jigig. A Dream-Vision Song used in War Dances. The first singer went out from the village into the chilly prairie, and this song came to him as the sun warmed the grass.[52]

Neshnabek   I delight in the grass, the green grass.
                               I delight in living to this day.
                               I rejoice to see buffalo wallow again,
                               The buffalo grass growing on the plains,
                               To see the flowers, to see beauty everywhere.[53]

                    ᘚ   Stanza 1 of Buffalo Bundle Chant 6.

Havasuwapay   In red, the beautiful girl,
                                  Beautiful in red!
                               In yellow, the beautiful World,
                                  Beautiful in yellow.[54]

Inuit   Beast of the Sea,
                               Come and offer yourself
                               In the beautiful early morning!
                                   Beast of the plain,
                               Come and offer yourself
                               In the beautiful early morning![55]

Aa'shi'wi   Now this day my Sun father,
                       Now that you have come out standing to your sacred place,
                               That from which we draw the water of life,
                                      Prayer meal here I give to you.

                                    Your long life, your old age,
                                      Your waters, your seeds,
                               Your riches, your power, your strong spirit,
                                   All these to me may you grant.[56]

Inuit   Aja-ha aja-ha,
                               I was out in my kayak
                               And went ashore.
                                   Aja-ha aja-ha,
                               Here I found a snow-drift
                               Beginning to melt.

    Aja-hai-ja aja-hai-ja,
And we'd lived through the winter!
    Aja-hai-ja aja-hai-ja,
I feared my eyes
Would be far too weak,
To see all the beautiful things.
Aja-hai-ja aja-hai-ja aja-ha.[57]

The singers said the composer made this Angmagssalik song about spring when the people were starving after a hard winter. A hunter kayaking, hunting for seal holes in the ice, landed, climbed a hill, and stood on a drift the rising sun had warmed to slipperiness. When he slipped, he burst into joyous song.

Dakota

This day is good.[58]

The unknown singer, an old man, sat in the sunshine alone on the prairie, singing this song.

Yurok

In the morning, when it's beautiful,
Beautiful sun rising back there early,
    You watch over me.
Take care of my children too!
    Don't deny me,
Don't think I'm someone else.
    I'm related to you.[59]

SINGER: Ella Norris. A morning prayer.

Havasuwapay

Sun, my relative, be good coming out.
    Do something good for us.
Make me work so I can do anything in the garden.
    I hoe, I plant corn, I irrigate.
You, Sun, be good going down at sunset.
We lie down to sleep. I want to feel good.
    While I sleep, come up.

Go on your course many times.
Make things good for us.
Make me always the same as I am now.[60]

SINGER: Sinyella.

NOTES

Introduction

1. Viola, *After Columbus*, 29.
2. Waldman and Braun, *Atlas*, 66–69. Waldman depends on the work of C. F. and F. M. Voegelin and Joseph Greenberg.
3. Curtis, *North American Indian* (hereafter cited as *NAI*), 17:56.
4. Fletcher and La Flésche, *Omaha Tribe*, 475.
5. Jenny Leading Cloud, in Erdoes and Ortiz, *American Indian Myths*, 257.
6. Skinner, *Mascoutens*, 145–46.
7. Opler, *Apache Life*, 121.
8. Opler, *Apache Life*, 59.
9. Zolbrod, *Reading the Voice*, 101–5.
10. Opler, *Apache Life Way*, 121.
11. Densmore, *Nootka*, 269.
12. Luckert and Cook, *Coyoteway*, 47–48. Luckert describes the entire ceremony in detail.
13. Effie Blain, in Densmore, *Pawnee Music*, 61.
14. Boas, "Eskimo Tales and Songs," 50.
15. Luckert, *Navajo Hunter Tradition*, throughout.
16. Bogoras, "Ideas of Space," 237.
17. Olson, *Book of the Omaha*, 1.
18. Baker, *On the Music*, 124.
19. Grinnell, *Fighting Cheyennes*, 178; Hyde, *Life of George Bent*, 155.
20. Rhodes, "American Indian Music: Kiowa," 18.
21. Marriott, *Ten Grandmothers*, 34.
22. Mooney, "Calendar History," 329.
23. Giglio, *Southern Cheyenne*, 141.
24. Densmore, *Cheyenne*, 35.
25. Sandoz, *Cheyenne Autumn*, 76.
26. Densmore, *Mandan*, 50.
27. Densmore, *Teton Sioux*, 357.
28. Black Elk, *Black Elk Speaks*, 101.
29. Powell, *Sweet Medicine*, 1:351.
30. Powell, *Anthropology of the Numa*, 121, col. 4.
31. Black Elk, *Black Elk Speaks*, 4.
32. Densmore, *Teton Sioux*, 68.
33. Rasmussen, *Netsilik*, 321.
34. Parker, *Code of Handsome Lake*, 83, Midwinter ceremony. Third day, the Ganio`dai'io song.
35. Cushing, "Zuni Fetishes," 33–34.
36. Underhill, *Red Man's Religion*, 23.
37. Sword, in Tedlock and Tedlock, *Teachings*, 214. See also Kehoe, *The Ghost Dance*.
38. Bailey, *Wovoka*, 169.
39. Trowbridge, *Meearmeear [Miami] Traditions*, 56.
40. Michelson, "Notes on the Fox Society," 519.
41. Caswell, *Shadows*, 28.
42. Deans, "Story of the Bear," 259.
43. Fletcher and La Flésche, *Omaha Tribe*, 279.
44. Fletcher, *Indian Story and Song*, 78–79.
45. Densmore, *Pawnee Music*, 43.
46. Jones, *Ojibwa Texts*, 60.
47. Bierhorst, *Four Masterworks*, 152–53.
48. Fletcher, *The Hako*, 366; my italics.
49. See Skinner, "Songs of the Menomini Medicine Ceremony," 292; Hofmann, *Frances Densmore*, 86.
50. Curtis, *NAI*, 8:58.
51. Black Elk, *Sacred Pipe*, 64, n. 1.

I In a Sacred Manner

1. A. Kroeber, *Handbook*, 321; Gatschet, *Klamath*, 156.
2. Kroeber, *Traditional*, 105.
3. Densmore, *Teton Sioux*, 41 and 169.
4. Densmore, *Nootka*, 276.
5. Densmore, *Chippewa*, 162–63.
6. Skinner, *Mascoutens*, 177.

7. Densmore, *Chippewa II*, 272.

8. Jenness and Roberts, *Eskimo Songs*, 439–40.

9. Skinner, *Mascoutens*, 177.

10. Rasmussen, *Iglulik*, 123. See also Rasmussen, *Eskimo Poems*, 27.

11. Skinner, "Political Organization," 507.

12. Coolidge and Coolidge, *Seris*, 244.

13. Densmore, *Papago*, 110. Also Densmore, *American Indians*, 64.

14. Underhill, *Singing*, 144.

15. Fletcher, *Hako*, 120.

16. Olson, *Book*, 10.

17. Densmore, *Papago*, 86.

18. After Rink, *Tales*, 68.

19. Densmore, *Papago*, 107.

20. Densmore, *Chippewa II*, 273.

21. Matthews, *Night*, 279–80.

22. Haile, *Waterway*, 53.

23. Austin, "Path," 7.

24. Matthews, *Mountain*, 393.

25. Densmore, *Chippewa*, 76.

26. Densmore, *Papago*, 133.

27. O'Bryan, *Navajo*, 156.

28. Spinden, *Tewa*, 94.

29. Densmore, *Papago*, 165.

30. Boas, "Eskimo Tales," 50.

31. Swanton, *Haida*, 16.

32. Densmore, *Teton Sioux*, 517.

II Thunder

1. Coolidge and Coolidge, *Seris*, 80.

2. Laguna, *Elias*, 1173.

3. Densmore, *Papago*, 140.

4. Russell, *Pima*, 324–25.

5. Densmore, *Chippewa*, 129.

6. Burton, *Songs*, 102, 227.

7. Black Elk, *Black Elk Speaks*, 62.

8. Fowler and Fowler, *Numa*, 126, col. 2.

9. Haeberlin and Roberts, "Salish," 518.

10. Boas, *Social Organization*, 711, 476.

11. Marsden, "Northern Paiute," 185.

12. Goddard, *Navajo Texts*, 176–78.

13. Boas, "Songs of the Kwakiutl," 9.

14. Kitsepawit, *Eye*, 82.

15. Skinner, *Mascoutens*, 165.

16. Curtis, *NAI*, 18:197.

17. Barbeau, "Tsimshian Songs," 151.

18. Gatschet, *Klamath*, 158.

19. Curtis, *NAI*, 17:56.

20. Russell, *Pima*, 332–33.

21. Fletcher and La Flésche, *Omaha Tribe*, 124. See also Olson, *Omaha*, 11–12.

22. Tedlock and Tedlock, *Teachings*, 206.

23. Densmore, *Pawnee*, 61. Densmore freely translates: "Beloved, it is good, / He is saying quietly, / The thunder, it is good."

24. Gatschet, *Klamath*, 169.

25. Bunzel, *Ceremonialism*, 626–27.

26. Sapir, "Religious Ideas," 38.

27. Densmore, *Chippewa*, 112. Desmore reads "Verily" rather than "Truly," "sounds" rather than "rumbles" and "thunders."

28. Schultz–Lorentzen, *Intellectual Culture*, 241. See also Rasmussen, *Eskimo Poems*, 100.

29. Matthews, *Mountain*, 459.

30. Densmore, *Acoma*, 65. Densmore uses "pretty" for "beautiful."

31. Goddard, *White Mountain Apache*, 129.

32. Laguna, *Elias*, 1172.

33. Opler, *Apache Life Way*, 108.

III Creation and Emergence

1. Dixon, *Maidu*, 8.

2. Jenness and Roberts, *Eskimo Songs*, 440.

3. Goddard, *Navajo Texts*, 137.

4. Voegelin, *Walam Olum*, 9–25.

5. Boas, "On Certain Songs," 55.

6. Kroeber, *Handbook*, 194.

7. Densmore, *Yuman*, 145.

8. Ballard, *Mythology*, 55.

9. Laguna, *Elias*, 1153.

10. Boas, "Mythology of the Bella Coola," 37.

11. Densmore, *Papago*, 20.

12. Hulsey [Woiche], *Annikadel*, 2.

13. Harrington, "Yuma," 328.

14. Dixon, *Maidu*, 7–8.

15. Curtis, *NAI*, 20:215.

16. Gatschet, *Klamath*, 192.

17. Laird, *Chemehuevis*, 15.

18. Harrington, *Yuma*, 342.

19. Gifford, *World Renewal*, 24, col. 1.

20. Ballard, *Mythology*, 52.

21. Chafe, *Thanksgiving*, 27–29.

22. Zolbrod, "Cosmos," 25–51.

23. Spinden, *Tewa*, 94.
24. Curtis, *Indians' Book*, 316, 551.
25. Spinden, *Tewa*, 93.
26. Mooney, *Ghost-Dance*, 1086.
27. Rasmussen, *Netsilik*, 288.
28. Benedict, "Serrano," 2.
29. Spinden, *Tewa*, 97.
30. Densmore, *Acoma*, 46. Densmore's translation uses "water pool" and other phrases.
31. Rasmussen, *Copper*, 133–34, 155–57.
32. Stevenson, *Sia*, 126–27.
33. Densmore, *Acoma*, 92.
34. Radin, *Road*, 254.
35. Wheelwright, *Navajo Creation*, 135.
36. Goddard, *San Carlos*, 56.
37. Wheelwright, *Navajo Creation*, 134.

IV   Initiation

1. Rasmussen, *Iglulik*, 47.
2. Densmore, *Seminole*, 172.
3. Johnson, *Stories*, 319.
4. Loeb, *Folkways*, 253.
5. Barbeau, "Tsimshian Songs," 142.
6. Boas, *Ethnology of the Kwakiutl*, 1310.
7. Grey, *Tales*, 18; stanza one of four.
8. Boas, *Ethnology of the Kwakiutl*, 1311.
9. Spinden, *Tewa*, 106.
10. Boas, *Ethnology of the Kwakiutl*, 1313.
11. Densmore, *Papago*, 166.
12. Mary C. Wheelwright, "Creation Chant MS," 211–14, printed in Frisbie, *Kinaalda*, 274–75.
13. Spier, *Southern Diegueño*, 342.
14. Densmore, *Chippewa*, 38. Densmore reads "am about to" instead of "start."
15. Kroeber, *Handbook*, 194.
16. Converse, *Myths*, 180–81.
17. Waterman, "Religious Practices," 296.
18. Curtis, *NAI*, 10:191.
19. Curtis, *NAI*, 10:320.
20. White, *New Material*, 335.
21. Densmore, *Santo Domingo*, 142.
22. Spinden, *Tewa*, 86–87.
23. Underhill, *Singing*, 110.
24. Hoffman, *Mide*, 263–64.
25. Michelson, "Mythical Origin," 107.
26. Densmore, *Chippewa*, 64.
27. Densmore, *Cheyenne*, 56.

28. Curtis, *NAI*, 2:55.
29. Skinner, "Societies of the Iowa," 708.
30. Hofmann, *Frances Densmore*, 86.
31. Opler, *Apache Life*, 119, 128, 130.
32. Bunzel, "Ritual Poetry," 635.
33. Densmore, *Maidu*, 48.

V   Visions

1. Curtis, *NAI*, 9:100.
2. Densmore, *Seminole*, 202.
3. Olson, *Omaha*, 47.
4. Swanton, *Social*, 54.
5. Tinsley, *American Cowboy*, 5.
6. Laguna, *Elias*, 1162.
7. Rand, *Legends*, 315.
8. Spinden, *Tewa*, 72.
9. Swanton, *Tlingit Myths*, 401.
10. Densmore, *Chippewa*, 127. Densmore translates the second verse in the passive voice.
11. Densmore, *Belief*, 221.
12. Gayton, *Yokuts*, 397.
13. Russell, *Pima*, 292–97.
14. Spier, *Havasupai*, 265.
15. Coolidge and Coolidge, *Seris*, 241.
16. Ray, *Sanpoil*, 195.
17. Adamson, *Folk-tales*, 192.
18. Du Bois, "1870," 47.
19. Densmore, *Northern Ute*, 88.
20. Underhill, *Singing*, 131–32.
21. Leland, *Kuloskap*, 312, 313.
22. Densmore, *Chippewa*, 71.
23. Petitot, *Traditions*, 253.
24. Michelson, *Buffalo*, 105.
25. Densmore, *Pawnee*, 35. Densmore's free translation differs.
26. Brinton, *Essays*, 292.
27. Spinden, *Tewa*, 109.
28. Underhill, *Singing*, 144.
29. Gayton, *Yokuts I*, 33, col. 2.
30. Fowler and Fowler, *Numa*, 124, col. 1.
31. Kroeber, *Handbook*, 471.
32. Densmore, *Northern Ute*, 192.
33. Demetracopoulou, "Wintu Songs," 485.
34. Hulesey [Woiche], *Annikadel*, 78.
35. Densmore, *Pawnee*, 49.
36. Underhill, *Singing*, 56.
37. Demetracopoulou, "Wintu Songs," 485.

38. Curtis, *Indians' Book*, 317, 551.
39. Fowler and Fowler, *Numa*, 125, col. 2.
40. Demetracopoulou, "Wintu Songs," 485.
41. Kroeber, *More Mohave Myths*, 118, col. 2.
42. Hinton, *Havasupai*, 210.
43. Kurath, *Iroquois*, 107.
44. La Flesche, *Osage III*, 634–35.
45. Densmore, *Pawnee*, 57.
46. Rasmussen, *Iglulik*, 119.
47. Fletcher and La Flésche, *Omaha Tribe*, 506.
48. Matthews, *Mountain*, 458.
49. Young, "Ute," 12.
50. Rasmussen, *Copper*, 93.
51. Russell, *Pima*, 321.
52. Underhill, *Singing*, 133–34.
53. Laguna, *Elias*, 1296–97.
54. Rasmussen, *Copper*, 164–66.
55. Curtis, *NAI*, 4:147.
56. Murie, *Ceremonies*, 324–25.
57. Curtis, *NAI*, 8:58.
58. Clark, *Guardian*, 6.
59. Wissler, "Blackfoot Indians," 408.
60. Jenness, *Carrier*, 548.
61. Haile, *Flintway*, 199.
62. Anon., in Jenness, *Carrier*, 569.
63. Petitot, *Traditions*, 300.
64. Curtis, *NAI*, 10:323.
65. Curtis, *NAI*, 10:158.
66. Luckert, *Navajo Mountain*, 125.
67. Luckert, *Navajo Mountain*, 17.
68. Curtis, *NAI*, 2:55.
69. Kroeber, *Seven Mohave Myths*, 46, col. 2.
70. Russell, *Pima*, 327–28.
71. Densmore, *Chippewa*, 89.
72. Densmore, *Chippewa*, 114.

VI The Great Ceremonies

1. Goddard, *Hupa Texts*, 232.
2. Herzog, "Comparison," 327.
3. Curtis, *NAI*, 12:153.
4. Stevenson, *Sia*, 130.
5. Herzog, "Comparison," 327.
6. Coolidge and Coolidge, *Seris*, 232.
7. Spinden, *Tewa*, 99.
8. Laski, *Seeking*, 64.
9. Bunzel, "Ritual," 622–23.
10. Spinden, *Tewa*, 98.

11. Russell, *Pima*, 283–98.
12. Coolidge and Coolidge, *Seris*, 222.
13. Russell, *Pima*, 306.
14. Bahr, *Pima*, 319.
15. Boas, *Social Organization*, 483, 714.
16. Curtis, *NAI*, 10:223.
17. Boas, *Social Organization*.
18. Curtis, *NAI*, 10:160.
19. Goldman, *Mouth*.
20. Curtis, *NAI*, 10:315.
21. Boas, *Social Organization*, 326.
22. Barbeau, "Tsimshian Songs," 136.
23. Boas, *Social Organization*, 460.
24. Laguna, *Elias*, 1245.
25. Walker, *Sun*, 129.
26. Barbeau, "Tsimshian Songs," 133.
27. Gatschet, *Klamath*, 167.
28. Bunzel, *Zuni Ceremonialism*, 484.
29. Du Bois, *Feather Cult*, 8, col. 2 (Washat Drum Song).
30. Brown and Ry, *Dreamer-Prophets*, 45.
31. Rasmussen, *Iglulik*, 243. *Eskimo Poems*, 28, also contains a translation.
32. Densmore, *Mandan*, 93.
33. Densmore, *Chippewa II*, 206.
34. Skinner, *Mascoutens*, 122.
35. Densmore, *Chippewa II*, 204.
36. Goddard, "Cree in Alberta," 302.
37. Wallis, "Sun–Dance," 333.
38. Curtis, *NAI*, 3:129.
39. Scott, "Notes," 345.
40. Wallis, "Sun–Dance," 333.
41. Shimkin, "Wind River," 418.
42. Sword, in Tedlock and Tedlock, *Teachings*, 214.
43. Fortune, *Omaha*, 78. Dorsey, *Traditions*, 471.
44. Mooney, *Ghost-Dance*, 1086.
45. Mooney, *Ghost-Dance*, 1102.
46. Mooney, *Ghost-Dance*, 1028.
47. Mooney, *Ghost-Dance*, 978–79.
48. Rand, *Legends*, 256.
49. Mooney, *Ghost-Dance*, 911, 921.
50. Turner, *Reader*, 139–40; Skinner, *Mascoutens*, 203.
51. Mooney, *Ghost-Dance*, 1055.
52. Black Elk, *Black Elk Speaks*, 34.
53. Voget, *Shoshone*, 62, 249; Mooney, *Ghost-Dance*, 13.
54. Young, "Ute," 12.

55. Mooney, *Ghost-Dance*, 990.
56. Trenholm, *Arapahoes*, 80.
57. Mooney, *Ghost-Dance*, 1082–83.
58. Mooney, *Ghost-Dance*, 984–85.
59. Underhill, *Singing*, 100.
60. Mooney, *Ghost-Dance*, 1038.
61. Clark, *Northern*, 127–28.
62. Mooney, *Ghost-Dance*, 1070.
63. Curtis, *Indians' Book*, 45.
64. Paige, *Songs*, 142.
65. Mooney, *Ghost-Dance*, 1074–75.
66. Mooney, *Ghost-Dance*, 999.
67. Mooney, *Ghost-Dance*, 966–67; Densmore, *Cheyenne*, 107.
68. Fletcher and La Flésche, *Omaha Tribe*, 306.
69. Black Elk, *Black Elk Speaks*, 53–59.
70. Mooney, *Ghost-Dance*, 300–301.
71. Mooney, *Ghost-Dance*, 1086–87.
72. Mooney, *Ghost-Dance*, 995–96.
73. Galler, *Tales*, 176.
74. Mooney, *Ghost-Dance*, 1030.
75. Mooney, *Ghost-Dance*, 224–25.
76. Mooney, *Ghost-Dance*, 1032. See also Mooney, *Ghost-Dance*, 964.
77. Mooney, *Ghost-Dance*, 1005.
78. Mooney, *Ghost-Dance*, 1055.
79. Mooney, *Ghost-Dance*, 1054.
80. Mooney, *Ghost-Dance*, 1052–53.
81. Mooney, *Ghost-Dance*, 1087.
82. Densmore, *Cheyenne*, 54–55.
83. Mooney, *Ghost-Dance*, 290–91.
84. Kroeber, *Handbook*, 509.
85. Gifford and Kroeber, *World Renewal*, 15, col. 1.
86. Densmore, *Santo Domingo*, 86–87.
87. Kitsepawit, *Eye*, 74.
88. Waterman, "Religious Practices," 317.
89. Kitsepawit, *Eye*, 82–83.
90. Waterman, "Religious Practices," 309–10.
91. Gifford and Kroeber, *World Renewal*, 25, col. 1.
92. Matthews, *Night*, 143–45.
93. Luckert and Cook, *Coyoteway*, 47–48.

VII Medicine

1. Gatschet, *Klamath*, 153–59. Kroeber, *Handbook*, 321.
2. Boas, *Social Organization*, 484.
3. Boas, *Social Organization*, 411–12.
4. Kroeber, *Handbook*, 758.
5. Coolidge and Coolidge, *Seris*, 230.
6. Russell, *Pima*, 307.
7. Fowler and Fowler, *Numa*, 125, col. 2.
8. Buckley, "Yurok," 153.
9. Skinner, *Mascoutens*, 151–52.
10. La Flesche, *Osage Tribe II*, 74.
11. Spier, *Havasupai*, 285.
12. Marriott, *Ten Grandmothers*, 234.
13. Densmore, *Teton Sioux*, 264.
14. Rasmussen, *Iglulik*, 115.
15. Mixco, *Kiliwa*, 102.
16. Densmore, *Cheyenne*, 64.
17. Rasmussen, *Netsilik*, 517. A freer version appears on 511.
18. Densmore, *Yuman*, 162. Densmore reads "is sitting" as "singing."
19. Russell, *Pima*, 310.
20. Boas, *Tsimshian Texts*, 231.
21. Goddard, "Chipewyan Texts," 58.
22. Densmore, *Pawnee*, 20.
23. Curtis, *NAI*, 10:63.
24. Fowler and Fowler, *Numa*, 124, col. 2.
25. Russell, *Pima*, 303.
26. Russell, *Pima*, 307–8.
27. Boas, "Eskimo," 49.
28. Underhill, *Red Man's Religion*, 23.
29. Olson, *Omaha*, 3. See also Fletcher and La Flésche, *Omaha Tribe*, 570.
30. Olson, *Omaha*, 1.
31. Capron, "Medicine," 167.
32. Densmore, *Teton Sioux*, 222–23.
33. Loeb, *Pomo*, 309.
34. Yates, "Charmstones," 299.
35. Russell, *Pima*, 212, 275.
36. Boas, "Eskimo," 49.
37. Densmore, *Cheyenne*, 35.
38. Jenny Leading Cloud, in Erdoes and Ortiz, *Myths*, 257.
39. Densmore, *Mandan*, 50.
40. Densmore, *Teton Sioux*, 357.
41. Underhill, *Singing*, 59.
42. Densmore, *Chippewa*, 76.
43. Densmore, *Chippewa*, 65.
44. Mooney, *Ghost-Dance*, 1001.
45. Barbeau, "Tsimshian Songs," 111.
46. Bahr, "Pima Swallow," 181 (song 19).
47. Underhill, *Singing*, 41. See also 40.

48. Russell, *Pima*, 284, 300, et passim.

49. Jacobs, *Coos Myth*, 137.

50. Swanton, *Tlingit Myths*, 409–10.

51. Fowler and Fowler, *Numa*, 123, col. 1.

52. Kurath, *Iroquois*, 108.

53. Blackburn, *December's Child*, 239.

54. Ballard, *Mythology*, 105.

55. Boas, *Tsimshian Texts* (n.s.), 239.

56. Adamson, *Folk-tales*, 52.

57. Boas and Hunt, *Kwakiutl Texts 2*, 223.

58. Densmore, *Papago*, 88.

59. Benedict, "Eight Stories," 69.

60. Benedict, "Eight Stories," 70.

61. Rasmussen, *People*, 142.

62. Espinosa, "Tales," 74.

63. Kitsepawit, *Eye*, 7.

64. Petitot, *Traditions*, 281.

65. Kroeber, *Handbook*, 511.

66. Kroeber, *Handbook*, 623.

67. Swanton, "Religious," 646.

68. Rasmussen, *Netsilik*, 284–85.

69. Densmore, *Teton Sioux*, 256.

70. Curtis, *NAI*, 17:68.

71. Barbeau, *Medicine-men*, 50.

72. Barbeau, *Medicine-men*, 54.

73. Densmore, *Santo Domingo*, 62.

74. Kroeber and Gifford, *Karok*, 288.

75. Jenness, *Sekani*, 76–77.

76. Underhill, *Singing*, 150.

77. Mooney, *Sacred*, 359–60.

78. Curtis, *NAI*, 10:320–22.

79. Densmore, *Papago*, 126; see also 115–16.

80. Underhill, *Singing*, 140.

81. Kroeber, *More*, 118, col. 2.

82. Kelly, *Ethnography*, 192.

83. Herzog, "Comparison," 332.

84. Luckert, *A Navajo*, 102.

VIII Love

1. Curtis, *Indians' Book*, 262, 550.

2. Wissler, "Societies and Dance," 92–94.

3. Rice, *Deer Women*, 33–46.

4. Kilpatrick and Kilpatrick, *Walk*, 86–87.

5. Densmore, *Yuman*, 49.

6. Hinton, *Havasupai*, 277–78.

7. Hinton, *Havasupai*, 284–88.

8. Densmore, *Yuman*, 200. Densmore reads "is" not "lives."

9. Herzog, "Comparison," 331.

10. Russell, *Pima*, 316–17.

11. Sapir, *Kaibab*, 435.

12. Laird, *Chemehuevis*, 149.

13. Curtis, *Indians' Book*, 483, 559.

14. Underhill, *Singing*, 139–40.

15. Streit, *Songs*, 2–3.

16. Densmore, *Chippewa II*, 300.

17. Burton, *American Primitive Music*, 274.

18. Densmore, *Chippewa*, 90.

19. Gatschet, *Klamath*, 183.

20. Gatschet, *Klamath*, 190.

21. Gayton, *Yokuts I*, 32, col. 1.

22. Gatschet, *Klamath*, 184.

23. White, "Acoma," 347.

24. Benedict, "Eight Stories," 67.

25. Haile, *Love-Magic*, 33–34.

26. Opler, *Apache Life Way*, 124.

27. Fletcher and La Flésche, *Omaha Tribe*, 322.

28. Bright, *Karok*, 251.

29. Sapir, "Song," 469.

30. Curtis, *Indians' Book*, 224, 546.

31. Swanton, *Tlingit Myths*, 415.

32. Curtis, *NAI*, 10:325.

33. Densmore, *Chippewa*, 150–51.

34. Bimboni, *Songs*, 2.

35. Burton, *American*, 97–99.

36. Vizenor, *Nogamon*, 24.

37. Uldall and Shipley, *Nisenan*, 163.

38. Rink, *Tales*, 19.

39. Deans, "Bear," 259.

40. Laguna, *Elias*, 1298.

41. Goddard, *Hupa Texts*, 309.

42. Laguna, *Elias*, 1291.

43. Densmore, *Teton Sioux*, 497.

44. Densmore, *Teton Sioux*, 372.

45. Olden, *Karok*, 91.

46. Blackburn, *December's Child*, 252.

47. Densmore, *Yuman*, 148.

48. Burns, "Digger," 397.

49. Chamberlain, "Primitive Woman," 208, from Boas, *Sixth Report*.

50. Curtis, *NAI*, 6:57.

51. Demetracopoulou, "Wintu Songs," 493.

52. Densmore, *Acoma*, 25.

IX Hunting

1. Chafe, *Thanksgiving*, 26–27, ll. 62–71.
2. Boas, *Social Organization*, 713, 482.
3. Kroeber and Gifford, *Karok*, 133.
4. Bunzel, "Katcinas," 1043.
5. Spier, *Havasupai*, 110.
6. Densmore, *Chippewa*, 84.
7. Densmore, *Teton Sioux*, 288.
8. Coolidge and Coolidge, *Seris*, 9.
9. Goddard, *San Carlos*, 62.
10. Rasmussen, *Iglulik*, 168.
11. Skinner, "Political," 526.
12. Curtis, *NAI*, 13:193.
13. Loeb, *Folkways*, 307.
14. Cushing, "Zuni Fetishes," 33–34.
15. Kurath, *Iroquois*, 105–6.
16. Curtis, *NAI*, 12:140.
17. Bunzel, "Zuni Ritual," 835.
18. Sapir, *Takelma Texts*, 511.
19. Spinden, *Tewa*, 102.
20. Gatschet, *Klamath*, 167.
21. Wicita Blain, in Densmore, *Pawnee*, 33.
22. Fowler and Fowler, *Numa*, 124, col. 1.
23. Daniels, *Ute*, 61–63.
24. Fletcher and La Flésche, *Omaha Tribe*, 300.
25. Dorsey, *Pawnee*, 200–201.
26. Fletcher and La Flésche, *Omaha Tribe*, 304.
27. Underhill, *Singing*, 57.
28. Luckert, *Hunter*, 24–25.
29. Densmore, *Pawnee*, 27.
30. Fletcher and La Flésche, *Omaha Tribe*, 299.
31. Dorsey, *Pawnee*, 462–63.
32. Weerhae, in Barbeau, "Tsimshian Songs," 149–50.
33. Tahirassuwichi, in Fletcher, *Hako*, 74.
34. Boas, *Social Organization*, 709, 475.
35. Goddard, *Jicarilla*, 269.
36. Spinden, *Tewa*, 103.
37. Laguna, *Elias*, 1310–11.
38. Hill and Hill, "Navajo Coyote Tales," 319.
39. A'yu'nni, in Mooney, *Sacred Formulas*, 373.
40. Densmore, *Chippewa*, 77.
41. O'Bryan, *Diné*, 67.
42. Gatschet, *Klamath*, 164.
43. O'Bryan, *Diné*, 66.
44. Norman, "Wesucechak," 409.
45. Gene Weltfish, "Music of the Pawnee," 6.
46. Rasmussen, *Iglulik*, 237–38.
47. Densmore, *Chippewa II*, 201 (song 97).
48. Bierhorst, *Trail*, 53.
49. Adamson, *Folk-tales*, 367.
50. Spinden, "Nez Perce," 150.
51. Beaglehole, *Hopi*, 19–20.
52. La Flesche, *Osage III*, 642.
53. Densmore, *Chippewa II*, 202 (song 98).
54. Jenness and Roberts, *Eskimo Songs*, 426.
55. Bunzel, *Zuni Texts*, 149.
56. Barbeau, "Tsimshian Songs," 136.
57. Mason, *Language*, 111.
58. Loeb, *Pomo Folkways*, 172.
59. Densmore, *Chippewa*, 84.
60. Thalbitzer, *Ammassalik*, 258.
61. Blackburn, *December's Child*, 314.
62. Blackburn, *December's Child*, 230.
63. Curtis, *Indians' Book*, 370, 555.
64. Densmore, *Teton Sioux*, 190.
65. Fletcher, *Hako*, 81.
66. Underhill, *Singing*, 60.
67. Luckert, *Hunter*, 37.
68. Adamson, *Folk-tales*, 33.
69. Curtis, *NAI*, 14:41.
70. Densmore, *Chippewa*, 86.
71. Boas, "Bella Coola," 29.
72. Gatschet, *Klamath*, 162.
73. Rasmussen, *Iglulik*, 18–19.
74. Wicita Blain, in Densmore, *Pawnee*, 31 (Buffalo Dance, song 6). This song suggests the hunter's trick of wearing a buffalo skin and moving like a buffalo and the myth of Buffalo Calf Woman. The historical woman about whom this song was made was shot in the back, but not killed.
75. Densmore, *Chippewa II*, 203 (song 99).
76. Densmore, *Pawnee*, 30.
77. Laguna, *Elias*, 1164.
78. Goddard, *Navajo Texts*, 163.
79. Russell, *Pima*, 317–18.
80. La Flésche, *Osage II*, 124.
81. Fletcher and La Flésche, *Omaha Tribe*, 633.
82. Russell, *Pima*, 299–300.
83. Rasmussen, *Copper*, 163.
84. Curtis, *NAI*, 20:250.
85. Kroeber, *Handbook*, 529.
86. Ray, *Sanpoil*, 84.
87. Coolidge and Coolidge, *Seris*, 219.
88. Goddard, *San Carlos*, 58.

89. Rasmussen, *Copper*, 132–33; a literal version, 151–52.
90. Goddard, *San Carlos*, 60.
91. Barbeau, "Tsimshian Songs," 131.
92. Densmore, *Cheyenne*, 107.
93. Densmore, *Teton Sioux*, 182.
94. Russell, *Pima*, 301.
95. Densmore, *Papago*, 201.
96. Howard, *American Indian Poetry*, 22.
97. Paige, *Songs*, 60.

X War

1. La Flesche, *War Ceremony*, 38.
2. Curtis, *Indians' Book*, 224, 546.
3. Underhill, *Singing*, 68.
4. Haile, *Enemy Way*, 304.
5. Haile, *Enemy Way*, 69.
6. Densmore, *Cheyenne*, 43.
7. Densmore, *Pawnee*, 50.
8. Curtis, *NAI*, 9:100.
9. Wissler, "Societies and Ceremonial," 15.
10. Erdoes and Ortiz, *Myths*, 248.
11. Fewkes, "A Contribution," 264–65.
12. Schoolcraft, *Historical*, 1:401.
13. Belden, *White Chief*, 43.
14. Schoolcraft, *Oneota*, 347, *Historical*, 402.
15. Coolidge and Coolidge, *Seris*, 245.
16. Lowie, *Societies of the Crow*, 305.
17. Schultz, *Blackfeet*, 156.
18. Gunther and Haeberlin, "Indians of Puget Sound," 14.
19. Parker, *Parker*, 3:53.
20. Densmore, *Santo Domingo*, 127.
21. Coolidge and Coolidge, *Navajo*, 2 (the War God's Horse Song).
22. McAllester, "The War God's Horse Song," 1–21.
23. Boas, "Songs of the Kwakiutl," 9.
24. Densmore, *Chippewa II*, 102.
25. Desmore, *Poems*, 13.
26. La Flesche, *Osage II*, 209.
27. Skinner, "Societies of the Iowa," 716.
28. Boas, *Social Organization*, 705, 468.
29. Curtis, *NAI*, 9:76.
30. Skinner, *Mascoutens*, 201.
31. Densmore, "Choctaw," 125.
32. Boas, "Songs of the Kwakiutl," 8.
33. Courlander, *Fourth World*, 137.
34. Cushing, "Zuni Fetishes," 42.
35. Densmore, *Teton Sioux*, 351.
36. Densmore, *Teton Sioux*, 299.
37. Fletcher and La Flésche, *Omaha Tribe*, 417–18.
38. Lowie, "Societies of the Arikara," 673.
39. Fletcher and La Flésche, *Omaha Tribe*, 477–78.
40. Underhill, *Singing*, 80.
41. Campbell [Vestal], *New Sources*, 168.
42. Fletcher and La Flésche, *Omaha Tribe*, 472–73.
43. Lowie, *Crow Texts*, 37–38.
44. Lowie, *Primitive*, 417.
45. Black Elk, *Black Elk Speaks*, 101.
46. Lame Deer, *Seeker*, 11.
47. Lame Deer, *Seeker*, 10.
48. Sandoz, *Cheyenne*, 76.
49. Erdoes and Ortiz, *Myths*, 266.
50. Fletcher and La Flésche, *Omaha Tribe*, 475.
51. Spinden, *Tewa*, 78.
52. Densmore, *Papago*, 181.
53. Russell, *Pima*, 227, 281.
54. Laird, *Chemehuevis*, 175.
55. Densmore, *Chippewa*, 198.
56. Austin, *American Rhythm*, 125.
57. Marriott, *Kiowa Years*, 118.
58. Marriott, *Ten Grandmothers*, 34.
59. Mooney, "Calendar," 329.
60. Rhodes, "Kiowa," 18.
61. Mayhall, *Kiowas*, 275, 300.
62. Fowler and Fowler, *Numa*, 123, col. 1.
63. Densmore, *Menominee*, 74.
64. Schlesier, *Wolves*, 3.
65. Underhill, *Singing*, 79.
66. Densmore, *Chippewa II*, 131.
67. Densmore, *Papago*, 193.
68. Densmore, *Chippewa II*, 112.
69. Barbeau, "Tsimshian Songs," 129.
70. Densmore, *Chippewa II*, 116.
71. Black Elk, *Pipe*, 127–38.
72. Curtis, *NAI*, 8:60.
73. Curtis, *NAI*, 14:27.
74. Swanton, *Tlingit Myths*, 413.
75. Grinnell, *Fighting Cheyennes*, 178.
76. Mooney, *Ghost-Dance*, 233.
77. Matthews, "Myths," 61.
78. Densmore, *Teton Sioux*, 394.
79. Black Bear, *Songs*, 57.
80. Eh–Ros–Ka, in Skinner, "Societies of the Iowa," 696.

81. Coolidge and Coolidge, *Seris*, 192.
82. Underhill, *Singing*, 91–92.
83. Boas, *Ethnology*, 1380–81.
84. Spinden, *Tewa*, 108.
85. Russell, *Pima*, 325–26.
86. Hooper, "Cahuilla," 345.
87. Adamson, *Folk-tales*, 77.
88. Spence, *Myths*, 71.
89. Underhill, *Autobiography*, 22–23.
90. Densmore, *Chippewa II*, 81.
91. Densmore, *Cheyenne*, 45. Cf. *Teton Sioux*, 109.
92. Densmore, *Chippewa II*, 179.
93. Densmore, *Chippewa*, 99.
94. Vizenor, *Nogamon*, 87.
95. Sarett, *Covenant*, xviii.
96. Haile, *Enemy Way*, 299.
97. Bunzel, *Zuni Ceremonialism*, 676–77.
98. Haile, *Enemy Way*, 272.
99. Haile, *Enemy Way*, 197.
100. Barbeau, "Tsimshian Songs," 141.
101. Sapir, *Takelma Texts*, 509.
102. Jacobs, *Coos Myth*, 233. Ediphone recording, Washington State Museum, 14:14580:j.
103. Rasmussen, *Copper*, 187–89. See also *Eskimo Poems*, 19–20.
104. Petitot, *Traditions*, 273.
105. Densmore, *Teton Sioux*, 365. Densmore reads: "It has come to pass!"
106. Spinden, *Tewa*, 108.
107. Laguna, *Elias*, 1161.
108. Petitot, *Traditions*, 273.

XI Death

1. Parks, *Caddoan Texts*, 8.
2. Hinton, *Havasupai*, 275.
3. Paige, *Songs*, 72.
4. McKenney, *Sketches*, 5:186.
5. Skinner, *Mascoutens*, 146–47.
6. Opler, *Apache Life*, 471.
7. Curtis, *Indians' Book*, 540.
8. Loskiel, *History*, 1:150.
9. Gilmore, *Smoke*, 207.
10. Alexander, *World's Rim*, 194.
11. Rasmussen, *Hudson Bay*, 7:70.
12. Densmore, *Chippewa II*, 114.
13. Curtis, *Indians' Book*, 225, 546.

14. Densmore, *Chippewa II*, 89.
15. Gatschet, *Klamath*, 165.
16. Gatschet, *Klamath*, 192.
17. Opler, *Apache Life Way*, 127–28.
18. Goddard, *Chilula*, 379.
19. Densmore, *Papago*, 215.
20. Fowler and Fowler, *Numa*, 123, col. 1.
21. Sapir, *Takelma Texts*, 51.
22. Loeb, *Folkways*, 227.
23. Laguna, *Elias*, 1160.
24. Barbeau, "Tsimshian Songs," 113.
25. Swanton, *Tlingit*, 408.
26. Petitot, *Traditions*, 273.
27. Swanton, *Tlingit*, 408.
28. Demetracopoulou, "Wintu Songs," 487.
29. Matthews, *Mountain*, 467.
30. Laguna, *Elias*, 1157.
31. Curtis, *NAI*, 9:85.
32. Kroeber, *Handbook*, 509.
33. Ortiz, *Tewa*, 54.
34. Fortune, *Omaha*, 130.
35. Du Bois, *Wintu*, 79.
36. Kroeber and Gifford, *Karok*, 315.
37. Michelson, "Notes," 507.
38. Ortiz, *Tewa*, 54.
39. Demetracopoulou, "Wintu Songs," 484.
40. Du Bois, "Religion," 110.
41. Laguna, *Elias*, 1281.
42. Swanton, *Tlingit*, 319.
43. Densmore, *Santo Domingo*, 68.
44. Rasmussen, *Copper*, 184–87. The last stanza comes from a different version, 136–38.
45. Densmore, *Santo Domingo*, 69.
46. Gatschet, *Klamath*, 165.
47. Demetracopoulou, "Wintu Songs," 487.
48. Densmore, *Chippewa II*, 278.
49. Densmore, "Words," 451.
50. Densmore, *Menominee*, 83.
51. Boas, *Ethnology*, 1307–8.
52. Adamson, *Folk-tales*, 295.
53. Adamson, *Folk-tales*, 23.
54. Parker, *Code*, 84–85.
55. Boas, *Ethnology*, 1292.
56. Curtis, *NAI*, 10:235.
57. Curtis, *NAI*, 10:239.
58. Barbeau, "Tsimshian Songs," 132.
59. Fletcher, *Indian Story*, 39–44.
60. Harrington, "Yuma," 340.

61. Densmore, *Yuman*, 132. Also Densmore, *American Indians*, 70.
62. Kroeber, *More*, 118, col. 1.
63. Kroeber, *More*, 118, col. 2.
64. Fowler and Fowler, *Numa*, 123, col. 2.
65. Opler, *Apache Life*, 128.
66. Johnston, *Gabrieliño*, 42.
67. Voth, *Oraibi*, 53.

XII Rain

1. Coolidge and Coolidge, *Seris*, 81.
2. Luckert, *Navajo Mountain*, 144.
3. Jenness and Roberts, *Eskimo Songs*, 493.
4. Bunzel, "Zuñi Ritual," 658.
5. Goddard, *White Mountain*, 131.
6. Densmore, *Papago*, 93.
7. Curtis, *Indians' Book*, 488, 560.
8. Hill, "Agricultural," 79–80.
9. Gill, *Sacred Words*, 66–85.
10. Densmore, *Papago*, 163.
11. Curtis, *Indians' Book*, 489, 560.
12. Skinner, *Mascoutens*, 132–33.
13. Stevenson, *Sia*, 123.
14. Curtis, *NAI*, 17:77.
15. Fletcher, *Hako*, 104.
16. Densmore, *Papago*, 92.
17. Gunther, "Klallam Folktales," 119.
18. Blackburn, *December's Child*, 226.
19. Bunzel, "An Introduction," 483–84.
20. Ballard, *Puget Sound*, 52.
21. Frachtenberg, "Siuslawan," 628.
22. Spier, *Klamath*, 119.
23. Densmore, *Chippewa*, 134.
24. Mooney, *Sacred Formulas*, 387.
25. La Flesche, *Osage II*, 350.
26. Densmore, *Chippewa II*, 158.
27. Densmore, *Maidu*, 27.
28. Ballard, *Puget Sound*, 81.
29. Densmore, *Acoma*, 103.
30. Densmore, *Chippewa II*, 124.
31. Densmore, *Menominee*, 76.
32. Densmore, *Teton Sioux*, 162. Densmore reads "erratic" rather than "darting."
33. Curtis, *NAI*, 17:48.
34. Bunzel, *Zuni Ceremonialism*, 484.
35. Haile, *Beautyway*, 64.
36. Densmore, *Papago*, 173.

37. Fletcher and Philmore, "A Study," 280.
38. La Flesche, *Osage II*, 354.
39. Fowler and Fowler, *Numa*, 126, col. 1.
40. Curtis, *NAI*, 4:157.
41. Densmore, *Acoma*, 38.
42. Ray, *Pragmatists*, 71.
43. Russell, *Pima*, 318.
44. Fletcher, *Indian Story*, 95–96.
45. Skinner, *Mascoutens*, 111.
46. Curtis, *NAI*, 17:52.
47. Densmore, *Papago*, 150.
48. Curtis, *Indians' Book*, 485, 559.
49. Densmore, *Acoma*, 48.
50. Fowler and Fowler, *Numa*, 128, col. 2.
51. Curtis, *Indians' Book*, 365–66.
52. Densmore, *Acoma*, 43.
53. Goddard, *White Mountain*, 130.
54. Sapir, *Takelma Texts*, 513.
55. Spier, *Klamath*, 119.
56. Skinner, *Mascoutens*, 251.
57. Densmore, *Yuman*, 161. Densmore reads "That is the time that" rather than "then."
58. Fowler and Fowler, *Numa*, 125, col. 2.
59. Hinton, *Havasupai*, 305.
60. Fowler and Fowler, *Numa*, 124, col. 1.
61. Boas, "Bella Coola," 29.

XIII Planting and Harvesting

1. La Flesche, *Osage III*, 636–37.
2. Dorsey, *Pawnee*, 235–36.
3. Bunzel, *Zuni Ceremonialism*, 483–84.
4. Densmore, *Maidu*, 41; Powers, *Tribes*, also prints a version.
5. Densmore, *Acoma*, 90.
6. Spier, *Havasupai*, 102.
7. Spinden, *Tewa*, 96.
8. La Flesche, *Osage Tribe IIa*, 58.
9. Curtis, *Indians' Book*, 479, 558.
10. Benedict, "Eight Stories," 74.
11. Harrington, "Karuk," 134, col. 2.
12. Curtis, *NAI*, 17:56.
13. Densmore, *Papago*, 141.
14. Densmore, *Acoma*, 33.
15. Curtis, *NAI*, 17:52.
16. Densmore, *Cheyenne*, 106.
17. Underhill, *Singing*, 44–45.
18. Curtis, *Indians' Book*, 304.

19. Underhill, *Singing*, 27.
20. Kurath, *Iroquois*, 195.
21. Waheenee–wea (Buffalo Bird Woman), in Buffalo Bird Woman [Waheenee], *Story*, 9.
22. Coolidge and Coolidge, *Seris*, 233.
23. Curtis, *Indians' Book*, 484–85, 559.
24. Buffalo Bird Woman, *Story*, 96.
25. Kurath, *Iroquois*, 111.
26. Spinden, *Tewa*, 83.
27. Barbeau, "Tsimshian Songs," 145.
28. Curtis, *NAI*, 14:51.
29. Du Bois, "Ceremonies," 228–29.
30. Boas, "Songs of the Kwakiutl," 3.
31. Densmore, *Mandan*, 44.
32. Adamson, *Folk-tales*, 374.
33. Densmore, "Choctaw," 177.
34. Goddard, *White Mountain*, 131.
35. Goddard, *White Mountain*, 131.
36. Matthews, "Songs of Sequence," 185–94.

XIV Dawn

1. La Flesche, *Osage III*, 699.
2. Rasmussen, *Iglulik*, 166.
3. Boas, *Social Organization*, 731, 631.
4. Densmore, *Yuman*, 150. Densmore, *American Indians*, 70, gives a shorter version.
5. Curtis, *NAI*, 8:54–55.
6. Fletcher, *Story*, 78–79.
7. Russell, *Pima*, 308–9.
8. Hoskinson, "Saguaro," 134–36.
9. Fletcher and La Flésche, *Omaha Tribe*, 505.
10. Hinton, *Havasupai*, 312.
11. Curtis, *NAI*, 14:114.
12. Densmore, *Acoma*, 64.
13. Goddard, *Hupa*, 274.
14. Hinton, *Havasupai*, 307.
15. Densmore, *Pawnee*, 43.
16. Densmore, *Acoma*, 103.
17. Fowler and Fowler, *Numa*, 122, col. 2.
18. Coolidge and Coolidge, *Seris*, 238.
19. Underhill, *Singing*, 140.
20. Hulsey [Woiche], *Annikadel*, 26.
21. Matthews, "Navaho Gambling Songs," 8. Haile, *Waterway*, 65, prints a more literal version.

22. O'Bryan, *Diné*, 67.
23. Goddard, "Gotal," 392.
24. Bunzel, "Zuni Katcinas," 891.
25. Densmore, *Northern Ute*, 66.
26. Densmore, *Yuman*, 162. Densmore reads "is coming up" for "rises."
27. Curtis, *Indians' Book*, 487, 560.
28. Laird, *Chemehuevis*, 18.
29. Densmore, *Yuman*, 156.
30. Haeberlin and Roberts, "Some Songs," 496.
31. Collins, *Valley*, 153.
32. Densmore, *Nootka*, 285.
33. Curtis, *NAI*, 8:57.
34. Black Bear, *Songs*, 127.
35. Schoolcraft gives various versions in *Red Race*, 411; *Oneota*, 347; *Historical*, 1:402. Walter Hoffman gives still another, in Schoolcraft, *Red Race*, 412.
36. Wyman, *Red Antway*, 205.
37. Densmore, *Cheyenne*, 55.
38. Boas, "Mythology of the Bella Coola," 36.
39. Du Bois, "Chaup," 230.
40. Gatschet, *Klamath*, 192.
41. Swanton, *Tlingit Myths*, 409.
42. Fowler and Fowler, *Numa*, 124, col. 1.
43. Laguna, *Elias*, 1306.
44. Densmore, *Acoma*, 45.
45. Goddard, "Masked Dancers," 134–35.
46. Densmore, *Acoma*, 30.
47. Barbeau, "Tsimshian Songs," 131.
48. Spinden, *Tewa*, 80.
49. Densmore, *Yuman*, 154.
50. Densmore, *Papago*, 137.
51. Densmore, *Chippewa II*, 254.
52. C. H. Beaulieu, in Densmore, "Words," 451.
53. Skinner, *Mascoutens*, 132.
54. Hinton, *Havasupai*, 301 (a Dance Song).
55. Rasmussen, *Iglulik*, 168.
56. Bunzel, *Zuni Ceremonialism*, 635.
57. Schultz–Lorentzen, *Intellectual*, 265, quoting Rasmussen.
58. Paige, *Songs*, 61.
59. Buckley, "Yurok Doctors," 153.
60. Spier, *Havasupai*, 286–87.

NAME	MEANING	ENGLISH	DERIVATION	TERRITORY
Aa'shi'wi	Zunian	Zuni	Spanish from K'eresan *sunyyitsi*	N bank of upper Zuni River, Valencia Co., New Mexico
A'a'tam A'kimult	River People	Pima	From *pimahaitu*, "nothing," incorrectly applied by missionaries	Gila and Salt River valleys
Absaroke	Crow-, Sparrowhawk-, Bird-People	Crow	From the French *gens de corbeaux*, for their name	On the Yellowstone from the Musselshell in the N to the Platte in the S
Achomawi	River People		From *adzuma* or *achoma*, "river"	NW California
Akume	Acoman	Acoma		Acoma Mesa, 60 miles W of Rio Grande, Valencia Co., New Mexico
A'nish'inabeg	Human	Chippewa, Ojibwa	Chippewa, "puckered moccasins"	Northern Lake Huron, Lake Superior, to North Dakota
Ani'Yun'wiya	Real People	Cherokee	Possibly from Creek *tciloki*, "different language speakers"	S Appalachians, from Tennessee and Virginia to Georgia and Alabama
[Assiniboin]		Assiniboin	Chippewa name meaning "cooks with stones"	N of Milk River and along Saskatchewan and Assiniboin Rivers in Canada

NAME	MEANING	ENGLISH	DERIVATION	TERRITORY
Bana'kwut		Bannock		SE Idaho, W Montana, down Snake River
[Carrier]	A general name referring to several bands	Carrier	From the custom of widows carrying their husbands' ashes in a basket	Headwaters of Frasier River, Canada
Chahiksichahiks	Manliest men	Pawnee	From *parisu*, "hunter," or *pariki*, "horn"	Middle Platte and Republican River valleys
Chehalis	Sand	Chehalis	From a village at the entrance to Grays Harbor	Central Washington coast
Choctaw		Choctaw, Flatheads	Unknown; Flathead, from the custom of flattening infants' heads	SE Mississippi
[Coos]	Southerner	Coos	From a Hanis word meaning "South"	S Oregon coast
Cowichan	Warm the Back Mountain People	Cowichan		SE coast of Vancouver Island
Cowlitz	Cowlitz River People	Cowlitz		Middle and lower Cowlitz River, Washington
Creek		Creek		Central Georgia and Alabama
Dakota, Lakota, Nakota	Allies	Sioux	From Chippewa *nadouessioux*, "snakes"	North and South Dakota, Nebraska
Dene		Chipewayan	From a Cree word meaning "pointed skins"	From Hudson Bay to Great Slave Lake, sub-arctic Canada
Dindzhu	People	Kutchin	Flats dwellers, dwellers furthest downstream	Along Chandelar and Yukon Rivers, Alaska
Diné	People	Navajo	From Tewa *navahu*, "cultivated land," through Spanish, *apaches de navajoa*	Four Corners, SW Colorado, NW New Mexico, NE Arizona, SE Utah

NAME	MEANING	ENGLISH	DERIVATION	TERRITORY
Ennesen	Ennesenners	Salinan	From the Salinas River	Headwaters of Salinas River N to Santa Lucia Peak and Soledad, and the sea to Coast Range
Haida	Humans	Hade	Humans, people	Queen Charlotte Islands, Prince of Wales Island, off British Columbia and S Alaska
Hamakhav	Three Mountains	Mohave	From *hamakhava*, "needles," "three mountains"	Colorado River Valley from Needles to Black Canyon, Arizona
Havasuwapay	Green (Blue) Water People	Havasupai		Cataract Canyon on Colorado River in NW Arizona
Hidatsa	Willows			Missouri River between Heart and Little Missouri Rivers
Hopitu	Most Peaceful People	Hopi	Peaceful, wise, good	Moshongnovi, Oraibi, Shipaulove, Shongopovi, Sichomovi, and Walpi Pueblos, on First, Second, and Third Mesas in NE Arizona
Hotcangara	Big Voice Speakers	Winnebago	From Sauk and Fox, "people of the dirty water"	S of Green Bay, Wisconsin, to Nebraska and S Dakota
Hum'a'luh	People	Skagit	Meaning unknown	Skagit and Stilliguamish River valleys, except deltas
Humptulip	Chilly Land			Humptulips River, central Washington
Ikaniuksalgi	Peninsula People	Seminole	Perhaps from Spanish *cimarrón*, "wild"	Central Florida, around Apalachicola River, and Everglades
Inuit	People	Eskimo	From Algonkin for "eaters of raw meat"	E Arctic Greenland to W Arctic Alaska

NAME	MEANING	ENGLISH	DERIVATION	TERRITORY
Inuna'ina'	Our People	Arapaho	From Pawnee *tirapihu*, "traders"	NE Wyoming, E and central Colorado
Ipay		Diegueño	From San Diego Mission	San Diego, California
Isonkuaili	Our People	Okanagon	From a place on the Okanagon River	N central Washington, S central British Columbia
Ivitem	Iviat Speaker	Cahuilla	From unidentified Spanish	Basin between San Bernardinos and Mount San Jacinto, S California
Iyiniwok	The First People	Cree	From French *kristinaux*, a corruption of Cree *kenistenoag*	Central Canada from James Bay to Saskatchewan
Ka'dohada'cho	Real Chiefs	Caddo	Abbreviation of name	NE Texas, SW Arkansas, Red River Valley
Ka'igwu	Principal People	Kiowa	Probably from the Kaigwu Band	Plains in W Kansas, Oklahoma, Texas Panhandle, E Colorado, New Mexico
[Karuk]	Upstream People	Karok		Middle of Klamath River drainage, N California
Kasogotine	Big Willow People	Hare Indians	From their dependence on the hare for food and clothing	W and NW of Great Bear Lake in NW Canada
[Keres]	[K'eresan Speakers]	Keres		Acoma, Cochiti, Laguna, San Felipe, Santa Ana, Santo Domingo, and Sia Pueblos
Kiliwa		Kiliwa		N Baja California
Kitksan	Skeena River People	Gitksan		Central British Columbia, Upper Skeena River
Konhiak	People	Seri	Spanish: derivation unknown	Tiburon Island in Gulf of California

NAME	MEANING	ENGLISH	DERIVATION	TERRITORY
Kumarik	Easterners	Gabrielino	From Mission San Gabriel	San Gabriel River Drainage, from Los Angeles S to Orange County, California
Kutiti	Cochitian	Cochiti		27 miles SW of Santa Fe, New Mexico, on W bank of Rio Grande
Kwagutl	Smoke of the World	Kwakiutl		Queen Charlotte Sound and S Vancouver
Kwatsan	Those Who Descended	Yuma	From a Piman or Papagan word through Spanish	Colorado River Valley, from Gila River junction to 50 miles N of mouth
Lenni Lenape	True Men	Delaware	From the Delaware River	New Jersey, New York W of Hudson, E Pennsylvania, N Delaware
Lku'ngen		Songish	English for a sept name, "scanges"	S Vancouver Island, San Juan Island, Washington
[Luiseño]		Luiseño	From the Mission San Luis Rey	SW California
Maidu	Person	Maidu		Feather and American Rivers drainage, W central California
Maklaks	Lake People	Klamath		Upper Klamath Lake, Williamson and Sprague Rivers, Oregon
Meshkwakihugi	Red Earth People	Foxes	Translation of a clan name, misapplied to the entire people	From Lake Winnebago along Fox River, Wisconsin, Minnesota, Illinois, and Iowa
Micmac	Allies	Micmac	From Migmag	Nova Scotia, Cape Breton, and Prince Edward Islands, E New Brunswick, Newfoundland

NAME	MEANING	ENGLISH	DERIVATION	TERRITORY
Miwok	People	Miwok		N California, N of San Francisco, along San Joaquin and Sacramento Rivers and in Clear Lake Basin
Modoc	Southerners	Modoc	From "Moatakni"	N California, Klamath, Tule, Clear Lakes
Nanbe	Nambean	Nambe	Spanish *nambé*, name for the Pueblo	On Nambe River, 16 miles N of Santa Fe, New Mexico
Natinnoh-hoi	Trinity River People	Hupa	From Yurok *hupo*, for the river valley	Middle Trinity River in N California
Nekanni		Wailaki	From the Wintun word for "northern speakers"	Upper Eel River valley, N California
Nimic		Snake Indians, Shoshone	English translation of Chippewa, Mandan, Omaha, Yankton Sioux names, meaning "snake people"	Northern Shoshone; E Idaho, W Wyoming, NE Utah: W Shoshone; Nevada, and Death and Panamint Valleys in California as well
Nimipu	People	Nez Perce	From French for "pierced noses"	Central Idaho, SE Washington, NE Oregon
[Noam-Kekhl]	From Wintun for "westerners"	Yuki	From Wintun for "stranger," "enemy"	Eel River drainage, NW central California
No-ochi	Persons	Ute		Central and W Colorado, E Utah, NW New Mexico
Nuchalnulth	Dwellers along the Mountains	Nootka	Mistranslation of the word for circling	From Cape Flattery in Washington to Port San Juan in Vancouver
Nukhstlhayum		Clallam	From S'Klallam, Tla'lem, Nu-sklaim, "strong people"	S side of Strait of Juan de Fuca, S Vancouver Island
Numa	People	Southern Paiute	Perhaps from the word for "water Ute"	W Utah, NW Arizona, SE Nevada, SE California

NAME	MEANING	ENGLISH	DERIVATION	TERRITORY
Numakaki (after 1837, Metutahanke)	People (from the name of their old village)	Mandan	Corruption of Sioux *mawatani*	Between Heart and Little Missouri Rivers, on Missouri River
Nuxalk	Bellacoola Valley People	Bellacoola	From Bellabella *bi'luxula*	N Bentinck, S Bentick Arms, Dean River and Channel and Bella Coola River, British Columbia
Omaha	Goers against the Current	Omaha		NE Nebraska
Oma'nomeni'wuk	Wild Rice People	Menominee		Menominee River Valley, Wisconsin
Ontinonsionni	Extended Lodge People	Iroquois	From Algonkin *irinakhoiw*, "real adders," through French	Mohawk Valley and Lake region of central New York
[Ottawa]	From a word meaning "traders"	Ottawa		S Ontario, N Michigan
Pahodja	Dusty or Pierced Noses	Iowa	From *ayuha*, their Dakota name, through French	Iowa, and small areas in neighboring states
Paviotso	Water Ute	Northern Paiute		W Nevada, SE Oregon, NE California to Owens Valley
Pestamokatiyak	Pollock Catchers	Passamaquoddy		N Maine, Canada
Pomo	Red Earthers	Pomo	from the suffix *-pomo*, "dwellers"	California coast N of San Francisco Bay
Potawatomi	Fire Keepers	Potawatomi		Michigan, Lower Peninsula
Qwulh-hwaipum	Prairie People	Klickitat	From Chinook, meaning "beyond," referring to the Cascade Range	Yakima and Columbia Rivers in central Washington
[Salish]	Dwellers at . . .	Flatheads	From the custom of letting children's heads grow into natural shape, rather than binding them into sloping foreheads	W Montana, from Flathead Lake to Crazy Mountain and Little Belt ranges

NAME	MEANING	ENGLISH	DERIVATION	TERRITORY
Sanish	Real Person	Arikara	Horn or Elk People	Missouri River valley from Cheyenne River, South Dakota, to Fort Berthold in North Dakota
[Sanpoil]		Sanpoil	Meaning unknown	Sanpoil River and Columbia below Big Bend in Washington
Sekani	Mountain Dwellers	Sekani	Probably originally a band name	E central British Columbia
Shis-Inde, Inde, Nde	Forest-People, People	Apache	From Zuni *apachu*, "enemy," through Spanish *apaches*	S New Mexico and Arizona, W Texas, SE Colorado, N Mexico
Siehwib-ag	Flint Place People	Isleta	From Spanish for "island"	W bank of Rio Grande, 12 miles S of Albuquerque
Siksika, also Ahhitape	Blackfeet, Blood People	Blackfeet, Bloods	Moccasins dyed black; Bloods derivation uncertain	N Saskatchewan to Missouri headwaters, 105 degrees W to Rockies
Sitsime	Lagunan	Laguna	From Spanish *laguna*, "lake"	On S bank of San Jose River, Valencia Co., New Mexico
Siuslaw	Siuslawan	Siuslaw	From the Siuslaw River region	On and near Siuslaw River, Oregon
Snohomish	Probably a place name	Snohomish		Central Washington Coast, Snohomish River, and Whidbey Island
Sulatelik	Sulat Speakers	Wiyot; Humboldt Bay Indians	Place names	Lower Mad and Eel Rivers, Humboldt Bay, N California
Suquamish		Suquamish	A place name	W side of Puget Sound
Takelma	Rogue River Dwellers	Takelma		Rogue River drainage, Oregon, south to N California

NAME	MEANING	ENGLISH	DERIVATION	TERRITORY
Takhtahm	Men	Serraño	From Spanish meaning "mountaineers"	San Bernardinos, San Gabriels, Sierra Madre, central S California
Ta'n-ta'wats	Northerners	Chemehuevi	Yuman name, meaning unknown	E Mohave Desert, Chemehuevi Valley and Colorado River valley, S California
[Tewa]	[Speakers of the Tewan branch of Kiowa-Tanoan]	Tewa	From K'eres for "moccasins"	Hano, Nambe, Tesuque, San Ildefonso, San Juan, and Santa Clara Pueblos in Rio Grande Valley, New Mexico
[Tiwa]	[Speakers of the Tiwan branch of Kiowa-Tanoan]			Isleta, Picuris, Sandia, and Taos Pueblos in Upper Rio Grande Valley, New Mexico
Tiwame	Tiwanan	Santo Domingo	The name of the Spanish Mission	18 miles above Bernallilo, New Mexico, on E bank of Rio Grande
Tlingit	People	Tlingit		Coast and islands of Alaska from Yakutat Bay S
Tohono Au'autam	Desert People	Papago	Bean People, from the Spanish translation of the Papago word *papabotas*	S and SW of Gila, into Sonora
Tsimshian	Skeena River People	Tsimshian		Lower Skeena River and adjoining coast, Alaska
Tsistsi'stas		Cheyenne		Moved from Minnesota to Missouri Valley and Black Hills in Dakotas
Tsiyame	Sian	Sia	From the Spanish spelling of Tsiya	16 miles NW of Bernalillo, New Mexico, on Jemez River
[Tsulu-la]	Bald Hill People	Chilula	From Yurok *tsulu*, Bald Hills	Lower Redwood Creek, N California

NAME	MEANING	ENGLISH	DERIVATION	TERRITORY
Tua'dhu		Twana; Skokomish	Tua'dhu word for "portage"	S inlets to Puget Sound, Washington
Walwarena		Santa Barbara Indians		Santa Barbara Islands and adjacent river valleys
Wazhazhe		Osage	English mispronunciation of Wazhazhe	Osage River in Missouri and Missouri River
[Wintu]	People	Wintu	From the Wintun word for "people"	Upper Sacramento and Trinity Rivers, N California
Yoemi		Yaqui		N Sonora, S Arizona
[Yokuts]	People	Yokuts	A general name for 40 groups, who name themselves from localities	From mouth of San Joaquin River to Tehachapi in California

NOTE: the information in this glossary derives from William C. Sturtevant, ed., *Handbook of North American Indians* (Washington, D.C.: Smithsonian Institution, 1978–), and John R. Swanton, *The Indian Tribes of North America*, Bulletins of the American Bureau of Ethnography, no. 145 (Washington, D.C.: Smithsonian Institution, 1952).

Adamson, Thelma. *Folk-tales of the Coast Salish.* Memoirs of the American Folk-Lore Society 27. New York: G. E. Stechert & Co., 1934.

Alexander, Hartley Burr. *The World's Rim: Great Mysteries of the North American Indians.* Lincoln: University of Nebraska Press, 1953.

Astrov, Margot, ed. *American Indian Prose and Poetry: An Anthology.* New York: Putnam, 1946. New York: John Day Co., 1972.

Austin, Mary Hunter. *The American Rhythm: Studies and Re-expressions of Amerindian Songs.* 2nd ed. Boston and New York: Houghton Mifflin Co., 1930.

———. "The Path on the Rainbow." Introduction to *The Path on the Rainbow: An Anthology of Songs and Chants from the Indians of North America*, ed. George W. Cronyn, introduction by Mary Austin. New York: Liveright Publishing Corp., 1934.

Bahr, Donald M., et al. *Pima Shamanism and Staying Sickness: Kácim Múmkidag.* Tucson: University of Arizona Press, 1974.

———. "Pima Swallow Songs." *Cultural Anthropology* 1/2 (1956): 171–87.

Bailey, Paul. *Wovoka, the Indian Messiah.* Great West and Indian Series 10. Los Angeles: Westernlore, 1957.

Baker, Theodore. *On the Music of the North American Indians/Über die Musik der Nordamerikanischen Wilden.* Trans. Ann Buckley. New York: Da Capo Press, 1977.

Ballard, Arthur C., ed. *Mythology of Southern Puget Sound.* Publications in Anthropology. Seattle: University of Washington Press, 1929.

Barbeau, Charles Marius. *Medicine-men on the North Pacific Coast.* Bulletins of the National Museum of Man, no. 152. Ottawa: National Museum of Canada, 1958.

———. "Tsimshian Songs." In *The Tsimshian: Their Arts and Music*, ed. Viola E. Garfield and Paul S. Wingert, 97–281. Publications of the American Ethnological Society 18, part 3. Leyden: E. J. Brill, 1951.

Beaglehole, Ernest. *Hopi Hunting and Hunting Ritual.* Publications in Anthropology, no. 4. New Haven: Yale University, Department of Anthropology, 1936.

Belden, George P., Lt. *Belden, the White Chief or, Twelve Years among the Wild Indians of the Plains.* Ed. James S. Gen. Brisbin. New York: C. F. Vent, 1870.

Benedict, Ruth. "Eight Stories from Acoma." *Journal of American Folklore* 43 (1930): 59–87.

———. "Serrano Tales." *JAF* 39 (1926): 1–17.

Bierhorst, John, ed. and comp. *Four Masterworks of American Indian Literature.* New York: Farrar, Straus & Giroux, 1974.

———. *In the Trail of the Wind: American Indian Poems and Ritual Orations.* New York: Farrar, Straus & Giroux, 1972.

———. *The Sacred Path: Spells, Prayers and Power Songs of the American Indians.* New York: Quill–William Morrow and Co., 1983.

Bimboni, A. *Songs of the American Indians.* Adapted by Frances Densmore. Trans. Robert Higheagle and Mary Warren English. New York: G. Schirmer, 1917.

Black Bear, Ben. *Songs and Dances of the Lakota.* Ed. R. D. Theisz. Rosebud: Sinte Gleska College–North Plains Press, 1976.

Blackburn, Thomas C., ed. *December's Child: A Book of Chumash Oral Narratives.* Berkeley: University of California Press, 1975.

Black Elk, Nicholas [Hehaka Sapa]. *Black Elk Speaks: Being the Life Story of a Holy Man of the Oglala*

Sioux. Ed. and comp. John G. Neihardt. Introd. by Vine Deloria, Jr. Lincoln: University of Nebraska Press, 1979.

———. *The Sacred Pipe: Black Elk's Account of the Seven Rites of the Oglala Sioux*. Ed. and comp. Joseph Epes Brown. New York: Penguin Books, 1971.

Boas, Franz. "Eskimo Tales and Songs." *JAF* 7 (1894): 45–50.

———. *Ethnology of the Kwakiutl*. 2 vols. Thirty–fifth Annual Report of the Bureau of American Ethnology (AR:BAE) (1913–14). Washington, D.C.: Smithsonian Institution, 1921.

———. *The Indians of British Columbia: Lku'ngen, Nootka, Kwakiutl, Shuswap: Sixth Report on the Northwestern Tribes of Canada 1890*. Reports of the British Association for the Advancement of Science, 1891.

———. "Mythology of the Bella Coola Indians." In *Publications of the Jesup North Pacific Expedition*, 25–127. Anthropological Papers 2. New York: American Museum of Natural History: 1900.

———. "On Certain Songs and Dances of the Kwakiutl." *JAF* 1 (1888): 49–64.

———. *The Social Organization and Secret Societies of the Kwakiutl: Report of the United States National Museum, 1895*. New York: Johnson Reprints, 1970.

———. "Songs of the Kwakiutl Indians." *Internationales Archiv für Ethnographie* 9, supplement 1 (1896): 1–9. Leiden: E. J. Brill.

———. *Tsimshian Texts*. Bulletin 27 of the Bureau of American Ethnology (B:BAE). Washington, D.C.: Smithsonian Institution, 1902.

———. *Tsimshian Texts* (new series). Publications of the American Ethnological Society. Leyden: E. J. Brill, 1912.

Boas, Franz, and George Hunt, eds. *Kwakiutl Texts: Second Series*. Memoirs 14. New York: American Museum of Natural History, 1908.

Bogoras, Waldemar. "Ideas of Space and Time in the Conception of Primitive Religion." *American Anthropologist* 27, no. 2 (April 1925): 205–66.

Boscana, Geronimo. *Chinigchinich*. Trans. Alfred Robinson. Annotated by J. P. Harrington. Foreword by Frederick Webb Hodge. Ed. Phil T. Hanna. Santa Ana: California Farmer, 1933.

Bright, William. *The Karok Language*. Publications in

Linguistics 13. Berkeley: University of California Press, 1957.

Brinton, Daniel Garrison. *Essays of an Americanist: Ethnographic and Archaeologic*. Philadelphia, 1890. New York: Johnson Reprint Co., 1970.

Brown, John Arthur, and Robert H. Ry. *Dreamer-Prophets of the Columbia Plateau: Smohalla and Skolaskin*. Foreword by Herman J. Viola. Norman: University of Oklahoma Press, 1989.

Buckley, Thomas. "Yurok Doctors and the Concept of Shamanism." In *California Indian Shamanism*, ed. Lowell John Bean and Sylvia Brakke Vane, 117–61. Ballena Press Anthropological Papers. Menlo Park: Ballena, 1992.

Buffalo Bird Woman [Waheenee]. *An Indian Girl's Story*. Ed. Gilbert L. Wilson. Lincoln: University of Nebraska Press, 1981.

Bunzel, Ruth Leah. "An Introduction to Zuñi Ceremonialism." In *AR:BAE 47* (1929–30), 467–544. Washington, D.C.: Smithsonian Institution, 1932.

———. *Zuni Ceremonialism*. Introd. by Nancy J. Parezo. Albuquerque: University of New Mexico Press, 1992.

———. "Zuni Katcinas: An Analytical Study." In *AR:BAE 47* (1929–30), 837–1086. Washington, D.C.: Smithsonian Institution, 1932.

———. "Zuni Ritual Poetry." In *AR:BAE 47* (1929–30), 611–835. Washington, D.C.: Smithsonian Institution, 1932.

———, ed. *Zuni Texts*. Publications of the American Ethnological Society. New York: G. E. Stechert, 1933.

Burns, L. M. "Digger Indian Legends." *Land of Sunshine* 14 (1901): 130–34, 223–26, 310–14, 397–402.

Burton, Frederick Russell. *American Primitive Music with Especial Reference to the Songs of the Ojibways*. New York: Moffat, 1909.

Campbell, William S. [Stanley Vestal, pseud.]. *New Sources of Indian History 1850–1891*. Norman: University of Oklahoma Press, 1934.

Capron, Louis. "The Medicine Bundles of the Florida Seminole and the Green Corn Dance." In *Anthropological Papers 33–42*, 155–210. B:BAE 151. Washington, D.C.: GPO, 1953.

Carpenter, Edmund Snow. *Anerca*. Illust. Enooesweetok. Toronto: J. M. Dent & Sons, 1959.

Caswell, Helen, ed. *Shadows from the Singing House: Eskimo Folktales Retold by Helen Caswell*. Illust. Robert Mayokok. Rutland: Charles E. Tuttle Co., 1968.

Chafe, Wallace L. *Seneca Thanksgiving Rituals*. B:BAE 183. Washington, D.C.: Smithsonian Institution, 1961.

Chamberlain, Alexander F. "Primitive Woman as Poet." *JAF* 16 (1903): 207–21.

Chapman, Abraham, ed. *Literature of the American Indians: Views and Interpretations*. New York: Meridian–New American Library, 1975.

Clark, Ella Elizabeth. *The Guardian Spirit Quest*. Montana Indian Publication 45. Billings: Montana Indian Publication Fund, 1974.

———. *Indian Legends from the Northern Rockies*. Norman: University of Oklahoma Press, 1966.

Collins, June McCormick. *Valley of the Spirits: The Upper Skagit Indians of Western Washington*. Seattle: University of Washington Press, 1974.

Converse, Harriet Maxwell Clarke. *Myths and Legends of the New York State Iroquois*. Ed. Arthur Caswell Parker. Albany, New York State Museum Bulletin 125, no. 437, 1908. Port Washington: New York State Museum, 1962.

Coolidge, Dane, and Mary Roberts Coolidge. *The Last of the Seris*. New York: Dutton, 1939.

———. *The Navajo Indians*. Boston: Houghton & Mifflin, 1930.

Courlander, Harold, ed. and comp. *The Fourth World of the Hopis*. New York: Crown, 1971.

Culin, Stewart. *Games of the North American Indians*. New York: Dover, 1975.

Curtis, Edward S. *The North American Indian*. Ed. Weston La Barre. 1907–30. 20 vols. New York: Johnson Reprint Co., 1970.

Curtis, Natalie [Burlin], ed. *The Indians' Book: Songs and Legends of the American Indians*. New York: Dover, 1968.

Cushing, Frank Hamilton. "Zuni Fetishes." In *AR:BAE* 2 (1880–81), 3–45. Washington, D.C.: Smithsonian Institution, 1883.

Daniels, Helen Sloan. *The Ute Indians of Southwestern Colorado*. Durango: Durango Public Library, 1941.

Day, Arthur Grove. *The Sky Clears: Poetry of the American Indians*. New York: Macmillan, 1951. Lincoln: University of Nebraska Press, 1964.

Deans, James. "The Story of the Bear and His Indian Wife." *JAF* 11 (1899): 255–60.

DeMallie, Raymond J. *The Sixth Grandfather*. Lincoln: University of Nebraska Press, 1984.

Demetracopoulou, Dorothy. "Wintu Songs." *Anthropos* 30 (1935): 483–94.

Densmore, Frances. *The American Indians and Their Music*. 1926. New York: Johnson Reprint Society, 1970.

———. "The Belief of the Indian in a Connection between Song and the Supernatural." In *Anthropological Papers 33–42*, 217–23. B:BAE 151. Washington, D.C.: Smithsonian Institution, 1953.

———. "The Words of Indian Song as Unwritten Literature." *JAF* 63 (1950): 450–58.

———, ed. and comp. *Cheyenne and Arapaho Music*. Southwest Museum Papers 10. Los Angeles: Southwest Museum, 1936.

———, ed. and comp. *Chippewa Music*. B:BAE 45. Washington, D.C.: Smithsonian Institution, 1910.

———, ed. and comp. *Chippewa Music II*. B:BAE 53. Washington, D.C.: Smithsonian Institution, 1913.

———, ed. and comp. "Choctaw Music: Anthropological Paper 28." In *B:BAE* 136, 101–88. Washington, D.C.: Smithsonian Institution, 1943.

———, ed. and comp. *Mandan and Hidatsa Music*. B:BAE 80. Washington, D.C.: Smithsonian Institution, 1923.

———, ed. and comp. *Menominee Music*. B:BAE 102. Washington, D.C.: Smithsonian Institution, 1932.

———, ed. and comp. *Music of Acoma, Isleta, Cochiti and Zuñi Pueblos*. B:BAE 117. Washington, D.C.: Smithsonian Institution, 1957.

———, ed. and comp. *Music of the Maidu Indians of California*. Publications of the Frederick Webb Hodge Anniversary Publication Fund 7. Los Angeles: Southwest Museum, 1958.

———, ed. and comp. *Music of Santo Domingo Pueblo, New Mexico*. Southwest Museum Papers, no. 12. Los Angeles: Southwest Museum, 1938.

———, ed. and comp. *Nootka and Quileute Music*. B:BAE 124. Washington, D.C.: Smithsonian Institution, 1939.

———, ed. and comp. *Northern Ute Music*. B:BAE 75. Washington, D.C.: Smithsonian Institution, 1922.

———. ed. and comp. *Papago Music.* B:BAE 90. Washington, D.C.: Smithsonian Institution, 1929.

———, ed. and comp. *Pawnee Music.* B:BAE 93. Washington, D.C.: Smithsonian Institution, 1929.

———. *Poems from Sioux and Chippewa Songs.* Washington, D.C.: n.p., [1917].

———, ed. and comp. *Seminole Music.* B:BAE 161. Washington, D.C.: Smithsonian Institution, 1956.

———, ed. and comp. *Teton Sioux Music.* B:BAE 61. Washington, D.C.: Smithsonian Institution, 1918.

———, ed. and comp. *Yuman and Yaqui Music.* B:BAE 110. Washington, D.C.: Smithsonian Institution, 1932.

Dixon, Roland Burrage. *Maidu Texts.* Narr. Tom Young. Publications of the American Ethnological Society 4. Leyden: E. J. Brill, 1912.

Dorsey, George Amos. *The Pawnee: Mythology Part 1.* New York: AMS, 1974.

———. *Traditions of the Caddo.* Washington, D.C.: Carnegie Institute, 1905.

Du Bois, Constance Goddard. "Ceremonies and Traditions of the Diegueños." *JAF* 21 (1908): 228–36.

———. "The Religion of the Luiseño and Diegueño Indians." In *University of California Publications in American Archaeology and Ethnology 8, no. 3,* 69–186. Berkeley: University of California Press, 1908.

———. "The Story of the Chaup: A Myth of the Diegueños." *JAF* 17 (1904): 217–42.

Du Bois, Cora. "The 1870 Ghost Dance." In *Anthropological Records 3,* part 1, 1–151. Berkeley: University of California Press, 1939.

———. *The Feather Cult of the Middle Columbia.* General Series in Anthropology 7. Menasha: George Banta, 1938.

———. *Wintu Ethnography.* Publications in American Archaeology and Ethnology 36, no. 1. Berkeley: University of California Press, 1935.

Erdoes, Richard, and. Alfonso Ortiz, eds. *American Indian Myths and Legends.* Pantheon Fairy Tale and Folklore Library. New York: Random House, 1984.

Espinosa, Aurelio M. "Pueblo Indian Folk Tales." *JAF* 49 (1936): 69–131.

Fewkes, Jesse Walter. "A Contribution to Passama-quoddy Folklore." *JAF* 3, no. 9 (1890): 257–80.

Fletcher, Alice Cunningham. *The Hako, a Pawnee Ceremony.* Performer Tahirassuwichi. Assisted by James R. Murie. Transcribed by Edwin S. Tracy. AR:BAE 22 (1900–1901). Washington, D.C.: Smithsonian Institution, 1904.

———. *Indian Ceremonies: I White Buffalo Festival, II Elk Mystery, III Four Winds Ceremony, IV Shadow or Ghost Lodge, V Wa-Wan or Pipe Dance.* Sixteenth and Seventeenth Annual Reports of the Peabody Museum of Natural History, 3, nos. 3 and 4. Cambridge: John Wilson & Son, 1884.

———. *Indian Story and Song from North America.* Boston: Small, Maynard & Co., 1900. University of Minnnesota Series in American Studies. New York: Johnson Reprint Society, 1970.

Fletcher, Alice Cunningham, and Francis La Flésche, eds. and trans. *The Omaha Tribe.* AR:BAE 27 (1905–6). Washington, D.C.: Smithsonian Institution, 1911.

Fletcher, Alice Cunningham, and John Comfort Philmore. "A Study of Omaha Indian Music." In *Papers of the Peabody Museum of American Archaeology and Ethnology,* vol. 1, no. 5, 231–382. Cambridge, Mass.: Peabody Museum, 1893.

Fortune, Reo Franklin. *Omaha Secret Societies.* Contributions to Anthropology 14. New York: Columbia University Press, 1932.

Fowler, Catherine S., and Don D. Fowler. *Anthropology of the Numa: John Wesley Powell's Manuscripts on the Numic Peoples of Western North America.* Contributions to Anthropology 14. Washington, D.C.: Smithsonian Institution, 1971.

Frachtenberg, Leo Joaquim. "Siuslawan." In *Handbook of American Indian Languages,* ed. Franz Boas, 2:431–629. B:BAE 40. Washington, D.C.: Smithsonian Institution, 1922.

Frisbie, Charlotte Johnson. *Kinaaldá: A Study of the Navaho Girl's Puberty Ceremony.* Salt Lake City: University of Utah Press, 1993.

Galler, Cristal McCleod [Humishuma]. *The Tales of the Okanogons.* Fairfield: Ye Galleon, 1976.

Gatschet, Albert Samuel. *The Klamath Indians of Southwest Oregon.* Contributions to North American Ethnology; BAE 2, parts 1 and 2. Washington, D.C.: GPO, 1890.

Gayton, Anna H. *(1) Yokuts and Western Mono Ethnography: I: Tulare Lake, Southern Valley and Central Foothill Yokuts.* Anthropological Records. Berkeley: University of California Press, 1948.

———. *(2) Yokuts and Western Mono Ethnography: II: Northern Foothill Yokuts and Western Mono.* Anthropological Records. Berkeley: University of California Press, 1948.

———. "Yokuts–Mono Chiefs and Shamans." In *University of California Publications in American Archaeology and Ethnology 24*, 361–420. Berkeley: University of California Press, 1930.

Gifford, Edward Winslow, and Alfred Kroeber. *World Renewal: A Cult System of Native Northwest California.* Anthropological Records. Berkeley: University of California Press, 1949.

Giglio, Virginia. *Southern Cheyenne Women's Songs.* Norman: University of Oklahoma Press, 1994.

Gill, Sam D. *Sacred Words: A Study of Navajo Religion.* Contributions in Intercultural and Comparative Studies 4. Westport: Greenwood, 1981.

Gilmore, Melvin R. *Prairie Smoke.* New York: Columbia University Press, 1929.

Goddard, Pliny Earle, ed. and trans. *Chilula Texts.* Publications in American Archaeology and Ethnology. Berkeley: University of California Press, 1914.

———. "Chipewyan Texts." In *Anthropological Papers of the American Museum of Natural History 10*, 3–65. New York: American Museum of Natural History, 1912.

———. "Gotal—a Mescalero Apache Ceremony." In *Putnam Anniversary Volume: Anthropological Essays Presented to Frederic Ward Putnam in Honor of His 70th Birthday*, ed. Franz Boas, 385–95. New York: AMS, 1976.

———. *Hupa Texts.* Publications on American Archaeology and Ethnology 1, no. 2. Berkeley: University of California Press, 1904.

———. *Jicarilla Apache Texts.* Anthropological Papers 8. New York: American Museum of Natural History, 1911.

———. "The Masked Dancers of the Apache." In *Holmes Anniversary Volume 132–36.* Washington, D.C.: privately published, 1916.

———. *Myths and Tales from the San Carlos Apache.* Anthropological Papers 24, part 1. New York: American Museum of Natural History, 1918.

———. *Myths and Tales from the White Mountain Apache.* Anthropological Papers 24, part 2. New York: American Museum of Natural History, 1918.

———. *Navajo Texts.* Anthropological Papers 34, part 1. New York: American Museum of Natural History, 1933.

———. "Notes on the Sun–Dance of the Cree in Alberta." Anthropological Papers 16, no. 4. New York: American Museum of Natural History, 1919.

Goldman, Irving. *The Mouth of Heaven: An Introduction to Kwakiutl Religious Thought.* New York: John Wiley & Sons, 1975.

Grey, Herman, trans. and ed. *Tales from the Mohaves.* Foreword by Alice Marriott. Norman: University of Oklahoma Press, 1970.

Grinnell, George Bird. *Blackfoot Lodge Tales: The Story of a Prairie People.* Lincoln: University of Nebraska Press, 1969.

———. *The Fighting Cheyennes.* Norman: University of Oklahoma Press, 1985.

Gunther, Erna. "Klallam Folk Tales." In *University of Washington Publications in Anthropology 1*, 113–70. Seattle: University of Washington Press, 1925.

Gunther, Erna, and Herman Haeberlin. "The Indians of Puget Sound." In *University of Washington Publications in Anthropology 4*, 1–84. Seattle: University of Washington Press, 1927.

Haeberlin, Herman K., and Helen H. Roberts. "Some Songs of the Puget Sound Salish." *JAF* 31 (1918): 496–520.

Haile, Fr. Berard, ed. and trans. *Beautyway: A Navaho Ceremonial.* Ed. Leland C. Wyman. Bollingen Series. New York: Pantheon, 1957.

———. *Love-Magic and Butterfly People: The Slim Curley Version of the Ajilee and Mothway Myths.* Narr. Slim Curley. Linguist Irvy W. Goossen. Ed. Karl W. Luckert. American Tribal Religions. Flagstaff: Museum of Northern Arizona, 1978.

———. *Origin Legend of the Navajo Enemy Way: Text and Translation.* Publications in Anthropology 17. New Haven: Yale University Press, 1938.

———. *Origin Legend of the Navaho Flintway: Text and Translation.* Chicago: University of Chicago Press, 1943.

———. *Waterway: A Navajo Ceremonial Myth Told by Black Moustache Circle.* Narr. Black Mustache Circle. Orthographer Irvy W. Goossens. Appendix Karl W. Luckert. American Tribal Religions. Flagstaff: Museum of Northern Arizona, 1979.

Harrington, John Peabody. "Karuk Texts."

International Journal of American Linguistics 6, no. 2 (1930): 121–61.

———. "A Yuma Account of Origins." *JAF* 21 (1908): 324–48.

Herzog, George. "A Comparison of Pueblo and Pima Musical Styles." *JAF* 49 (1936): 283–418.

Hill, Dorothy W., and W. W. Hill. "Navaho Coyote Tales and Their Position in the Southern Athabascan Group." *JAF* 58 (1945): 317–43.

Hill, Willard W. *The Agricultural and Hunting Methods of the Navaho Indians*. Publications in Anthropology 18. New Haven: Yale University Press, 1938.

Hinton, Leanne. *Havasupai Songs: A Linguistic Perspective*. Ars Linguistica. Tübingen: Gunter Narr Verlag, 1984.

Hinton, Leanne, and Lucille J. Watahomigie, eds. *Spirit Mountain: an Anthology of Yuman Story and Song*. Tucson: University of Arizona Press, 1984.

Hoffman, Walter James, comp. and ed. *The Midéwiwin or "Grand Medicine Society" of the Ojibwa*. AR:BAE 7 (1885–86). Washington, D.C.: Smithsonian Institution, 1891.

Hofmann, Charles, ed. *Frances Densmore and American Indian Music: A Memorial Volume*. Contributions from the Museum of the American Indian Heye Foundation. New York: Museum of the American Indian Heye Foundation, 1968.

Hooper, Lucile. "The Cahuilla Indians." In *University of California Publications in Archaeology and Ethnology 16.10*, 315–80 (1920). New York: Kraus Reprint, 1965.

Hoskinson, Tom. "Saguaro Wine, Ground Figures, and Power Mountains: Investigations at Sears Point, Arizona." In *Earth and Sky: Visions of the Cosmos in Native American Folklore*, ed. Claire R. Farrer and Ray A. Williamson, 131–61. Albuquerque: University of New Mexico Press, 1992.

Howard, Helen Addison. *American Indian Poetry*. Ed. Sylvia E. Bowman. United States Authors Series. Boston: Twayne Publishers, 1979.

Hulsey, William [Istet Woiche]. *Annikadel: The History of the Universe as Told by the Achumawi Indians of California*. Tucson: University of Arizona Press, 1992.

Hyde, George E. *Life of George Bent: Written from His Letters*. Norman: University of Oklahoma Press, 1968.

Jacobs, Melville, ed. *Coos Myth Texts*. Publications in Anthropology 8, part 2. Seattle: University of Washington Press, 1940.

Jenness, Diamond. *The Carrier Indians of the Bulkley River: Their Social and Religious Life*. B:BAE. Washington, D.C.: Smithsonian Institution, 1943.

———. *The Sekani Indians of British Columbia*. Bulletin of the National Museum of Canada. Ottawa: National Museum of Canada, 1937.

Jenness, Diamond, and Helen Roberts. *Eskimo Songs: Songs of the Copper Eskimos*. Vol. 14 of *The Report of the Canadian Arctic Expedition (1913–1918)*. Ottawa: n.p., 1925.

Johnson, Broderick H., ed. *Stories of Traditional Navajo Life and Culture by Twenty-two Navajo Men and Women*. Tsaile: Navajo Community College, 1977.

Johnston, Bernice E. *California's Gabrielino Indians*. Southwest Museum Papers. Los Angeles: Southwest Museum, 1962.

Jones, William, ed. and trans. *Ojibwa Texts*. Ed. Truman Michelson. New York: AMS, 1973.

Kehoe, Alice Beck. *The Ghost Dance: Ethnohistory and Revitalization*. Case Studies in Cultural Anthropology. Chicago: Holt, Rinehart & Winston, 1989.

Kelly, Charles. *The Ethnography of the Surprise Valley Paiute*. Publications in American Archaeology and Ethnology 31, part 3. Berkeley: University of California Press, 1932.

Kilpatrick, Jack Frederick, and Anna Gritts Kilpatrick. *Walk in Your Soul: Love Incantations of the Oklahoma Cherokees*. Dallas: Southern Methodist University Press, 1965.

Kitsepawit [Fernando Librado]. *The Eye of the Flute: Chumash Traditional History and Ritual as Told by Fernando Librado [Kitsepawit] to John P. Harrington*. Ed. and annot. Thomas Blackburn et al. Santa Barbara Bicentennial Historical Series. Santa Barbara: Santa Barbara Museum of Natural History, 1977.

Kroeber, Alfred Lewis. *Handbook of the Indians of California*. B:BAE 78. Washington, D.C.: Smithsonian Institution, 1925.

———. *More Mohave Myths*. Anthropological Records 27. Berkeley: University of California Press, 1972.

————. *Seven Mohave Myths*. Anthropological Records 11. Berkeley: University of California Press, 1948.

Kroeber, Alfred Lewis, and E. W. Gifford. *Karok Myths*. Ed. Grace Buzaliko. Foreword by Theodora Kroeber. Folklore commentary by Alan Dundes. Berkeley: University of California Press, 1980.

Kroeber, Karl, ed. and comp. *Traditional American Indian Literatures: Texts and Interpretations*. Lincoln: University of Nebraska Press, 1981.

Kurath, Gertrude Prokosch. *Iroquois Music and Dance: Ceremonial Arts of Two Seneca Longhouses*. B:BAE. Washington, D.C.: Smithsonian Institution, 1964.

La Flesche [La Flésche], Francis. *The Osage Tribe I: Rite of the Chiefs, Sayings of the Ancient Men*. AR:BAE 36 (1914–15). Washington, D.C.: Smithsonian Institution, 1921.

————. *The Osage Tribe II: The Rite of Vigil*. AR:BAE 39 (1918–19). Washington, D.C.: Smithsonian Institution, 1925.

————. *The Osage Tribe IIa: Two Versions of the Child-Naming Rite*. AR:BAE 43 (1925–26). Washington, D.C.: Smithsonian Institution, 1928.

————. *The Osage Tribe III: Rite of the Wa-xo'-be*. AR:BAE 45 (1927–28). Washington, D.C.: Smithsonian Institution, 1930.

————. *The War Ceremony and Peace Ceremony of the Osage Indians*. B:BAE 101. Washington, D.C.: Smithsonian Institution, 1939.

Laguna, Fredericka de, ed. and comp. *Under Mount Saint Elias: The History and Culture of the Yakutat Tlingit*. 3 parts. Smithsonian Contributions to Anthropology 7. Washington, D.C.: GPO, 1972.

Laird, Carobeth. *The Chemehuevis*. Banning: Malki Museum, 1976.

Lame Deer [John Fire], narrator. *Lame Deer: Seeker of Visions*. New York: Washington Square Press–Pocket Books, 1976.

Laski, Vera. *Seeking Life*. Foreword by John Collier. Philadelphia: American Folklore Society, 1958.

Leland, Charles Godfrey, and John Dyneley Prince. *Kuloskap the Master and Other Algonkin Poems*. New York: Funk & Wagnalls, 1902.

Levitas, Gloria, Frank R. Vivelo, and Jaqueline J. Vivelo, eds. *American Indian Prose and Poetry: We Wait in the Darkness*. New York: Capricorn-Putnam, 1974.

Loeb, Edwin M. *Pomo Folkways*. Publications in American Archaeology and Ethnology 19, no. 2. Berkeley: University of California Press, 1926.

Loskiel, George Henry. *History of the Mission of the United Bretheren among the Indians of North America*. Trans. Christian I. La Trobe. London: n.p., 1794.

Lowie, Robert Harry. *Crow Texts*. Berkeley: University of California Press, 1960.

————. *Primitive Religion*. New York: Grosset & Dunlap, 1952.

————. *The Religion of the Crow Indians*. Anthropological Papers 25, part 2. New York: American Museum of Natural History, 1923.

————. *Societies of the Arikara Indians*. Anthropological Papers 11, no. 8. New York: American Museum of Natural History, 1915.

————. *Societies of the Crow, Hidatsa and Mandan Indians*. Anthropological Papers 11, part 3. New York: American Museum of Natural History, 1913.

Luckert, Karl W. *A Navajo Bringing Home Ceremony: The Claus Chee Sonny Version of Deerway Ajilee*. Flagstaff: Museum of Northern Arizona, 1978.

————. *The Navajo Hunter Tradition*. Trans. John Cook et al. Tucson: University of Arizona Press, 1975.

————. *Navajo Mountain and Rainbow Bridge Religion*. Flagstaff: Museum of Northern Arizona, 1977.

Luckert, Karl W., and Johnny C. Cook, trans. *Coyoteway: A Navajo Healing Ceremonial*. Tucson: University of Arizona Press, 1979.

McAllester, David P. " 'The War God's Horse Song': An Exegesis in Native American Humanities." In *Selected Reports in Ethnomusicology*, ed. Charlotte Heth, 1–21. Department of Music: Program in Ethnomusicology. Los Angeles: UCLA, 1980.

McKennan, Robert A. *The Upper Tanana Indians*. Publications in Anthropology 55. New Haven: Yale University Press, 1959.

McKenney, Thomas L. *Sketches of a Tour to the Lakes, of the Character and Customs of the Chippeway Indians, and of Incidents Connected with the Treaty of Fond Du Lac*. Baltimore: Fielding Lucas, 1827. Barre: Imprint Society, 1972.

Mallery, Garrick. *Picture Writing of the American Indians*. AR:BAE 10. Washington, D.C.: Smithsonian Institution, 1893.

Marriott, Alice. *Kiowa Years: A Study in Culture Impact*. New York: Macmillan, 1968.

———. *The Ten Grandmothers*. Norman: University of Oklahoma Press, 1945.

Marriott, Alice, and Carol K. Rachlin, eds. *American Indian Mythology*. New York: Mentor–New American Library, 1968.

Marsden, W. L. "The Northern Paiute Language of Oregon." Publications in American Archaeology and Ethnology 20. Berkeley: University of California Press, 1923.

Mason, J. Alden. *The Language of the Salinan Indians*. Publications in American Archaeology and Ethnology 14, no. 1. Berkeley: University of California Press, 1918.

Matthews, Washington. *The Mountain Chant, a Navajo Ceremony*. AR:BAE 5. Washington, D.C.: Smithsonian Institution, 1887.

———. "Navaho Gambling Songs." *American Anthropologist* o.s. 2, no. 1 (1889): 1–20.

———. *Navajo Myths, Prayers and Songs with Texts and Translations*. Ed. Pliny Earle Goddard. Publications in American Archaeology and Ethnology 5, no. 2. Berkeley: University of California Press, 1907.

———. *The Night Chant: A Navajo Ceremony*. Memoirs 6. New York: American Museum of Natural History, 1902.

———. "Songs of Sequence of the Navahos." *JAF 7* (1894): 185–94.

Mayhall, Mildred P. *The Kiowas*. 2nd ed. Norman: University of Oklahoma Press, 1971.

Michelson, Truman, ed. "The Mythical Origin of the White Buffalo Dance of the Fox Indians." Kapayou, speaker. Ed. Alfred Kiyana. Trans. Horace Poweshiek and Thomas Brown. In *AR:BAE 40* (1918–19), 23–289. Washington, D.C.: Smithsonian Institution, 1925.

———, ed. "Notes on the Fox Society Known as 'Those Who Worship the Little Spotted Buffalo' " By Sam Peters. Trans. George Young Bear and Harry Lincoln. In *AR:BAE 40* (1918–19), 497–539. Washington, D.C.: Smithsonian Institution, 1925.

Mixco, Mauricio J. *Kiliwa Texts*. Anthropological Papers. Salt Lake: University of Utah Press, 1983.

Mooney, James. "Calendar History of the Kiowa Indians." In *AR:BAE 17* (1898–1901), 129–445. Washington, D.C.: Smithsonian Institution, 1900.

———. *The Ghost-Dance Religion and the Sioux Outbreak of 1890*. AR:BAE 14, pt. 2 (1892–93). Washington, D.C.: Smithsonian Institution, GPO, 1896. Rpr. Chicago: University of Chicago Press, 1965.

———. *The Sacred Formulas of the Cherokees*. AR:BAE 7 (1886–87). Washington, D.C.: Smithsonian Institution, 1891.

Murie, James R. [Pawnee]. *Ceremonies of the Pawnee*. Ed. Douglas R. Parks. Contributions to Anthropology 27. Washington, D.C.: Smithsonian Institution, 1981.

Norman, Howard. "Wesucechak Becomes a Deer and Steals Language: An Anecdotal Linguistics concerning the Swampy Cree Trickster." In *Recovering the Word: Essays on Native American Literature*, ed. Arnold Krupat and Brian Swann, 402–21. Berkeley: University of California Press, 1987.

O'Bryan, Aileen, comp. and ed. *The Diné: Origin Myths of the Navajo Indians*. B:BAE 163. Washington, D.C.: GPO, 1956.

Olden, Sarah Emilia, ed. *Karok Indian Stories*. San Francisco: Harr Wagner Publishing Co., 1923.

Olson, Paul A., ed. and trans. *The Book of the Omaha*. Lincoln: Nebraska Curriculum Development Center, 1979.

Opler, Morris Edward. *An Apache Life Way: The Economic, Social, and Religious Institutions of the Chiricahua Indians*. Publications in Anthropology, Ethnological Series. Chicago: University of Chicago Press, 1969.

Ortiz, Alfonso. *The Tewa World: Space, Time, Being and Becoming in a Pueblo Society*. Chicago: University of Chicago Press, 1969.

Paige, Harry W., trans. and ed. *Songs of the Teton Sioux*. Great West and Indian Series. Los Angeles: Westernlore, 1970.

Parker, Arthur C. *Parker on the Iroquois: Iroquois Uses of Maize and Other Food Plants: The Code of Handsome Lake, the Seneca Prophet: The Constitution of the Five Nations*. Ed. William N. Fenton. New York State Studies. Syracuse: Syracuse University Press, 1968.

Parks, Douglas R., ed. *Caddoan Texts*. Vol. 2. International Journal of American Linguistics 2.1. Native American Texts Series. Chicago: University of Chicago Press, 1977.

Petitot, Rev. Emile Fortune Stanislas Joseph, S.J. *Traditions Indiennes du Canada Nord-Ouest.* Les littératures populaires de toutes les nations. Paris: Maisonneuve Frère & Ch. LeClerc, 1886.

Powell, John Wesley. *Anthropology of the Numa: John Wesley Powell's Manuscripts on the Numic Peoples of Western North America.* Ed. Catherine S. Fowler and Don D. Fowler. Contributions to Anthropology 14. Washington, D.C.: Smithsonian Institution, 1971.

Powell, Peter J. *Sweet Medicine: The Continuing Role of the Sacred Arrows, the Sun Dance and the Sacred Buffalo Hat in Northern Cheyenne History.* Norman: University of Oklahoma Press, 1979.

Powers, Stephen. *Tribes of California.* Contributions to North American Ethnology, vol. 3. Washington, D.C.: Smithsonian Institution, 1877.

Radin, Paul. *The Road of Life and Death: A Ritual Drama of the American Indians.* Bollingen Series 5. New York: Pantheon, 1945.

———. *The Trickster: A Study in American Indian Mythology.* New York: Schocken, 1972.

Rand, Silas Tertius. *Legends of the Micmacs.* Wellesley College Philological Publications. New York: Johnson Reprint Corporation, 1971.

Rasmussen, Knud Johan Viktor, ed. and trans. *Eskimo Poems from Canada and Greenland.* Translation of *Snehyttens Sange* (Danish). Trans. Tom Lowenstein. Pittsburgh: University of Pittsburgh Press, 1973.

———. *Intellectual Culture of the Copper Eskimos.* Vol. 9 of *The Report of the Fifth Thule Expedition (1921–24).* New York: AMS, 1976.

———. *The Intellectual Culture of the Hudson Bay Eskimos, Iglulik and Caribou Eskimos.* Vol. 7 of *The Report of the Fifth Thule Expedition (1921–24), nos. 1–3.* Trans W. E. Worster and W. Calvert. Copenhagen: Gyldendalske Boghandel, 1930.

———. *Intellectual Culture of the Iglulik Eskimos.* Trans. W. Worster. Vol. 7, no. 1, of the *Report of the Fifth Thule Expedition (1921–24).* New York: AMS, 1976.

———. *The Netsilik Eskimos: Social Life and Spiritual Culture.* Trans. W. E. Calvert. Vol. 8 of *Report of the Fifth Thule Expedition (1921–24)* (1931). New York: AMS, 1976.

———. *The People of the Polar North.* London: Kegan Paul, Trench, Tubner, 1908.

Ray, Verne F. *Primitive Pragmatists: The Modoc Indians of Northern California.* American Ethnological Society. Seattle: University of Washington Press, 1963.

———. *The Sanpoil and Nespelem: Salishan Peoples of Northeastern Washington.* University of Washington Publications in Anthropology 5. New Haven: Human Relations Area Files, 1954.

Revard, Carter. "Traditional Osage Naming Ceremonies: Entering the Circle of Being." In *Recovering the Word: Essays on Native American Literature,* ed. Arnold Krupat and Brian Swann, 446–66. Berkeley: University of California Press, 1987.

Rhodes, Willard. "American Indian Music: Kiowa." Introd. to *Music of the American Indian: Kiowa.* Archive of Folk Song LP. Washington, D.C.: Library of Congress, n.d.

Rice, Julian. *Deer Women and Elk Men: Lakota Narratives of Ella Deloria.* Albuquerque: University of New Mexico Press, 1992.

Rink, Hinrich, comp., ed., and trans. *Tales and Traditions of the Eskimo, with a Sketch of Their Habits, Religion, Language and Other Peculiarities.* Ed. Robert Brown. London and Edinburgh: W. Blackwood and Sons, 1875.

Russell, Frank. *The Pima Indians.* AR:BAE 26 (1904–5). Washington, D.C.: Smithsonian Institution, 1908.

Sandoz, Mari. *Cheyenne Autumn.* New York: Avon, 1964. Rpt. Lincoln: University of Nebraska Press, 1992.

Sapir, Edward S. "The Religious Ideas of the Takelma Indians." *JAF* 20 (1908): 33–49.

———. "Song Recitative in Paiute Mythology." *JAF* 23 (1910): 455–72.

———. *Takelma Texts.* Vol. 7 of *The Collected Works of Edward Sapir.* Ed. Victor Golla. Berlin: Mouton de Gruyter, 1990.

———. *Texts of the Kaibab Paiutes and Uintah Utes.* Proceedings 65, no. 2. American Academy of Arts and Sciences, 1930.

Sarett, Lew. *Covenant with Earth: A Selection from the Poetry of Lew Sarett.* Comp. Alma Johnson Sarett. Foreword by Carl Sandburg. Gainesville: University of Florida Press, 1956.

Schlesier, Karl H. *The Wolves of Heaven: Cheyenne Shamanism, Ceremonies and Prehistoric Origins.* Norman: University of Oklahoma Press, 1987.

Schoolcraft, Henry R[owe]. *Historical and Statistical Information Respecting the History, Condition and Prospects of the Indian Tribes of the United States.* Illust. Capt. S. Eastman. 6 vols. Philadelphia: Lippincott [Bureau of Indian Affairs], 1851–57.

———. *Oneota, or Characteristics of the Red Race of America: Their History, Traditions, Customs, Poetry, Picture Writing &c.* New York: Wiley & Putnam, 1845.

———. *The Red Race of America: Their History, Traditions, Customs, Poetry, Picture Writing &c.* New York: W. H. Graham, 1847.

Schultz, James Willard [pseud. Apikuni]. *Blackfeet and Buffalo: Memories of Life among the Indians.* Ed. and introduction by Keith C. Seele. Norman: University of Oklahoma Press, 1962.

Schultz-Lorentzen, Christian Wilhem. *The Intellectual Culture of the Greenlanders.* Vol. 2 of *Greenland: The Report of the Commission for the Direction of the Geological and Geographical Investigations in Greenland.* London: H. Milford, 1928.

Scott, Hugh Lenox. "Notes on the Kado, or Sun Dance of the Kiowa." *American Anthropologist* 13, n.s. 3 (1911): 345–79.

Shimkin, D. B. "The Wind River Shoshone Sun Dance." In *Anthropological papers 33–42*, 397–487. B:BAE 151, paper 41. Washington, D.C.: Smithsonian Institution, 1953.

Skinner, Alanson. *The Mascoutens or Prairie Potawatomi Indians.* Bulletins of the Public Museum of the City of Milwaukee. Milwaukee: Public Museum of the City of Milwaukee, 1924.

———. "Political Organization, Cults, and Ceremonies of the Plains–Ojibway Indians." *American Museum of Natural History Anthropological Papers* (1914): 475–511.

———. "Political Organizations, Cults and Ceremonies of the Plains Cree Indians." In *Anthropological Papers of the American Museum of Natural History*, vol. 2, part 4, 513–42. New York: American Museum of Natural History, 1914.

———. "Societies of the Iowa, Kansa and Ponca Indians." *American Museum of Natural History Anthropological Papers* (1915): 679–740 (ed. Clark Wissler).

Spence, Lewis, ed. *The Myths of the North American Indians.* Mineola: Dover, 1989.

Spier, Leslie. *Havasupai Ethnography.* Anthropolog-ical Papers 29. New York: Trustees of the American Museum of Natural History, 1928.

———. *Klamath Ethnography.* Publications in American Archaeology and Ethnology 30. Berkeley: University of California Press, 1930.

———. *Southern Diegueño Customs.* Publications in American Archaeology and Ethnology 20. Berkeley: University of California Press, 1923.

Spinden, Herbert Joseph. "Myths of the Nez Perce Indians II." *Journal of American Folk-lore* 21 (1928): 149–58.

———, ed. and trans. *Songs of the Tewa.* New York: Exposition of Indian Tribal Arts, 1933.

Stevenson, Matilda Cox [Tilly E.]. *The Sia.* AR:BAE 11 (1889–90). Washington, D.C.: Smithsonian Institution, 1894.

Streit, Eloise. *Sepass Poems: The Songs of Y-ail-mihth.* New York: Vantage, 1963.

Swanton, John R., ed. *Haida Songs.* Publications of the American Ethnological Society 3. Leyden: American Ethnological Society, 1912.

———. *Myths and Tales of the Southeastern Indians.* B:BAE 88. Washington, D.C.: Smithsonian Institution, 1929.

———. "Religious Beliefs and Medical Practices of the Creek Indians." In *Forty-second Annual Report of the Bureau of American Ethnology (1920–21)*, 473–672. Washington, D.C.: Smithsonian Institution, 1928.

———. "Social Conditions, Beliefs and Linguistic Relationship of the Tlingit Indians." In *Twenty-sixth Annual Report of the Bureau of American Ethnology (1904–5)*, 391–485. Washington, D.C.: Smithsonian Institution, 1909.

———. *Tlingit Myths and Texts.* B:BAE 39. Washington, D.C.: Smithsonian Institution, GPO, 1909.

Tedlock, Dennis, and Barbara Tedlock, eds. *Teachings from the American Earth: Indian Religion and Philosophy.* New York: Liveright, 1975.

Thalbitzer, William. *The Ammassalik Eskimo: Contributions to the Ethnology of East Greenland Natives in Two Parts: Part 2, Number 4.* Meddelelser om gronland; udgivne af kommissionen for ledelsen af de geologiske og geografiske undersogelser i gronland, 40. Copenhagen: C. A. Reitzel, 1941.

Tinsley, Jim Bob. *He Was Singin' This Song: A Collection of Forty-eight Traditional Songs of the American Cowboy, with Words, Music, Pictures and*

Stories. Transcribed by Elizabeth Orth. Orlando: University Presses of Florida, 1981

Trenholm, Virginia Cole. *The Arapahoes, Our People.* Norman: University of Oklahoma Press, 1970.

Trowbridge, C. C. *Meearmeear [Miami] Traditions.* Ed. Vernon Kinietz. Occasional Contributions from the Museum of Anthropology. Ann Arbor: University of Michigan Press, 1938.

Turner, Frederick W., III, ed. *The Portable North American Indian Reader.* New York: Viking, 1973.

Uldall, Hans Jorgen, and William Shipley. *Nisenan Texts and Dictionary.* Narr. William Joseph. Publications in Linguistics 46. Berkeley: University of California Press, 1966.

Underhill, Ruth M., ed. *The Autobiography of a Papago Woman.* By Maria Chona. Memoirs of the American Anthropological Association 46. Menasha, 1936. Millwood: Kraus, 1974.

———. *Red Man's Religion: Beliefs and Practices of the Indians North of Mexico.* Chicago: University of Chicago Press, 1965.

———. *Singing for Power: The Song Magic of the Papago Indians of Southern Arizona.* Berkeley: University of California Press, 1968.

Velie, Alan R., comp. and ed. *American Indian Literature: An Anthology.* Illust. Danny Timmons. Norman: University of Oklahoma Press, 1979.

Viola, Herman J. *After Columbus: The Smithsonian Chronicle of the North American Indians.* Smithsonian Institution. Washington, D.C.: Smithsonian Books, 1990.

Vizenor, Gerald [Robert], trans. and ed. *Anishinabe Nogamon: Songs of the People.* Minneapolis: Nodin, 1970.

Voegelin, Charles F., ed. and trans. *Walam Olum or Red Score: The Migration Legend of the Lenni Lenape or Delaware Indians.* Indiana Historical Society. Chicago: Lakeside, 1954.

Voget, Fred W. *The Shoshone-Crow Sun Dance.* Norman: University of Oklahoma Press, 1984.

Voth, Henry R. *Oraibi Natal Customs and Ceremonies.* Anthropological Series 6, no. 2. Chicago: Field Columbian Museum, 1905.

Waldman, Carl, and Molly Braun, illustrators. *Atlas of the North American Indian.* New York: Facts on File Publications, 1985.

Walker, James R. *The Sun Dance and Other Ceremonies of the Oglala Division of the Teton Dakota.* Anthropological Papers 16, part 2 (1917). New York: American Museum of Natural History, 1979.

Wallis, W. D. *The Sun-Dance of the Canadian Dakota.* Anthropological Papers 16, no. 4. New York: American Museum of Natural History, 1919.

Waterman, Thomas T. *The Religious Practices of the Diegueño Indians.* Publications in American Archaeology and Ethnology 8, no. 6. Berkeley: University of California Press, 1910.

Weltfish, Gene. "Music of the Pawnee." In *Music of the Pawnee.* Folkways FE4334. New York: Folkways, 1965.

Wheelwright, Mary C., ed. and trans. *The Navajo Creation Myth: The Story of the Emergence, by Hosteen Klah.* Informant Hosteen Klah. Trans. Harry Hoijer. Ed. George Herzog. New York: AMS, 1980.

White, Leslie A. *New Material from Acoma.* B:BAE 136, paper 32. Washington, D.C.: Smithsonian Institution, 1943.

Wissler, Clark. *Indians of the United States.* Garden City: Doubleday, 1940.

———. "Societies and Ceremonial Associations in the Oglala Division of the Teton–Dakota." In *Societies of the Plains Indians,* ed. Clark Wissler. Anthropological Papers 11, no. 1. New York: American Museum of Natural History, 1912.

———. "Societies and Dance Associations of the Blackfoot Indians." In *Anthropological Papers of the American Museum of Natural History,* vol. 11, no. 4, 359–460. New York: American Museum of Natural History, 1913.

———. "The Sundance of the Blackfoot Indians." In *Anthropological Papers of the American Museum of Natural History,* vol. 16, part 3, 221–70. New York: American Museum of Natural History, 1918.

Wyman, Leland Clifton. *The Red Antway of the Navaho.* Tucson: University of Arizona Press, 1965.

Yates, Lorenzo G. "Charmstones: Notes on the So–called Plummets of Sinkers." In *Annual Report of the Smithsonian Institution to the End of June, 1886,* 296–305. Washington, D.C.: Smithsonian Institution, 1889.

Young, Levi Edgar. "Ute Poems and Legends." *Utah Education Review* 9 (1916): 10–15.

Zolbrod, Paul G. "Cosmos and Poesis in the Seneca Thank–You Prayer." In *Earth and Sky: Visions of the Cosmos in Native American Folklore*, ed. Claire R. Farrer and Ray A. Williamson, 25–51. Albuquerque: University of New Mexico Press, 1992.

———. *Reading the Voice: Native American Oral Poetry on the Written Page*. Salt Lake City: University of Utah Press, 1995.

PERMISSIONS

I wish to thank the following people and institutions for their gracious permission to reprint material whose copyright they own or control and to acknowledge their generosity:

The Ballena Press for "We Holy Persons," p. 153; "In the morning," p. 153: Thomas Buckley, "Yurok Doctors and the Concept of Shamanism." In *California Indian Shamanism*, ed. Lowell John Bean and Sylvia Brakke Vane, 117–61. Ballena Press Anthropological Papers. Menlo Park: Ballena, 1992. © 1992. Reprinted by permission from the Ballena Press.

The Canadian Museum of Civilization for "He will walk . . . behind the sky," p. 50: Charles Marius Barbeau, *Medicine-men on the North Pacific Coast*. Bulletins of the National Museum of Man of the National Museum of Canada, Bulletin 152. Ottawa: National Museum of Canada, 1958. Reprinted by permission from the Canadian Museum of Civilization.

Michael Courlander for "Houses will be wrapped," p. 137: Harold Courlander, ed. and comp., *The Fourth World of the Hopis*. New York: Crown, 1971. © 1971. Reprinted by permission from Michael Courlander.

Gunter Narr Verlag for "Flood's song," p. 305; "Hank Ward," pp. 277–78; "Rebel Girl," pp. 284–88; "Hunting Song," pp. 266–69; "Sinyella's healing song," pp. 250–52; "The icy ground," p. 312; "Sun Up Song," p. 307; "In red . . . Beautiful in yellow," p. 301; "Sinyella's song," p. 210; "Heart Horn's Song," p. 275: Leanne Hinton, *Havasupai Songs: A Linguistic Perspective*. Ars Linguistica. Tübingen: Gunter Narr Verlag, 1984 (a 1977 dissertation). Reprinted by permission from Gunter Narr Verlag.

The Indiana Historical Society for "At first, there, always," pp. 9–25: Charles F. Voegelin, ed. and trans., *Walam Olum or Red Score: The Migration Legend of the Lenni Lenape or Delaware Indians*. Indiana Historical Society. Chicago: Lakeside, 1954. Reprinted by permission from the Indiana Historical Society.

The Malki Museum for "Poo'wavi's song," p. 149; "Mosquito's war song," p. 175; "Pete Chile's Deer song," p. 15; "Pete Chile's song," p. 18: Carobeth Laird, *The Chemehuevis*. Banning: Malki Museum, 1976. Reprinted by permission from the Malki Museum.

The Museum of the American Indian Heye Foundation for "Brave Buffalo's Song," p. 86: Charles Hofmann, ed., *Frances Densmore and American Indian Music: A Memorial Volume.* Contributions from the Museum of the American Indian Heye Foundation. New York: Museum of the American Indian Heye Foundation, 1968. Reprinted by permission from the Museum of the American Indian Heye Foundation.

The Museum of Northern Arizona for "The medicine," p. 102: Karl W. Luckert, *A Navajo Bringing Home Ceremony: The Claus Chee Sonny Version of Deerway Ajilee.* Flagstaff: Museum of Northern Arizona, 1978. Reprinted by permission from the Museum of Northern Arizona.

The Museum of Northern Arizona for "Rainbow boy," p. 144; "This dream," p. 125: Karl W. Luckert, *Navajo Mountain and Rainbow Bridge Religion.* Flagstaff: Museum of Northern Arizona, 1977. Reprinted by permission from the Museum of Northern Arizona.

The Santa Barbara Museum of Natural History for "The little lizard." p. 7; "Seaweed Dance song," p. 74; "Bear Dance Song," pp. 82–83; "Bear Dance Song," p. 82: Kitsepawit [Fernando Librado], *The Eye of the Flute: Chumash Traditional History and Ritual as Told by Fernando Librado [Kitsepawit] to John P. Harrington.* Ed. and annot. Thomas Blackburn et al. Santa Barbara Bicentennial Historical Series. Santa Barbara: Santa Barbara Museum of Natural History, 1977. Reprinted by permission from the Santa Barbara Museum of Natural History.

The Smithsonian Institution for "White feather," p. 126, col. 1; "Rainwater," p. 128, col. 2; "On the sand," p. 125, col. 2; "As feathers," p. 124, col. 1; "In that ancient," p. 123, col. 1; "On the plain," p. 124, col. 1; "Over the land," p. 125, col. 2; "Our song," p. 124, col. 2; "My curved horns," p. 123, col. 1; "At sunrise," p. 122, col. 2; "Over the land," p. 124, col. 1; "Feathers," p. 124, col. 1; "The spirit," p. 125, col. 2; "On the peak," p. 126, col. 2; "Here, long," p. 123, col. 1; "Mountain crest," p. 123, col. 2: Catherine S. Fowler and Don D. Fowler, *Anthropology of the Numa: John Wesley Powell's Manuscripts on the Numic Peoples of Western North America.* Smithsonian Contributions to Anthropology 14. Washington, D.C.: Smithsonian Institution, 1971. Reprinted by permission from the Smithsonian Institution.

The Smithsonian Institution for "Raven went up," p. 1153; "Where does he paddle," p. 1157; "Your grandfathers," p. 1160; "Where is that Crane Canoe," p. 1161; "The pole drifts," p. 1162; "From inside the fishtrap's wings," p. 1164; "It always," p. 1172; "Over there," p. 1173; "I am going to go," p. 1281; "Ravens, he is your stone canoe," p. 1245; "Whenever I see," p. 1291; "For the last time," pp. 1296–97; "The world is rolling," p. 1298; "Storm bound," p. 1306; "I feel sad," pp. 1310–11: Fredericka de Laguna, ed. and comp., *Under Mount Saint Elias: The History and Culture of the Yakutat Tlingit.* 3 parts. Smithsonian Contributions to Anthropology 7. Washington, D.C.: GPO, 1972. Reprinted by permission from the Smithsonian Institution.

The Smithsonian Institution for "Big Star, Bear Ceremony, Song 2," pp. 324–25: James R. Murie [Pawnee], *Ceremonies of the Pawnee*, ed. Douglas R. Parks. Smithsonian Contributions to Anthropology 27. Washington, D.C.: Smithsonian Institution, 1981. Reprinted by permission from the Smithsonian Institution.

The University of Arizona Press for "Flies in sky," pp. 24–25; "Early in the morning," p. 37: Karl W. Luckert, *The Navajo Hunter Tradition*, trans. John Cook et al. Tucson: University of Arizona Press, 1975. Reprinted by permission from the University of Arizona Press.

The University of California Press for "I am traveling," p. 226; "Who is like me," p. 252; "Come out," p. 314; "Now I begin," p. 239: Thomas C. Blackburn, ed., *December's Child: A Book of Chumash Oral Narratives*. Berkeley: University of California Press, 1975. © The Regents of the University of California. Reprinted by permission from the University of California Press.

The University of California Press for "Walk around," p. 32.1; "Now I," p. 33.2: Anna Gayton, *(1) Yokuts and Western Mono Ethnography: I: Tulare Lake, Southern Valley and Central Foothill Yokuts*. University of California Anthropological Records. Berkeley: University of California Press, 1948. © The University of California Press. Reprinted by permission from the University of California Press.

The University of California Press for "Georgia Orcutt's hunting song," p. 133; "Wolf of Imam," p. 288; "Mary Ike's death formula," p. 315: Alfred Lewis Kroeber and Edward Winslow Gifford, *Karok Myths*, ed. Grace Buzaliko. Foreword by Theodora Kroeber. Folklore commentary by Alan Dundes. Berkeley: University of California Press, 1980. © The Regents of the University of California, 1980. Reprinted by permission from the University of California Press.

The University of California Press for "The night halfway," p. 118.2; "The sun is set," p. 118.2; "He has gone," p. 118.1; "See the white clouds," p. 118.2: Alfred Lewis Kroeber, *More Mohave Myths*. University of California Anthropological Records 27. Berkeley: University of California Press, 1972. © 1972. Reprinted by permission from the University of California Press.

The University of California Press for "I am the wire–grass queen," p. 163: Hans Jorgen Uldall and William Shipley, *Nisenan Texts and Dictionary*. Narr. William Joseph. University of California Publications in Linguistics 46. Berkeley: University of California Press, 1966. © 1966 The Regents of the University of California. Reprinted by permission from the University of California Press.

The University of California Press for "Where on Quijatoa," pp. 22–23; "Dizziness," p. 40; "Dizzy women," p. 41; "The wind smooths the ground," pp. 44–45; "A little gray whirlwind," p. 52; "Datura," p. 56; "Bird children," p. 57; "Over there," p. 59; "Lo, Surely I shall die," p. 60; "An old male deer," p. 60; "Is it for me," p. 68; "Morning began to run upon us," p. 79; "Grey owl," p. 80; "At the foot of the East," pp. 91–92; "Reed Mountain," p. 110; "Now I am ready," pp. 131–32; "Do you see," pp. 133–34; "On the flat land," pp. 139–40;